D1562933

North Carolina Wesleyan College
WISDOM AND COURAGE THROUGH CHRISTIAN EDUCATION
1956
ROCKY MOUNT, N.C.

YALE LAW LIBRARY SERIES IN
LEGAL HISTORY AND REFERENCE

The Face That Launched a Thousand Lawsuits

The American Women Who Forged a Right to Privacy

JESSICA LAKE

Yale UNIVERSITY PRESS
New Haven and London

Published with support from the Lillian Goldman Law Library, Yale Law School.
Published with assistance from the Mary Cady Tew Memorial Fund.

Yale University Press books may be purchased in quantity for educational, business, or promotional use. For information, please e-mail sales.press@yale.edu (U.S. office) or sales@yaleup.co.uk (U.K. office).

Set in Minion type by Westchester Publishing Services, Danbury, Connecticut.
Printed in the United States of America.

ISBN 978-0-300-21422-2 (hardcover : alk. paper)

Library of Congress Control Number: 2016939462

A catalogue record for this book is available from the British Library.

This paper meets the requirements of ANSI/NISO Z39.48–1992 (Permanence of Paper).

10 9 8 7 6 5 4 3 2 1

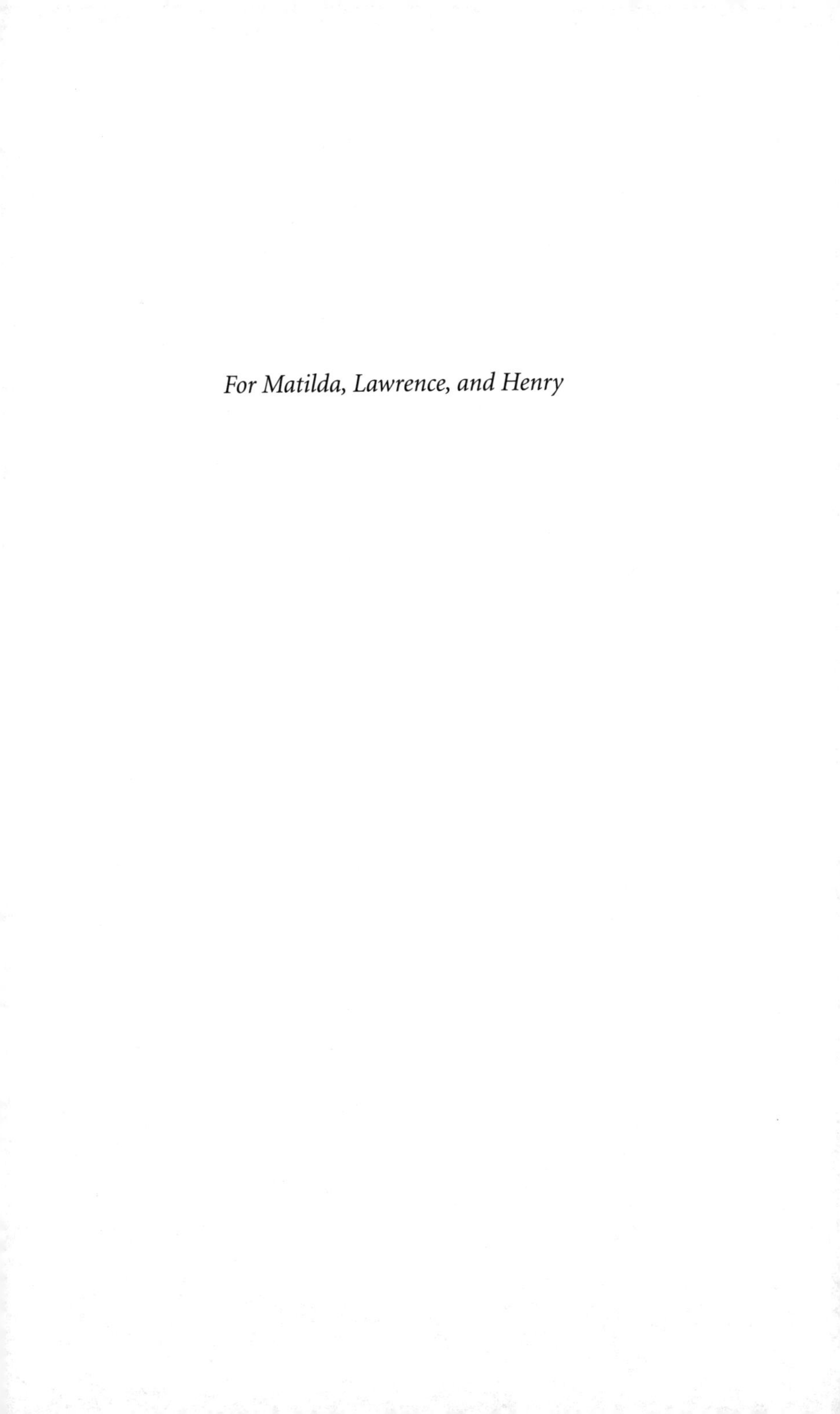

For Matilda, Lawrence, and Henry

Contents

Acknowledgments

This book began life as a doctoral dissertation in law and film studies at the University of Melbourne. The extensive research on which it is based would not have been possible without the generous assistance of numerous librarians and archivists across the United States. In particular I would like to sincerely thank Jenny Romero, Special Collections Department coordinator at the Academy of Motion Picture Arts and Sciences' Margaret Herrick Library (Beverly Hills, California), for helping me to locate and review folders of clipping files and production notes in Special Collections for the films subject to important privacy litigation. Also in California, I would like to acknowledge the enthusiastic efforts of Peter Dalgenos and other staff members at the Witkin State Law Library in Sacramento for transporting numerous case records and briefs from remote warehouses specially for my visit and subsequently providing me with further research assistance once I returned to Melbourne.

I also wish to thank the librarians in the Manuscripts Reading Room and the Newspaper Reading Room at the Library of Congress in Washington, D.C., who kept my spirits up as I nearly lost my sight straining to read microfiche for hours on end searching for one particular undated news article in the *Albany Journal.* In addition, I am very grateful for the assistance of the law librarians at the Library of Congress for helping me to locate and review the important 1888 Bill to Protect Ladies. Across town I also found valuable assistance at the National Archives, where the Legislative Archives consultant spent so much time with me reviewing limited clues relating to a nineteenth-century petition I was desperately trying to locate and, in the end, directed me to a number of dusty and fragile boxes from 1888, where in a wonderful eureka moment, I found the Petition against the Bill to Protect Ladies.

In Rochester I was offered cheerful assistance by Kathy Connor, George Eastman Legacy Curator at the George Eastman House International Museum of Photography and Film, and Nancy Martin, university archivist at the Rush Rhees Library of the University of Rochester, who helped me locate and review extensive early advertising material in the George Eastman Archives and the Kodak Historical Collection, respectively. I also offer special thanks to Shawn Purcell and other librarians in the Manuscripts and Special Collections Unit of the New York State Library in Albany, New York, who located a plethora of case records and briefs and looked after me during the long hours I spent at the library. During my research trip I was unfortunately not able to visit Topeka, Kansas, to review the primary court documents for one case in particular, *Kunz v. Allen,* and so I am particularly indebted to the generosity of Martin Wisneski from the Washburn University Law Library in Topeka for traveling to the Kansas Supreme Court Law Library, copying the entire thing, and sending it to me. This case was crucial to the development of my thesis, and I am forever grateful for his considerable efforts.

While I was in the United States I presented a paper at the Association for the Study of Law, Culture, and Humanities

(ASLCH) annual conference, held at the University of Nevada in Las Vegas. I would like to thank Professor Austin Sarat and other members of the Organizing Committee for ASLCH for taking an interest in this project, awarding me a Graduate Student Stipend that enabled me to travel to and participate in the conference, and encouraging me to submit an article to their respected journal. As a result an earlier version of chapter 2 was published in *Law, Culture, and Humanities* in December 2011.

The many months I spent conducting research for my project in the United States would not have been possible without the financial assistance of a number of organizations. First and foremost I would like to thank the Australian and New Zealand American Studies Association for awarding me the generous Paul Bourke Postgraduate Travel Fellowship and the University of Melbourne for the award of a Melbourne Abroad Traveling Scholarship. My research was also made possible, during the years of my Ph.D. enrollment, by an Australian Postgraduate Award from the Australian government. I would also like to thank the Centre for Media and Communications Law at Melbourne Law School, which provided me with a visiting research fellowship while I began to transform my dissertation into a book.

My Ph.D. degree at the University of Melbourne was a joint enrollment in the Melbourne Law School and the School of Culture and Communication. I would like to thank my supervisors Barbara Creed in the School of Culture and Communication and Megan Richardson in the Melbourne Law School for encouraging my project and dedicating their time and effort to discussing and reviewing my progress. The interdisciplinary nature of my topic may have been a challenge to traditional models of supervision, but my project benefited from the combination of their different areas of expertise and from our lively meetings. At the University of Melbourne, I was introduced to American history by David Goodman, to privacy law by Andrew Kenyon, and to cinema studies by Mark Nicholls and Angela Ndalianis. Their classes inspired my first interest in these fields.

I would like to thank my colleagues in the Law School at Swinburne University of Technology, especially the dean, Dan Hunter, for supporting my research and taking an interest in the development and progress of this project.

I also wish to acknowledge the dedicated work of my Ph.D. examiners, Kathy Bowrey and Sonia Katyal, whose keen insights, thoughtful comments, and positive feedback were important in helping me turn my dissertation into a book. This process also benefited from the enthusiastic response and valuable suggestions of two anonymous reviewers.

And warm thanks to my editor at Yale University Press, Jaya Chatterjee, for her encouragement and belief in this book.

Thank you to my friends for your ongoing curiosity about my work and for providing me with outings, distractions, and weekends away when I most needed them. Heartfelt thanks to my family for their continuing support, emotionally and materially, over the past several years. My parents, Marilyn and Sam Lake, have offered models of commitment to academic scholarship and much else besides. Both parents and parents-in-law, Eril and Teng Tan, helped cook our food, clean our house, and care for our children while I worked very long days to complete this book. My sister, Katherine Lake, has given me encouragement and made me laugh during hard times.

Above all I offer loving gratitude to my husband, Lachlan Tan, always wise, generous, and kind in the midst of chaos and sleep deprivation and during the many long hours I have spent researching and writing. And last, but certainly not least, warm thanks to my delightful daughter Matilda and her baby brothers, our twin boys Henry and Lawrence, who have all entered the world during a very busy and crowded few years. They have made it all worthwhile, and it is to them that I dedicate my book.

Introduction

On 10 July 2015, the New York Supreme Court convicted the rapper 50 Cent (Curtis James Jackson III) of breaching the privacy rights of a Florida mother, Lastonia Leviston, when he acquired and uploaded online a sexually explicit video of her.[1] The video went viral and attracted more than three million views in a matter of days. According to court documents, Leviston suffered depression, suicidal thoughts, and post-traumatic stress disorder as a result of the unauthorized circulation of the private sex tape. She sued Jackson under sections 50 and 51 of the New York Civil Rights laws, the statute forged in the wake of the action taken by young Abigail Roberson more than a hundred years earlier, when she brought a case against the unauthorized use of her photographic image in advertising material.[2]

The defeat of Roberson's suit in 1902 resulted in the passage of the New York privacy laws under which Jackson was ordered to pay Leviston seven million dollars in damages in 2015. "I've been served justice by the courts and vindicated by God," a victorious Leviston stated on the steps of the New York Supreme Court.[3] She might also thank the pioneering women, like Roberson, who first went to court to establish "a right to privacy" in the United States in protest against the unauthorized publication and circulation of their photographic and cinematic images.

In this book I offer a new history of the evolution of privacy law in the United States that places the legal activism of individual women front and center, women such as the feisty Abigail Roberson, Coney Island high diver Mabel Colyer, the private detective Grace Humiston, Kansas housewife Stella Kunz, Broadway star Gladys Loftus, African American dancer Pauline Myers, and Californian society matron Gabrielle Melvin. It was their bold and courageous action in seeking legal redress for the humiliation and harm caused by the wrongful use and circulation of their images, from the late nineteenth century into the twentieth century, that effectively established a right to privacy in United States law. Their collective stories, which until now lay buried in court and film archives, have not yet been told. Their action as plaintiffs is the key dynamic that drives this history of the establishment of the legal right of privacy in the United States.[4]

Today young women across the United States and around the world continue to seek redress for the unauthorized use and publication of their images that now circulate online. In August 2014, for example, five hundred private photographs of celebrities and others, nearly all women, were published via various platforms, such as Reddit, Imgur, and Tumblr. One of the high-profile victims, actress Jennifer Lawrence, angrily responded: "This is a flagrant violation of privacy." At the same time, the phenomenon of "revenge pornography," whereby a person (usually a man) uploads nude or otherwise explicit images of someone else (usually a woman) online in order to humiliate, shame, or ridicule the victim, is ruining lives. In 2009, Holly Jacobs (founder and executive director of the Cyber Civil Rights Initiative) discovered to her horror that her ex-boyfriend had posted numerous explicit photographs and videos of her across the Internet. Jacobs and other victims of revenge pornography and their lawyers are campaigning to have this behavior criminalized, and as a result twenty-six states have now outlawed it.

Nonetheless, justice often remains elusive. Victims face courts, lawyers, law enforcement agencies, and lawmakers who, often dismissing their grievances as trivial, prove unwilling to advocate, charge offenders, or enact changes to existing laws. Meanwhile, images of women's naked bodies continue to spread like an infection across the Internet. Today's victims might take heart from the determined action of their forebears who went to court, individually, to protest the use and abuse of their photographic and cinematic images by others. In bringing their cases those forebears put their voices, stories, and images on the public record, and it was their cases that worked to establish a right to privacy in the United States. They also raised legal and philosophical issues that in many cases are far from being resolved. These pioneers are as yet little known.

As traditionally understood, the invention of the right to privacy in the United States was the work of Harvard Law School graduates Samuel Warren and Louis Brandeis, who, provoked by the intrusion of photographers at the wedding of Warren's daughter, declared themselves in favor of a right to privacy in a famous article they cowrote in the *Harvard Law Review.*[5] As William Prosser, dean of University of California Law School, Berkeley, later put it in a survey of the history of privacy law, the press had a "field day" reporting the "blue-blood" Boston wedding, provoking Warren's extreme annoyance. Prosser wryly noted: "All this [was] a most marvelous tree to grow from the wedding of the daughter of

Mr. Samuel D. Warren. One is tempted to surmise that she must have been a very beautiful girl. Resembling, perhaps, that fabulous creature, the daughter of a Mr. Very, a confectioner in Regent Street, who was so wondrous fair that her presence in the shop caused three or four hundred people to assemble every day in the street before the window to look at her, so that her father was forced to send her out of town. . . . This was the face," concluded Dean Prosser of Warren's daughter, "that launched a thousand lawsuits."[6] It was a beguiling story but has since been proved apocryphal.[7]

Stories about the disruptive power of the beauty of young women have a legendary appeal. My book, unlike the books of most other legal scholars, including Prosser, and Warren and Brandeis before him, documents the legal and social disruptions produced by women (and a minority of men) who spoke out and publicly asserted their right to control the publication of images (both still and moving) of their faces and bodies. At a time when women formed the minority of general litigants and lacked basic civil and political rights, they nonetheless constituted the majority of privacy plaintiffs. *Hers* was indeed the face that launched a thousand lawsuits. What Prosser could not contemplate and few have acknowledged since was the historical agency of women—angry that their images were being circulated, exploited, and viewed by others without permission—whose actions established this right at law.[8] My book tells the stories of the women behind the faces and gives voice to those previously silenced by history. It also discusses some of the few cases brought by men, such as *Pavesich v. New England Life Insurance Co.* (Georgia, 1905). In an area of law dominated and shaped by female plaintiffs, it is notable that the first superior court case to recognize a right to privacy at common law was brought by a man.

Brandeis and Warren were not in fact the first to contemplate the possibility of a right to privacy. I show that the idea was being discussed more generally in the broader community before the publication of their academic article. When newspapers contemplated the implications of a new federal bill introduced in the House of Representatives in 1888 entitled a Bill to Protect Ladies, public attention was focused on the possibility that women might be protected from the unwanted use of their photographs. The bill, introduced by Congressman John Robert Thomas of Illinois, sought to prohibit publication of women's images in their capacity "as the wives, daughters, mothers and sisters of American citizens" for advertising purposes without their consent. The wording of the bill, inadvertently perhaps, highlighted the fact that American women were not yet citizens themselves. Congressman Thomas wrote the bill after becoming incensed that President Grover Cleveland's young wife, First Lady Frances Folsom, could not control the extensive use of her pretty face in advertisements for tobacco, pharmaceutical nostrums, beer, and other products. While the bill did not mention a right to privacy, local newspapers, as I show in chapter 2, introduced the idea into the debate that followed about the use and abuse of women's pictures. Oddly, Warren and Brandeis failed to mention this bill, or the first lady's predicament in their article, which is especially curious given that Warren's wife, Mabel, was a friend of the first lady during this period.

The advent of photography and the possibility that people's images might be used without their consent occasioned new kinds of harm that were felt especially acutely by women, whose "pretty faces" and "gorgeous forms" were more likely to be photographed, circulated, and exploited by others.[9]

The harms that people began to experience—the embarrassment, humiliation, sense of diminishment, and loss of control—seemed to be beyond the redress of the existing common law. I begin this new history with the historical and social context of the advent of photography and draw out the implications of film, both still and moving, for people's sense of self—its simultaneous effects of identification and alienation. I also point to the conflict of interest that arose between those who "shot" the pictures and those whose pictures were "taken."

Prior to the advent of the camera, the tradition of portraiture relied upon the capacity of artists to capture a "likeness" through the media of drawing and painting. The cosy circumstances of these practices defined their legal regulation. The execution of honorific portraits often required prolonged physical proximity between an artist and his subject, necessitating a relationship in which the terms and conditions of the portrait (such as who would possess it and hold copyright in it) could be negotiated subject to a legally binding contract and/or obligation of confidence. Further, if an artist were required to access a sitter by entering private property, lack of consent to do so could instantiate an action in trespass or nuisance. As legal historian Jonathan Hafetz has noted, insofar as there was a right to privacy, for most of the nineteenth century it was closely tied to the physical boundaries of real property—"the four walls of a man's home."[10]

The advent of photography in the 1830s altered the architecture and experience of seeing and being seen.[11] The profoundly intimate relationship between viewing and being viewed was disrupted. Via this new medium, the uncanny likeness of an individual could be lifted with relative ease from its possessor and cast upon paper, to be reproduced, handled, and owned by others. The image became simultaneously more authentic and more autonomous. Photography's transformation into an amateur pastime in the 1880s further changed the conditions and circumstances of visual representation. Portraits no longer required the skilled hand of an artist. Rather they could be captured, reproduced, disseminated, and published on an unprecedented scale. The established legal doctrines of contract, copyright, breach of confidence, and defamation, previously effective in regulating the rights of a "pictured subject," were found wanting. Debate began over how to remedy this situation and provide protection for individuals, particularly women, who seemed to experience the new harm most acutely, against the unauthorized circulation of their portraits.

One of the most enduring contributions to these debates, as noted above, was made by the Harvard law scholars Louis Brandeis and Samuel Warren, who argued for the common law to recognize a right to privacy in their article in the *Harvard Law Review* in 1890.[12] In what has since been labeled "the most influential law review article ever written,"[13] Warren and Brandeis pondered the legal implications of new technical "inventions" and "mechanical devices": "Recent inventions and business methods call attention to the next step which must be taken for the protection of the person, and for securing to the individual what Judge Cooley calls the right 'to be let alone.' Instantaneous photographs and newspaper enterprise have invaded the sacred precincts of private and domestic life; and numerous mechanical devices threaten to make good the prediction that 'what is whispered in the closet shall be proclaimed from the house-tops.'"[14] Warren and Brandeis argued that to remain relevant and effective the common law had to adapt to political, social, and economic change.

Already implicit within existing doctrines (such as copyright, contract, and breach of confidence), a right to privacy, they argued, should be recognized as a separate cause of action to deal with the increasing problem of the unauthorized circulation of photographic portraits and the "evil" invasion of the private lives of individuals by newspapers. Their article has been credited with launching hundreds of cases across the United States contesting a right to privacy. As I show, however, it was the issue of the unauthorized circulation of women's photographic portraits that first catapulted a right to privacy into public consciousness, and it was young women who brought the first cases that pushed for and established its legal recognition. The doctrine of a right to privacy offered women the legal power to rescue their images from public consumption and impede the desire of the voyeur, as it also allowed them to choose the terms upon which they presented themselves in their public and professional lives. When men called on "privacy" to protect their reputations from ridicule they invoked particular constructions of masculinity. A gendered analysis, I argue, is crucial to understanding how a right to privacy became enshrined in U.S. law.

To understand why these plaintiffs brought their actions, an examination of their social, cultural, and embodied experiences as women and men is necessary as well as an understanding of the ways in which they viewed and negotiated the new inventions of photography and film. This book thus places emphasis on the voices of plaintiffs, witnesses, and their legal attorneys as recorded in documents in court archives, rather than simply relying on the texts produced in official judicial decisions. Through an investigation of particular cases we can better understand how the advent of still and moving film changed the relationship of individuals to their own "form and features" and why their concerns were expressed in the language of privacy.[15] A gendered analysis is necessary to understand why the concept of privacy appealed especially to women plaintiffs and why the majority of plaintiffs were women. At the same time, we need to ask how the changing circumstances of women shaped the establishment of a legal right to privacy and the extent to which privacy became a feminine legal doctrine. An understanding of this history can clarify what's at stake in current debates concerning the unauthorized distribution and circulation of women's pictures on the Internet.

The foundational case that led to the establishment of a right to privacy in law was *Roberson v. Rochester Folding Box Co.*, brought by a feisty young woman, Abigail Roberson, in New York in 1900. Roberson, supported by her suffragist lawyer, Milton Gibbs, submitted that the defendants should be restrained from using her face without her consent on their advertisements for flour. In doing so, she asserted, they breached both her right to privacy and her property rights in her own beauty. Although defeated in court, Roberson's case led to the enactment of the first privacy laws in the United States in the state of New York in 1903. When Chief Justice Parker, who dismissed her case, later became a presidential candidate and complained about unwanted publicity, Roberson vented her outrage in a letter to the *New York Times:* "I take this opportunity to remind you that you have no such right as that which you assert. I have very high authority for my statement, being nothing less than a decision of the Court of Appeals of this State wherein you wrote the prevailing opinion. . . . [I]n an opinion sixteen pages long you arrived at the conclusion that I had no rights that could be protected by your tribunal. . . . I am forced to the conclusion that this incident well illustrates the truth of the old saying that it makes a lot of difference whose ox is gored."[16]

A right to privacy was pursued as a distinct cause of action in the United States from the beginning of the twentieth century, ahead of other common law jurisdictions such as the United Kingdom, Australia, Canada, and New Zealand. It is now established, in one form or another, via either case law or statute, in the vast majority of U.S. states and included within the *Second Restatement of Torts*.[17] The genesis story of a right to privacy has long fascinated legal scholars and historians, yet their considerable body of work has rarely examined the gendered history of the establishment of a right to privacy.[18] My interdisciplinary account based on extensive archival research in repositories across the country tells the story of why and how a right to privacy developed in the United States between the years 1880 and 1950 by addressing the conjuncture of three apparently separate developments: legal innovation, changes in the status of women and ideas of womanhood, and the invention of still and moving film. How these three developments intersected to change legal history can be traced in the actions, protests, and lawsuits of numerous individual women and some men and the inventive arguments of their lawyers. Although men also brought early cases asserting breach of privacy, deploying the doctrine creatively in an attempt to redress masculine grievances, I draw attention to the fact that it was women who accounted for the majority of the early privacy plaintiffs, and their cases proved the most significant in terms of shaping the doctrine's discourse, utility, and character.

The women responsible for forging a right to privacy hailed from a generation who envisaged lives very different from those of their mothers. At the beginning of the twentieth century, women enrolled in college education and entered the paid workforce in rapidly increasing numbers. At the same time, the proportion who chose never to marry, or to end their marriage in divorce, also grew rapidly. They were part of the generation that earned the description "New Women" and self-consciously rejected traditional gender roles and womanly traits such as passivity, modesty, and self-sacrifice in favor of greater freedom in their public, professional, and personal lives.

The New Woman was a controversial figure who encompassed a wide range of "types," including suffragettes, college girls, professionals, flappers, models, and actresses. The New Woman became a visual symbol of progress and modernity.[19] The right to privacy doctrine may have apparently espoused traditional gender norms, as some scholars have suggested,[20] but it also served to register the strong protests of women about the use of their images by others without their consent. My book suggests that "privacy" could work in ambiguous ways.

In an increasingly ocularcentric culture, images became the primary means by which shifting ideas of womanhood were expressed and negotiated.[21] Individual women could articulate their place within the gendered spectrum—whether as traditional "lady," modern woman, or stage actress—through their self-presentation and photographic images, often oscillating between "roles" depending upon the context and purpose of their appearance. Control over the production, reproduction, circulation, and publication of their pictures was critical for social and self-expression. Experimenting with New Womanhood could become problematic, however, if one's image slipped into the hands of the wrong viewer, whether it was a woman's husband or father, a salacious voyeur, or the reader of a men's magazine. How one appeared on celluloid influenced one's social reputation, familial position, and professional prospects.

My book includes the stories of almost thirty women who brought cases in the late nineteenth and early twentieth centuries to protest against the use of their images by others, located within their broader legal, historical, and cultural contexts. The case archives (affidavits, pleadings, testimonies) reveal a right to privacy not as an ill-defined grievance, as some have described it, but as a vehicle for redress. It shaped the articulation of new personal and proprietary rights (such as the right of publicity) and raised the possibility of further legal reforms. Without these case archives, we would have little, if any, evidence that those pictured as the silent subjects of photographs and on moving film during this period ever voiced their dissent. By placing the pictured, rather than the picture taker, at the heart of this history, I show the ways in which the doctrine also worked to challenge the largely masculine protections of copyright law. I also raise important questions about how the gender of law determines the subsistence and allocation of property. Why did the law accord so many rights to those behind the camera as opposed to those in front of it?

My interdisciplinary approach also introduces the legal concept of a right to privacy to film history. The relevant case law provides insights into how the advent of photography and cinema affected people's lived experiences and generated new social concerns and legal arguments. The case archives possess a wealth of valuable material, featuring the often-forgotten perspectives of those whose images were used and exploited by photographers and film producers. These records provide a counterdiscourse to the voices of filmmakers and audiences, of producers, artists, directors, and spectators that have tended to dominate traditional histories of photography and cinema. They illuminate the ways in which women and some men negotiated photographic and cinematic images of themselves in a bid to construct or consolidate their own sense of self. I show the ways in which those who were filmed struggled for control over their visual articulation.

I have arranged the arguments of the book in thematic and roughly chronological order. Chapter 1, "Setting the Scene: Proliferating Pictures and the Advent of Photography and Cinema," provides the historical context for the cases that follow, offering an analysis of the changes in visual technologies that were occurring in the nineteenth century and the ways in which these new "inventions" and "mechanical devices" (in the words of Warren and Brandeis) radically altered the experience of seeing and being seen by others. For the picture taker, this new medium offered many pleasures; for the pictured subject, however, photography created an acute tension between feelings of identification and alienation. I argue that the invention of photography and its fashioning as an amateur pastime from the 1880s, together with the development of cinema at the end of the nineteenth century, occasioned the potential for new harms to pictured subjects (especially as experienced by women) for which the law provided inadequate redress.

In chapter 2, "'Has a Beautiful Girl the Right to Her Own Face?': Privacy, Propriety, and Property," I investigate the ways in which concerns about the unauthorized publication of women's portraits in the United States led to the legal formulation of a right to privacy. I examine the history of the articulation of this right prior to Warren and Brandeis's seminal article and connect claims to a right to privacy to the advent of New Womanhood and women's broader struggle for equal citizenship. I argue that despite its emphasis on ladylike "modesty" and "reserve," the case of *Roberson v. Rochester Folding Box Co.* can be read as the protest of a courageous young woman—an orphan—against the use of her photograph that transformed her into an anonymous "pretty" object of mass consumption. I compare her objections to the masculine language of liberty and freedom espoused by the court in a significant privacy case brought by a man at much the same time: *Pavesich v. New England Life Insurance Co.* Pavesich sought to restrain the use of his photograph in connection with a false endorsement on the defendant's advertisement for life insurance. In most of the early cases a right to privacy was employed by young women who objected to their images being handled and circulated by others to assert ownership over images of their faces and forms.

Chapter 3, "Medical Men and Peeping Toms: Spectacles of Monstrosity and the Camera's Corporeal Violations," moves from cases concerning women's beauty to those in which a right to privacy was invoked by women to protest against violations of their bodies or the bodies of their newborn babies. This chapter offers a parallel history of a right to privacy that charts the ways in which the law traditionally "protected" women's bodies by treating them as male property and confining them to the home. The advent of the camera, its ability to penetrate physical and temporal boundaries, and its creation of movable as well as moving images brought into question the efficacy of laws such as trespass and nuisance grounded in physical structures. To highlight new invasions inflicted by the camera, I compare the cases of *DeMay v. Roberts* and *Feeney v. Young,* which involved the optic violation of a woman's reproductive body by a stranger's eyes and by a camera. I argue that women invoked a right to privacy to protest against the transformation of their bodies (and the bodies of their dead deformed newborn babies) into voyeuristic spectacles of "monstrosity."[22]

Chapter 4, "Privacy, the Celluloid City, and the Cinematic Eye," shifts our focus to the cinematic camera's recordings of women in public space. I examine claims to a right to privacy in relation to early nonfiction film in the form of cinema advertisements, newsreels, and documentaries. The cases discussed are significant for their contribution to the development of privacy law, but they also offer insight into the discomfort experienced by those caught unknowingly in a motion picture during this period. The plaintiffs tell vividly of their shock and distress at becoming the object of a mass gaze, with their movements and mannerisms looming larger than life on the big screen. The cases are important to the study of early film history, both for their impact upon the industry and for the historical, social, and cultural experiences they relay. The women fought for restrictions on the practices of early filmmaking, but the cases also reveal the limits of the doctrine of privacy when used in this context. Courts tended to frame the issue in terms of the public/private dichotomy, usually privileging the "public interest" in nonfiction filmmaking over an individual's right to privacy.

In chapter 5, "Privacy for Profit and a Right of Publicity," I chart the evolution of a right to privacy to a "right of publicity" in U.S. law. Legal scholars have often commented on the "puzzling" nature of this shift. I suggest that if a right to privacy is recognized as a doctrine primarily used by women to control images of their faces and bodies, the development of a right of publicity (the ability to profit from their own images) was in fact a logical extension of a right to privacy. In the

1930s, women found new professional opportunities in the emerging visual arts industries as dancers, models, and actresses. As the only legal doctrine offering individuals rights in the (still and moving) images of themselves, a right to privacy was employed by professional women to protect and profit from what Liz Conor has termed their "techniques of appearing." It was also invoked by men to protect and profit from what I call (in contradistinction to women's "techniques of appearing") their masculine "professions of performance."[23]

In chapter 6, "Hollywood Heroes and Shameful Hookers: Privacy Moves West," I examine the cases in which individuals used the doctrine of a right to privacy to claim ownership over their life stories, when appropriated by "fiction" films. I track the move of industrial image making from the East Coast to the West Coast of the United States and compare the different contexts of New York's privacy laws with California's, informed as they were by a utopian "pursuit of happiness" guaranteed by the California Constitution. I also examine the right of privacy in relation to the demands of the Hays Code and consider the onscreen celebration of men's heroic "public" lives compared to the shaming of women's "private" lives. I discuss the motion pictures *CQD or Saved by Wireless* (Vitagraph Company of America, 1911), *The Red Kimono* (Walter Lang, 1925), *Yankee Doodle Dandy* (Michael Curtiz, 1942), and *The Sands of Iwo Jima* (Allan Dwan, 1949). I conclude chapter 6 with an assessment of privacy law up to 1950.

In the Conclusion, I discuss the implications of privacy's gendered history and reflect on the ways in which this new history relates to and might inform contemporary debates about the circulation and publication of naked or sexually explicit images of women on the Internet. In many ways, the current attempts by women and their advocates to address the phenomenon of revenge pornography in the United States echoes the earlier struggles for image rights and the recognition of a right to privacy that began in the first years of the twentieth century. The unauthorized circulation and publication of still and moving images disproportionately harms young women even now, and privacy is the primary discourse in which protests are framed to protest such practices. Legal change is still advocated as a remedy. But there are also differences today, with lawyers and lawmakers now seeking to impose criminal rather than civil sanctions.

I also reflect in the Conclusion on the benefits of bringing together research in the fields of law, film studies, and women's history and suggest possible future directions for such work. Interdisciplinary scholarship is rewarding and illuminating in the ways it brings distinct and often disparate discursive fields into conversation to generate new perspectives and new questions. But there is also a challenge in seeking to address different readerships and engage different disciplines. As Austin Sarat, Lawrence Douglas, and Martha Umphrey have noted in their book *Law on the Screen,* study of the law/film relationship, in particular, is still relatively undeveloped.[24] By weaving together case studies in privacy law with the histories of women, photography, and cinema in the United States, my book aims to contribute to this growing field of scholarship.

1

Setting the Scene

Proliferating Pictures and the Advent of Photography and Cinema

In 1890, Marion Manola, a twenty-four-year-old singer and actress, went to court in New York to seek redress when the manager of the theater in which she was working surreptitiously took photographs of her that emphasized the attractive shape of her body in tights. She sought to restrain him from using and publishing the pictures because, as she told a newspaper journalist, she did "not want her photograph in costume to be common property, circulated from hand to hand, and treasured by every fellow who can raise the price demanded by the photographer for a copy of the picture."[1] Her case came to the attention of the legal community when Warren and Brandeis cited it in their famous *Harvard Law Review* article, but it was just one of a number of similar court actions in the late nineteenth and early twentieth centuries initiated by women whose photographic images were being circulated in public without their consent. As a performer, Manola appreciated an audience's admiration of her professional skills in the intimate setting of the theater, but she didn't want photographic images of her face and form to become "common property, circulated from hand to hand" in the public domain.

Just over fifty years before Manola faced the New York Supreme Court, the public unveiling of the modern photographic camera, in the form of Louis Daguerre's "daguerreotype" and William Henry Fox Talbot's "calotype" had marked a radical shift in the possibilities and perils of visual representation.[2] In a climate of growing positivist thought, photography promised the ability to create an "objective" visual record of the world, but in doing so, it removed the appearances of objects and people from their original contexts. It was this tension between presence and absence, the blurring between "representation" and "reality," and the simultaneous dislocation and manipulation of that "reality" that created new social concerns and legal challenges. As Jonathan Crary has noted, "Photographs may have some apparent similarities with older types of images, such as perspectival painting or drawings made with the aid of a camera obscura; but the vast systematic rupture of which photography is a part renders such similarities insignificant."[3] Photography transformed the nature of portraiture, the image becoming simultaneously more authentic and more autonomous. As a distraught Marion Manola realized, her photograph could take on a life of its own.

In his book *Visions of Modernity,* Scott McQuire has traced the history of modernism through the lens of the camera.[4] From its conception, photography as a form of writing with light (with all its theological and philosophical associations) occupied a unique relationship to "truth." It was not merely another form of representation but promised an "invisible umbilicus joining image and referent."[5] Whether in the realm of science or of social relations, the image *seen* promised the veracity of the *scene*. In the 1840s, Fox Talbot, speculating on the possibilities of photography, produced a calotype of several shelves of expensive china. He mused that "if a thief afterwards purloined the treasures—if the mute testimony of the picture were to be produced against him in court—it would certainly be evidence of a novel kind."[6] Unlike a painting, a photograph seemed to prove the existence and ownership of the objects depicted.

The law was, however, hesitant to embrace photography's evidentiary potential. As the law journal the *Western Jurist* remarked in 1879: "The law of the land is a wary old fox, and scrutinizes a new invention a long time before extending the paw to appropriate it."[7] In the United States and Britain, a legal debate began over the status of photography: what indeed did it or could it show, and how?[8] One jurist was confident: "The photographic apparatus never intentionally falsifies nor do its products ever so fade as to distort the image they present, as do figures of things committed to the treacherous memory of man."[9] Yet a contributor to the *Virginia Law Journal* was not so sure: "Can the sun lie? . . . Perhaps we may say that though the sun does not lie, the liar may use the sun as a tool."[10]

Even as the cracks in photography's guise of unmediated objectivity began to emerge, photography was established as one of the primary media for "exposing" the "real" world. It extended the capacities of the feeble eye and brought minute detail and distant happenings into view. In 1888, the astronomer P. J. C. Janssen pronounced: "The sensitive photographic film is the true retina of the scientist . . . for it possesses all the properties science could want: it faithfully preserves the images which depict themselves upon it, and reproduces and multiplies them indefinitely on request."[11] Photography enhanced the disciplines of science in its clear reflection of otherwise obscure objects, phenomena, and happenings. It also enabled those without access to the privileges of painted portraiture to possess and cherish images of their loved ones, distant or dead, and to surround themselves with "albums" or galleries of familiar belongings. "Blessed be the inventor of photography," enthused Jane Welsh Carlyle. "I set him even above the inventor of chloroform! It has given more positive pleasure to poor suffering humanity than anything that has been 'cast up' in my time . . . this art, by which even the poor can possess themselves of tolerable likenesses of their absent dear ones."[12] In a letter to a friend, the nineteenth-century poet Elizabeth Barrett indicated a preference for photography over portraiture: "It is not at all monstrous in me to say . . . that I would rather have such a [photographic] memorial of one I loved dearly than the noblest artist's work ever produced . . . it is not merely the likeness which is precious in such cases but the association and sense of nearness in the thing . . . the fact of the very shadow of the person lying there fixed forever."[13]

Photography promised the "nearness" of a loved one that portraiture, in its seemingly greater reliance upon artistic mediation, could not. A photograph was physically and spiritually connected to the subjects' bodies—light had touched them and cast their shadow upon paper. At the same time, however, Barrett's words suggest a sense of loss: the subject was preserved only as a "shadow" and a thing "fixed forever." The ability of photography to capture human subjects was problematic from its beginnings. On the one hand, a photograph of a loved one brought that person closer to those who loved him or her; on the other hand, photography detached the subject from himself or herself. The presence emphasized the absence. Barrett's reflection calls up Walter Benjamin's conception of photography as something "to pry an object from its shell, to destroy its aura"[14] and Roland Barthes's description of the alienating process of being photographed: "I am neither subject nor object but a subject who feels he is becoming an object."[15]

In his essay "The Body and the Archive," Allan Sekula argues that in the nineteenth century photography functioned as both an honorific and a repressive medium, taking over the portraiture of the bourgeoisie on the one hand and silencing the voices of immigrants, foreigners, and deviants with one frozen image on the other.[16] Every "proper portrait," Sekula observes, "has its lurking, objectifying inverse in the files of the police."[17] Sekula details the extent to which photography was used to document and discipline the "criminal body" (as corporeal entity and as collective) in the nineteenth century and to define it against the "social body." One of earliest organized applications of photography took place in Bristol, in England, in the 1840s, when police first began photographing offenders for the purposes of identification. Photographing prisoners provided the possibility of circulating an identical and replicable record to other police stations and authorities, to be used for the purposes of apprehension and conviction. Tom Gunning describes this use of photography as inscribing the deviant body with a "new mark" of individuality, which rested upon its structural differentiation from all other recorded individual bodies.[18] But it was not just the police who kept photographic records. A large range of other institutions of power—scientific, technical, medical, legal, and political—began to employ photography as a means of recording, categorizing, and controlling individuals.[19]

The medium of photography also operated as a democratic force. By "democratizing" likeness, photography brought together in one archive the portraits of "heroes, leaders, moral exemplars, celebrities, and those of the poor, the diseased, the insane, the criminal, the non-white, the female, and all other embodiments of the unworthy."[20] Furthermore, such photographic reflections floated freely, resisting traditional anchors of definition, context, and categorization. For just as images could be captured, developed, and presented to loved ones, so could they be stolen, lost, and trafficked.

Between the 1840s and 1870s, photographic portraiture, particularly using Daguerre's method, flourished in the United States. Luxurious studios offering Americans uncannily accurate pictures of themselves proliferated on the East Coast. At the studios of Southworth and Hawes in Boston, Robert Cornelius in Philadelphia, John Plumbe, Jeremiah Gurney, Matthew Brady, the Meade Brothers, and Charles Fredericks's "Temple of Art" in New York Americans came in the hundreds of thousands to be photographed.[21] The industry's rapid growth was fostered mainly by a demand for photographic portraits among the new middle classes, including shopkeepers, managers, clerks, and small traders of all kinds.[22]

By 1850, two thousand "daguerreotypists" existed in the United States, and Americans were spending between eight and twelve million dollars a year on photographic portraits. By 1853 more than three million portraits were produced each year.[23] Portraits constituted an astonishing 95 percent of photographic production. On the banks of the Hudson River in New York, a town responsible for manufacturing photographic plates was named "Daguerreville."[24] In 1854 the growth in professional photographic portraiture received a further boost with the introduction of the "carte de visite" format, a camera with multiple lenses and moving plate holder that produced a visiting card fixed with four or five small photographs of the sitter.

An industry of celebrity photographic portraits emerged, and studios sought to attract the most famous figures from show business, the aristocracy, and politics to sit for them, enhancing their profits by selling the resulting cartes de visite for a sizable sum. In 1850 studio owner Matthew Brady published a *Gallery of Illustrious Americans* featuring a lithographic portrait and biography of each prominent individual.[25] Soon celebrities and other high-profile figures began to demand more than one photographic print for the task of sitting so they could share in the profits.[26] Such arrangements could be negotiated, but when it came to legal enforcement, without a contrary agreement the professional photographer held the rights to the image through the expanding doctrine of copyright.

In 1862 the United Kingdom passed the Fine Arts Copyright Act recognizing photography alongside the other visual arts (painting, drawing, sculpture) and placing the right to reproduce and/or publish the article in the hands of the photographer. In 1865 the United States adopted the United Kingdom's copyright protections for photographs. This extension of copyright law privileged the image taker over the person photographed and ignored the differences between the processes of painting and photography. It treated photography as merely an extension of an existing artistic tradition. But I suggest that photography was a rupture with, rather than a continuation of, previous modes of creative representation.[27] Placing ownership of the image within the hands of the photographers recognized their effort and expenditure at a time when photographic equipment was both complicated to operate and expensive. But the need to make such an investment in the means of production would soon change with the arrival of the amateur apparatus.

"You Press the Button, We Do the Rest"

Until the 1880s, only those skilled in the science and mechanics of photography and able to afford the expensive equipment necessary for capturing an image could call themselves "photographers." Individuals desiring likenesses of themselves or their family members sat for professionals in their studios or shops. Such activity was not unlike commissioning a painted portrait. There was a relatively clear demarcation between picture makers and those pictured. This divide began to blur in the 1880s, however, as photography was refashioned as a "delightful pastime" for ordinary people.[28]

Though there were many photographic companies, George Eastman of Rochester, New York, led this change in the 1880s, and the Kodak trade name quickly became synonymous with amateur photography. In the United States, Eastman transformed the photographic camera from a complicated scientific device into a fashionable consumer item for everyman. As a young man in the early 1870s, Eastman worked at the Rochester Savings Bank to support his widowed mother. As the story goes, while at the bank he planned a holiday with friends to Santo Domingo, and a fellow worker suggested he make a record of his travels. Eastman agreed and purchased all the necessary photographic paraphernalia: a tripod, a heavy, bulky camera, glass plates, a glass plate holder, numerous pans for sensitizing the plates, and a dark tent. He then paid five dollars to a local photographer to instruct him how to use the equipment.

As it happened, Eastman's trip to Santo Domingo never eventuated, but the exercise ignited a fascination with photography and a mission to simplify the process for future travelers and enthusiasts. By day he worked at the bank, by night he experimented at home with photographic plates, until he discovered and launched his first product in the late 1870s: the Eastman (gelatin-coated) Dry Plates. An advertisement for the dry plates in *Anthony's Photographic Bulletin* in June 1881 claimed: "Their preeminent quality is extreme rapidity, by which they are especially adapted to gallery work for taking portraits."[29] The language and style of these early Eastman advertisements suggest that they were targeting professional photographers as their assumed market. They were heavy in text, with few if any illustrations, and employed extensive technical and scientific discourse. Many of them also included testimonials from a number of professional photographers.

In October 1884 an advertisement for the Eastman Dry Plates mentioned amateur photographers for the first time: "Dry Plate Outfits both for the Professional and the Amateur."[30] Eastman continued his photographic experiments and in 1885 added four new products to his range: machine-coated paper, a roll holder, paper film coated with gelatin, and stripping film coated with gelatine. Gradually he achieved his goal of packaging photography for ordinary people. In June 1886 he launched his "detective camera" and displayed a model of it at the St. Louis Photographic Convention. An advertisement in the *Photographic Times Annual* the following year promised: "This Camera is the latest advance in complete apparatus for photography. . . . The camera can be used for instantaneous or time exposures, with or without a tripod."[31] But still the camera cost the considerable sum of $45, and the advertisement relied on technical language. Eastman abandoned the detective camera and set to work on a model that would establish him as the father of modern photography. Thus was born the Kodak Camera, introduced to the world at the Convention of the Photographic Association of America in Minneapolis in 1888.

In less than a year, with the release of the lightweight and cheaper $25 Kodak Camera, Eastman's marketing changed. In September 1888 an advertisement for the new Kodak Camera appeared in the *Scientific American,* one of the first to expressly target novice photographers: "100 instantaneous pictures! Anybody can use it. No knowledge of photography is necessary. The latest and best outfit for amateurs."[32] A month later, another advertisement in the same journal was even more direct: "Makes 100 Instantaneous Pictures by simply pressing a button. Anybody can use it who can wind a watch. No focusing. No tripod. Rapid Rectilinear Lens. Photographs moving objects. Can be used indoors."[33] Within a year the Kodak trademark slogan—"You press the button, we do the rest"—was in circulation.[34]

The first Kodak and its successors were sold as "easy" portable devices to accompany the leisure pursuits of adults and the adventures of children. An advertisement in *Youth Companion* in November 1888 recommended the No.1 Kodak for "Tourists, Wheelmen and Yachtsmen," describing its "neat sole-leather carrying case with shoulder strap" as its most important, distinguishing feature.[35] Kodaks were marketed as the essential accompaniment to an active outdoors American life, documenting American landscapes as well as the exotic curiosities of foreign lands. Photographers were also shown taking pictures of other people.

In the early 1890s, an advertisement illustrated the uses of a Kodak with a man taking a photograph of two women playing tennis, a man taking a photograph through a train window of a number of women standing on the platform, a woman taking a photograph of a city as she and her companions depart on a ship, a man in uniform taking a photograph while on "pedestrian tour," and a man on a bicycle taking a photograph of people arriving on a boat.[36] One Kodak advertisement in December 1888 headed "Sports and Pastimes" focused primarily on pictures of men engaged in outdoor activities: a man photographing his friend diving into a lake ("Caught in the Air"), a man cycling and photographing simultaneously ("Rapid Transit Photography"), a man photographing his friend hauling in a fish on high seas ("Caught on the Fly"), and a woman posing aboard a ship ("On board ship").[37] Eastman not only stamped the Kodak brand with a bounding sense of adventure, he also educated consumers about the various applications for this novel technology.

The Kodak camera was also sold as a much-treasured family companion. The "At Home with The Kodak" advertising campaign linked the ability to document loved ones photographically with the warm hearth of cosy domesticity. One advertisement from the 1890s for "Home Portraiture," featuring a photograph of an angelic child, lulled the reader into a fantasy world: "Views of the snowy landscape, with its leafless trees and field of glistening ice, and flashlight pictures of congenial friends gathered about the warm fireside in long winter evenings, all add to the charms of amateur photography."[38] Other advertisements instructed customers, "Make Kodak your family historian" and "Make somebody happy with a Kodak this year," as the "pictures will serve to make many people happy in the years that follow."[39] Kodak had become the family's trusted, benevolent friend, which through a unique ability to record likenesses would bring happiness and appreciation in years to come.

For the image taker, the Kodak was undoubtedly a machine of many pleasures. Amateur photography became a leading hobby, reaching, in the words of the *New York Tribune* in 1889, the level of a "craze."[40] The next year, *Wilson's Photographic Magazine* reported: "It is the general opinion that there are more amateur photographers in our day than there have been since photography was first discovered. In no other branch of art or science can you find so many devoted and enthusiastic followers. There is no limit to their perseverance, nor difficulty they will not try to surmount in order to secure a picture."[41] By 1896 the Eastman Kodak Company had sold more than a hundred thousand of its hand-held cameras.

For the photographed subject captured in the lens of the Kodak, however, the implications of this craze were more problematic. The number of detective cameras on sale in the late nineteenth century point to the popularity of surreptitious photography. The theme of many advertisements was indeed the thrill of capturing the likeness of another person without their knowledge or consent. The design of cameras also allowed these possibilities. The detective camera first invented by Eastman was so called as its small size and ease of use allowed it to be more readily hidden from view. Later Kodaks were also manufactured and marketed to enhance their function as detective cameras. An 1890 edition of the *Detective* journal included a glowing review of the Kodak Camera: "This device enables us to obtain (instantaneously) perfect pictures of faces, objects, or scenes which may secured without the knowledge or exciting the suspicion of the person or persons whose picture is being taken. . . . As a detective Camera, the Kodak is unequalled; it is a silent but unimpeachable witness; its merits warrant its application for the purposes described. All Sheriffs and Police and Detective departments should provide themselves with one of these valuable aids in the prevention of crime."[42] Eastman wasn't the only manufacturer of the "detective" camera. Others included E. & H. T. Anthony & Company's "Schmid's Patent Detective camera" (1883), Tisdell & Whittlesey's "T. & W. Detective camera" (1887), the Boston Camera Company's "Hawk Eye" detective camera (1888), Paul Nadar's "Express Détective Nadar Tropical Model" (1888), and the American Camera Company's "Demon Detective Camera No. 1" (1889).[43]

Detective cameras were not, however, sold for use only by detectives. A number of advertisements and commentaries suggested that photographing people without their knowledge or consent was encouraged by camera companies as an exciting, titillating pursuit for ordinary people. Photographs could be taken anywhere, anytime. An early 1890s Kodak advertisement in an Australian publication featured a well-dressed man and woman attending a formal public event. He exclaims: "Hang it, I'm sure I heard one of those confounded Kodaks!" To which she replies: "Possibly; my brothers all have them, you know."[44] In an advertisement for the Boston Camera Company, a well-dressed woman passes a couple exiting a shop on a busy street. There is a mischievous glint in her eye, and we see that under her arm is concealed a camera with which she is secretly snapping their picture.[45] By the late nineteenth century, the potential conflict between amateur photographers and their unwilling and unknowing subjects was evident.

Yet public commentary on the objections that were beginning to be voiced—often by women—usually sided with the photographers, who were also the copyright holders. Press editorials dismissed the complaints of unconsenting subjects as "peculiar" expressions of "vanity" and were especially unsympathetic when the pictured subjects were women. As Robert Mensel has observed, the operating metaphor in discussion of such cases was that of a medieval hunt: amateur photographers were "knights of the camera," with "pretty girls" their "natural prey."[46]

But not all publications were unsympathetic to the plight of photographed subjects. The annoyance caused by intrusive amateur photographers was made clear in an article published in the *Ladies Home Journal* in 1900. The author framed the issue as one of "Kodak manners" but noted that "Kodak" was being used as a term for photographic cameras in general: "It must be confessed that the etiquette of the 'kodaker' has not kept pace with the development of the 'kodak.' It is difficult for some people to understand that there are those who have a strong prejudice against being promiscuously 'snapped at' through a camera. . . . [Amateur photographers] have an idea that everything and everybody may be considered as fair game for their cameras, and that no one should interpose objections to being 'snapped.' . . . Whenever this criticism of the 'kodaker' is advanced it is invariably met with the query, 'Where's the harm?' . . . Of course, no harm is done by the simple taking of a picture. But that is not the question. It should be enough for any self-respecting girl or boy, woman or man, that the objection exists."[47] The author acknowledged that the camera was indeed an excellent means of education and the "most potent handmaid of delight ever invented," but if abused it must bring discredit on its possessor. Above all, the author warned presciently, it "must not be employed in violation of private rights."[48]

By the turn of the century, "Kodaker" had become an unflattering term used to describe the impertinent and annoying behavior of chronic picture takers. Even photographic periodicals attempted to distance themselves from amateurs with bad photographic manners: "There is another class who call themselves amateurs, who have as much claim to the title as an Italian organ-grinder has to that of musician. These are the 'press-the-button-we-do-the-rest-amateurs.' No matter where you turn, one of these fiends is sure to bob up. In nearly every instance they annoy everybody with whom they come in contact; they are ridiculed by the press, caricatured by the comic papers, despised by the real amateur, and laughed at by everybody."[49]

To avoid causing annoyance, cameras were designed to be concealed by resembling the shape of everyday objects. Such disguises included imitations of hip flasks (C. P. Stirn's "Concealed Vest camera No. 2," 1888), pocket watches (J. Lancaster & Son's "Patent Watch Camera," 1886), a single book (H. Mackenstein's "Photo-Livre," 1889) or a stack of books (Scovill & Adams's "Book Camera," 1892), women's purses (Charles Alibert's "Kauffer Photo-Sac à Main," 1895), wooden carrying boxes (Max Jurnick's "Tom Thumb Camera," 1889), men's ties (E. Block's "Photo-Cravate," 1890), binoculars (Geymet & Alker's "Photo-Binocular," 1867), photo albums (A. Schaeffner's "Photo-Album," 1892), revolvers (A. Briois's "Thompson's Revolver camera," 1862; E. Enjalbert's "Photo-Revolver de Poche," 1882), and shotguns (Kodak's "Gun Camera," 1915).[50] All of these cameras promised the ability to capture the images of unsuspecting individuals. The shotgun or revolver cameras are particularly fascinating as detective devices, begging the question why it would be more disturbing to have a camera pointed at someone than a gun?

The gun/camera connection went further than gimmicky products. In 1895 Eastman released two new amateur cameras called "Bulls-eye" and "Bullet," and advertisements employed the camera-as-firearm association. Advertisements for the "Bulls-eye" featured a border of bull's-eye motifs, while the "Folding Pocket Kodak" was promoted by an illustration of a man drawing a Kodak from his pocket as he might draw a pistol from a holster.[51] Another Kodak advertisement published in the early 1900s featured a man walking through the woods, with the caption: "There are no game laws for those who hunt with a Kodak."[52] It was at this time that the phrase "to take a shot" entered public discourse to describe the act of photographing an animal, a view, or a woman. Advertisements from 1890 urged photographers to take "A Shot with Kodak."[53]

The camera-as-firearm theme highlighted the conception of the photographic camera as a tool or weapon for the picture taker, rather than an invention for the delight of the pictured subject. It also suggests the ways in which manhood and womanhood were being refashioned and imagined anew in relation to photography in the late nineteenth century. One article from the *New York Times* in 1889 described amateur photographers as "young knights of the camera" who sallied forth with "neat little russet boxes swung jauntily over their shoulders" to capture pictures of "pretty girls." The newspaper was unsympathetic to the plight of the young women "captured": "If the young lady refuses he will perhaps strive to get her picture when she is not on guard just out of spite."[54] Advertisements reinforced the masculinity of "taking a shot" with a Kodak, depicting men in the act of hunting and traveling. Four out of the five illustrations within the "Shot with Kodak" advertisement featured a man holding the camera. As described above, in the first a man photographs women playing tennis, in the second he surreptitiously photographs women on a train platform, in the third he takes a "landscape" shot when on a "pedestrian tour," and in the fourth he photographs people arriving on a boat while he simultaneously rides a bicycle. In the fifth illustration, a woman photographs a city receding into the distance as she and her companions depart on a ship. While a few late nineteenth-century promotions represented women as photographers, more often than not women were depicted as the objects in front of the lens, not the subjects creating pictures behind it.

The "Living Picture" Craze

The advent of cinema was not merely an extension or continuation of developments in photography. Moving pictures marked a point of departure from the image of a stationary, static object seen by a single viewer. Now mass audiences began to be introduced to the magic of moving images. Photography did not parent cinema so much as shape its future definition. Cinema became, aesthetically and culturally, that which photography was not: a medium traversing time and space. It was this temporal and geographical movement that transformed the experience of being a filmed subject. It also propelled cinema toward the function of narrative.

The invention of cinema in the 1890s, as with photography fifty years earlier, was the culmination of an international mix of research and experimentation. The desire to animate pictures derived largely from the industries of toys, magic tricks, and mass entertainment. The ability to do so rested upon numerous technological advances, largely within the medium of photography. In particular, George Eastman's development of celluloid roll film (in 1889), in place of singular plates, marked a significant step toward cinema. It enabled photographic negatives to be passed rapidly not only through a camera lens to capture images but also through a projector for display.

Throughout the nineteenth century, the properties of vision and the possibilities of optic illusion were explored by numerous scientists and entertainers. Certain devices were created that offered viewers the ability to see pictures dancing in front of their eyes, such as the Phenakistoscope, the Zoetrope, and the Praxinoscope.[55] The first images to be freed from static immobility, however, were drawings. Endeavors to display movement had yet to combine with photography. It was not until 1893 that Thomas Edison and W. K. L. Dickson first united these machines of movement with the uncanny clarity of photography to make "movies" with their "Kinetoscope." This breakthrough was followed swiftly by Louis and Auguste Lumière's "Cinematographe" in 1895, which set the speed of motion pictures at sixteen frames per second and elevated motion pictures from the realm of scientific experiment to a commercially viable entertainment industry.

Early cinema was overwhelmingly nonfiction in character. Cameras studied the way the natural world moved, and they traveled through cities and across continents for the delight of eager audiences at home. These roving cameras recorded for the sake of recording and reflected back to city audiences the dynamics and drama of city life. The camera as modern flaneur witnessed (and by doing so produced) spectacles of urban life and bustling street scenes that became highly popular entertainment. Tom Gunning has noted that "exoticism" is no explanation for the fascination with early movies, because while scenes of distant places were popular, early exhibitors' policy of projecting local scenes was equally successful, with crowds merrily applauding moving images of familiar faces and places.[56] The potential excitement of seeing one's own form and features on screen is evident in early motion picture advertising, which exhorted potential audiences, "See yourselves as others see you!"[57]

The history of early film tends to focus upon the experience of those making or viewing cinema, that is, directors, producers, and audiences. Very few scholars have studied how it felt to be recorded by this new medium, to be "caught" on film. And the few who have investigated this experience have generally concentrated on the accounts of professional actors, female and male. In his essay "The Work of Art in the Age of Mechanical Reproduction," Walter Benjamin quoted playwright Pirandello on what it meant to appear on film as opposed to on stage: "The film actor feels as if in exile—exiled not only from the stage but also from himself. With a vague sense of discomfort he feels an inexplicable emptiness; his body loses corporeality, it evaporates, it is deprived of reality, life, voice, and the noise caused by him moving about, in order to be changed into a mute image, flickering an instant on the screen, then vanishing into silence."[58]

Benjamin was one of the few theorists of his time interested in how an appearing subject is affected by his or her representation on film. In arguing that media of mechanical reproduction removed a reproduced object from its spatial and temporal context, from its unique existence, Benjamin conceived of both photography and film as doing a certain violence to the "thing" captured by the camera.[59] Turning his focus to the human subjects of these arts, he observed: "The feeling of strangeness that overcomes the actor before the camera . . . is basically the same kind of estrangement felt before one's own image in the mirror. But now the reflected image has become separable, transportable. And where is it transported? Before the public."[60] As will be demonstrated in the chapters that follow, the process of transporting images of people and making them public profoundly disturbed some of those thus filmed and led to claims for the right of privacy.

More recent work has cast both nineteenth-century photography and early cinema as tools of "detection" to discipline and "mark" the filmed body. Gunning has argued that these technologies attempted to trace, measure, and assign unique identity to the body at a time when it was being lost to the crowds and conditions of modernity: "The body itself appeared abolished, rendered immaterial, through the phantasmagoria of both still and motion photography. . . . The body, rather, became a transportable image fully adaptable to the systems of circulation and mobility that modernity demanded."[61] Gunning and Benjamin have both charged cinema and photography with rendering an assault upon the individual body of the filmed subject. But to conflate the effects of photography and cinema is to misunderstand the distinctive experience of being pictured within a photograph as opposed to being projected on the big screen. The evidence of women who sought redress in courts for embarrassment or humiliation makes clear that cinema has the added capacity to purloin and project a person's individual's movements, mannerisms, expressions, and way of being in the world.

Although early cinema depicted a host of landscapes and steam trains, it was primarily depictions of the human figure, as Jonathan Auerbach has claimed, that enabled cinema to make its impact.[62] In his examination of the screened body and its actions, poses and gestures, Auerbach has argued that early "actualities" and nonfiction films objectified selfhood and visualized self-consciousness. He points to a number of early actualities where the camera's presence compelled subjects to "self-consciously imitate" themselves.[63] Although insightful about the impact of photography on conceptions of selfhood, the work of Benjamin, Gunning, Auerbach, and others never questions the willingness of those captured by the early cinematic camera to be filmed. This book presents extensive evidence of that disturbing experience.

Without records to the contrary, it is easy to assume that those silent and ghostly subjects we see flickering in early documentary or actuality cinema either welcomed the regard of the camera or simply acquiesced in its presence. But not all individuals were happy for their likeness to be projected on the screen in front of millions of expectant and eager eyes. Early court cases involving claims to privacy reveal that the practices of pioneering filmmakers were often considered intrusive and unethical. These cases record vital, but often forgotten, debates involving the status and legal rights of filmed subjects. Rather than focus on the experiences of those who produced or consumed the film footage, *The Face That Launched a Thousand Lawsuits* gives voice to some of the otherwise silent filmed subjects, revealing their distress at finding themselves rendered larger than life on screens in front of large public audiences.

Cinema violated not only the privacy of individuals but also the integrity of individual life stories, through the construction of film narratives. In a lecture entitled "The Law of the Motion Picture Industry" in 1916, Gustavus A. Rogers of the New York Bar quoted the Harvard psychologist and early film theorist Professor Hugo Munsterberg on "what is a motion picture": "The massive outer world has lost its weight; it has been freed from place, time and causality and it has been clothed in the forms of our own consciousness. The mind has triumphed over matter and the pictures reel on with the ease of musical tones. It is a superb enjoyment which no other art can furnish us."[64] Munsterberg's work has been cited as the first comprehensive study of the effects of the film medium. Significantly, Munsterberg considered it a liberating development, freeing the outer world from physical limitations, to be reconstituted by the inner world of emotions, imagination, and memory.[65] Contemporary theorists influenced by Munsterberg, such as Giuliana Bruno, have argued that cinema's initial defining quality was movement, both in a physical (motion) and in a psychological (emotion) sense.[66] It was this capacity for spatial and temporal movement that propelled cinema toward narrative.

At the beginning of the twentieth century, cinema quickly became one of the most popular producers of stories for a mass audience, creating an insatiable market for intriguing and revealing tales. The plots of plays, novels, and historical events all became fodder for the fiction film industry. But so too did the achievements, tragedies, mistakes, and adventures of living individuals. Suddenly the lives of war veterans, naval heroes, and high-society ladies were not only featured in newspapers or books but also elaborated upon in color and detail in moving picture theaters. The line between fiction and nonfiction blurred as the imperatives of drama and suspense took over. The individuals at the center of the tales began to feel robbed of their lives, experiences, and reputations. In the courts privacy was invoked, particularly in the jurisdiction of California, where Hollywood was located, to reclaim ownership of those narratives.

The existential anxieties occasioned by becoming a filmed subject played themselves out as practical and legal challenges in the late nineteenth and early twentieth centuries. To become an image on film was to lose self-possession and self-determination, as an image taken for one purpose was appropriated and manipulated for another. In the United Sates, the unauthorized circulation of still and moving portraits emerged as a major legal issue in the late nineteenth century. As one *New York Times* author put it in 1889: "It is a question of debate what rights the amateur has in securing pictures, and of course there are some who consider a party of young women as free as subjects of photography as the waterfall or clump of trees."[67] People felt closer to and identified with filmed images but were disconnected from the production and reproduction of such images. The emotional stakes became higher, but regulation more difficult. Women, for reasons I explore in the ensuing chapters, experienced this tension between identification and dispossession most acutely.

In the rest of the book, I show how a right to privacy was appropriated as a legal discourse, primarily (but not always) by women, to assert rights to the filmed images of their faces and bodies—images that were being published, circulated, exploited, and denigrated by others in a variety of public domains. In the ocularcentric culture of this period, to be a modern woman meant cultivating a visual presence, as Liz Conor has argued, not simply in self-presentation but on paper and celluloid. If photography and cinema provided the means for such endeavors, the doctrine of privacy became a chosen weapon with which to define, limit, and assert one's rights over the resulting products. In the following chapters I introduce some of the women and men who pushed for recognition of the rights of pictured subjects and the diversity of their reasons for doing so. The cases demonstrate the importance of the doctrine of a right to privacy to early contestations over film and photography, and the activism of individual women in courts even as unenfranchised citizens. Their stories, as yet largely untold, form the basis of a vivid and compelling history of the establishment of the right to privacy within United States law.

2

"Has a Beautiful Girl the Right to Her Own Face?"

Privacy, Propriety, and Property

In 1900 the seventeen-year-old Rochester orphan Abigail Roberson suffered "severe nervous shock" and was "confined to her bed" and "compelled to employ a physician" when she recognized her own pretty face on a packet of flour purchased by her next-door neighbor.[1] The foundational case of *Roberson v. Rochester Folding Box* involved the unauthorized use of an image of an attractive young woman's face to sell flour at the end of the nineteenth century. It roused intense public interest in the vulnerability of photographed subjects, and although the case was defeated in court, it led to new privacy laws being passed in New York State.[2] In legal scholarship of the time and subsequently, Roberson became the pinup girl for privacy rights as much as she had been for flour.[3] She was not the first, however, to call for rights in relation to photographic portraits. From the 1860s discussion had already begun in newspapers, courtrooms, and law reviews concerning the novel harms being experienced by photographed individuals and appropriate legal protections.

It became clear that individuals did not suffer these harms equally. Case records and periodical articles indicate that women's pictures were used without their consent far more commonly than were men's. Developments in photography, the rise of shopping as a leisure pursuit, changes in graphic advertising, and the rise of the periodical press at the turn of the century combined to render a woman's beauty a valuable asset worthy of exploitation. Men's images were also used to sell products, but with far less frequency. Perhaps unsurprisingly, many women were not flattered by the unexpected appearance of their faces on a product advertisement, within a magazine or on a greeting card. They began to look for ways to resist such treatment. In this chapter I show that the mechanisms for prohibiting the use of women's pictures without their consent were influenced by changing discourses on womanhood, with a shift from concern about vulnerable "ladies" in need of male "protection" to assertions by women themselves demanding their own privacy rights and recognition of their autonomy.

Initially deployed to defend traditional womanly traits of modesty and reserve, the doctrine of privacy began to offer a level of legal control to aggrieved pictured subjects. By so doing it enabled women to remove themselves from public view if they wished to, but it also allowed them agency to articulate and negotiate the terms of their public representations. I argue that privacy can be understood as one of the many rights for which women campaigned at the end of the nineteenth and beginning of the twentieth centuries. There was no organized movement, but a group of individuals, who, by taking their demands to court, began to have a remarkable impact upon statutory and common law in the United States.

"A Bill to Protect Ladies"

In an 1869 piece entitled "The Legal Relations of Photographs" in the *American Law Register,* one jurist mused presciently: "So, if a likeness, once lawfully taken, were, without permission, to be multiplied for gain, the artist reckoning on the beauty or distinction of the original for extensive sale, it might be considered whether there was a natural copyright, possessed by every person of his or her own features, for which the courts would be bound to furnish redress."[4] The author referred to a recent case in Europe in which an artist photographed an attractive lady of high rank at the Austrian court in Vienna and sold copies in another city. Relaying the details from an unnamed newspaper, he noted that the "injured lady" successfully brought a suit against the artist, but that the grounds for, or nature and extent of, the recovery were not reported. He supposed "special damage" (financial loss) may have formed the basis of the claim, as "her right to control the market of her own beauty could not have been denied her by any court."[5] In hindsight, and in light of subsequent history, the early assumption that an individual, particularly a woman, should have exploitable rights to her own image seems surprising.

A decade later, the question of whether an individual should have rights to his or her own photographic likeness would touch the highest office in the United States. In 1885 Democratic President Grover Cleveland entered the White House as a bachelor but soon after married Frances Folsom, the pretty twenty-one-year-old daughter of a good friend.

Cleveland was the second president to marry in office and the only one to hold his wedding in the White House. Understandably, there was intense public interest in the new First Lady, and her picture circulated widely. So attractive was her countenance that her likeness soon began to appear, without her consent, on numerous product advertisements, from Pearline petroleum products (such as soap) to pianos and pharmaceutical nostrums and even advertisements for beer, cigarettes, and snuff tobacco.[6]

In early 1888 John Robert Thomas, a Republican Congressman from Illinois and lawyer by profession, was reportedly recovering from illness and visiting a drugstore in Washington, D.C., when he happened upon a nostrum advertisement picturing the First Lady.[7] He was apparently so incensed by the audacity of the advertisement and the inability of the First Lady to prevent the use of her picture that on 6 March 1888 he introduced a bill into the House of Representatives entitled "A Bill to Protect Ladies."[8] The preamble to the bill stated its purpose as follows: "To prohibit the use of likenesses, portraits, or representations of females for advertising purposes, without consent in writing. . . . Whereas the wives, daughters, mothers and sisters of American citizens . . . are entitled to protection from the vulgar and unauthorized use, for advertising purposes, of their likeness, portrait or representation, produced or reproduced by photographic, lithographic, chromographic or other means."[9]

It stipulated that any person who publicly exhibited, used, or employed the likeness, portrait, or representation of any female, living or dead, who was the "wife, daughter, mother or sister of any citizen of the United States," without consent in writing, would be guilty of a high misdemeanor and liable for a fine of between $500 and $5,000. The wording of the bill would echo years later in the "appropriation of name or likeness" laws first passed in New York State in 1903,[10] regarded by legal authorities as one of the four "common law privacy torts."[11] In 1888, however, the term "privacy" was notably absent from the bill. Rather, there was outrage at the offence caused to the female relatives of citizens of the United States.

The language of the bill reminded legislators that only men enjoyed rights of citizenship. Women were their dependents. For women fighting for equal rights in the late nineteenth century, the fact that women were defined via their familial relationships with male citizens was especially galling. It highlighted the enduring power of the English common law doctrine of coverture, inherited by the United States as former British colonies. Sir William Blackstone described it in the following terms: "By marriage, the husband and wife are one person in law; that is, the very being or legal existence of the woman is suspended during the marriage, or at least is incorporated and consolidated into that of the husband."[12] As a number of legal historians have argued, through coverture married women effectively lost their citizenship—the duties they owed to their husbands trumped those they owed to the state.[13] They also lost legal personhood, such as the ability to own or trade property or sue in their own names. This systematic subordination of women to men was usually dressed in the benevolent language of protection and privilege as occurred in a Bill to Protect Ladies.[14]

The use of the word "ladies" in the name of the bill was also significant. In *No Constitutional Right to Be Ladies*, Linda Kerber has pointed out that rather than shielding women from the burdens inherent in citizenship, the doctrine of coverture worked to conceal practices that made women more vulnerable to forms of private and public power. "As long as married women were understood to owe virtually all their obligation to their husbands," Kerber wrote, "they could make no claims of rights against the political community."[15] The Bill to Protect Ladies may have derived from Congressman Thomas's concern about the inability of ladies to control the use of their portraits, but it stopped short of providing American women with any rights as citizens themselves.

Nonetheless, it is important to note that by recognizing the rights of pictured subjects in photographic portraits, the bill did challenge the prevailing doctrine of copyright, which since 1865 had vested all rights in relation to a photograph in the photographer alone. For this reason, the bill swiftly attracted the attention of professional photographers, who were concerned that their practice of displaying the negatives of portraits to illustrate their artistic abilities was under threat. In a letter to the editor of the *Philadelphia Photographer* entitled "A Danger Ahead," one photographer warned: "I know that in years past you were always ready to defend photographers in their rights. . . . It seems to be thought here that the Bill will pass the House. As it reads, a photographer is prohibited from exhibiting photographs of ladies in his own gallery; we would be in a sad plight with such a law."[16]

It was clear that the interests—and proposed rights—of those in front of the camera's lens would potentially collide with the interests of those behind it. Granting rights to the "pretty faces" pictured would impede the ability of photographers to profit, as they would be restricted in reproducing, selling, and distributing their images. An association of thirty-five photographers and photographic studios in the thirty-second district of New York State went so far as to lodge an official petition against the bill with their local congressional representative, the Honorable John M. Farquhar, arguing: "The text [of the Bill] will prevent Photographers from exhibiting, even in the most proper way, any picture of any lady customer (a privilege which custom has always acceeded [*sic*] us, unless the lady makes objection). We do respectfully urge you to use your influence to secure some modification of said Bill, to exempt Photographers from its operations."[17] The proposed exemption was not necessary. The bill was referred to the Judiciary Committee, subsequently lost traction, and never went to a vote.

General press coverage of the bill was minimal, as it seems to be have been overshadowed by other political issues. One article in the *Albany Evening Journal* entitled "Our Representative Women" did, however, offer vehement opposition to the proposed law, suggesting that the First Lady might indeed be considered common property: "The bill whose main purpose is to prohibit the use of the President's wife's portrait for advertising purposes is not wise. It is inevitable that a pretty woman in public station should be advertised to some extent, and there is no harm in it."[18] The writer argued that the first lady of the land was the property of the people in "so far as the art of printing [was] concerned" and that nothing could destroy that right of possession. The use of her or any other woman's portrait in advertisements, the author contended, should be regarded as a "compliment" rather than an annoyance.

This article provoked the *Sacramento Daily Record-Union* to publish an editorial in March 1888 criticizing the *Albany Journal* for its "faulty views."[19] It is all very well, they argued, for the public to assert a property claim in the faces of women occupying public positions ("great singers and actresses, and the women notable as philanthropists or for beauty, daring or great works"), but such a claim must be secondary to the primary right of an individual to determine how and when her portrait would be used. "If one has not the *right to privacy* in this matter, as well as in other domestic concerns, then the limitation upon the use of portraits cannot be defined at all. Evidently the right to reproduce in portraiture one's features is a personal one and belongs to the owner of the face, or in case of minors, to the guardian. . . . The protest of the bill is not an evidence of snobbery, or of exclusiveness; it is simply a protest against making the *privacy* of life indecently public, and to just that extent it is proposed to fortify and protect the personal right to have one's features copied in print."[20] Thus two years before Warren and Brandeis published their article in the *Harvard Law Review* this Californian newspaper introduced the idea of a right to privacy to this debate for the first time.[21]

The introduction of the Bill to Protect Ladies and the subsequent discussion in which a right to privacy was invoked and a challenge to copyright law contemplated help contextualize the 1890 article by Warren and Brandeis. Their conception of a right to privacy, promoted, in part, to remedy the problems posed by photography and the unauthorized circulation of private portraits, was highly influential but not without precedent. Interestingly, their article failed to mention or to refer to the experience of President Cleveland's wife, the 1888 Bill to Protect Ladies, or the surrounding debate that first contemplated rights accruing to "the owner of the face" rather than to the photographer, giving rise to the idea of a right to privacy. This is especially odd given that Samuel Warren's wife, Mabel Bayard Warren, was a good friend of the First Lady's during the relevant period.[22]

In the same year as debate concerning the unauthorized use of "pretty portraits" intensified in the United States, it first reached the courts of the United Kingdom.[23] In 1888 Alice Pollard attended the studio and shop of the Photographic Company in Rochester, England, and "there had her photograph taken in various positions"[24] and "paid for likenesses of herself taken from negatives then made and for photographs of other members of her family."[25] Some months later, it came to her attention that Mr. Box, the photographer and proprietor, was exhibiting in his shop window, for sale, one of the photographic portraits of her "got up" as a Christmas card. Justice North described the card in the following terms: "[T]he photographic vignette has been decorated by the addition thereto, above and below the figure, of scrolls of what I suppose are intended for leaves, with the superscription, also in leafy letters, of the words 'A Merry Christmas and a Happy New Year.' "[26]

Pollard brought legal action against Mr. Box, demanding he desist from using her image to sell goods in his store. Evidence was given at trial that when Mr. Andrews, Pollard's attorney, visited Box's shop and asked about the photograph in the window, a copy was produced for sale. Andrews and Box gave conflicting stories as to their conversation regarding Box's authority to offer it for sale. Box claimed the photograph served as a specimen to invite orders for others to be taken in a similar manner, as a means of advertising his photographic ability. By displaying the photograph of Pollard in the window, Box used the beauty of her face to attract attention to his studio.

Alice Pollard won her suit. The court found for her on the grounds of breach of contract, breach of confidence, and copyright. Everything hinged on the relationship between Box and Pollard as vendor and customer, Justice North stating: "[T]he customer who sits for the negative thus puts the power of reproducing the object in the hands of the photographer: and in my opinion the photographer who uses the negative to produce other copies for his own use, without authority, is abusing the power confidentially placed in his hands . . . the [Copyright] Act provides that when the negative of any photograph is made or executed for or on behalf of another person for good or valuable consideration . . . copyright shall belong to the person for or on whose behalf the same shall have been made."[27] It is vital here to note that copyright refers to copyright in the photo, not Pollard's face. The fact that judgment in this case depended upon the relationship of trade between her and Box raised questions as to what would have occurred without such a clear commercial transaction. What if Pollard had been passing on the street outside the shop and had her photograph snapped by Box and then displayed? Without a relationship or prior agreement, Pollard would not have been able to stop Box using her likeness. Justice North stated definitively in his judgment that "a person has no property in *his* own features."[28]

The masculine language of the law, invoked here for its apparent universality, jars with the gendered circumstances of the grievance. As the Bill to Protect Ladies also suggested, this was an issue primarily affecting women. Thus, the *Ladies' Home Journal* warned its readers in 1890: "While the great majority of professional photographers are men of honor and responsibility . . . women should always know the standing of the man to whom they entrust their negatives. . . . The negative once in his possession (if he is so disposed), he has the means of causing them great mortification by using it for base purposes."[29] The author stated that the journal had repeatedly received the thanks of women for calling their attention to this "matter of great importance."[30]

The circumstances in *Pollard,* where a professional photographer reproduced and used the negative of a female client for an unauthorized purpose, were not uncommon in the United States and Europe in the nineteenth century. In 1890 the Supreme Court of Minnesota heard the case of *Moore v. Rugg,*[31] which was decided wholly on the basis of the *Pollard* decision. According to Justice Collins, the plaintiff, Moore, engaged the services of a professional photographer, Rugg, to take and make photographic portraits of her. The defendant did so, but he also struck off another photograph from the negatives, which he delivered to a detective for a purpose that was described by the court as "highly improper."[32] The defendant's action breached his agreement with the plaintiff, as "almost an unlimited number might also be printed from the negative but the contract included, by implication, an agreement that the negative for which the plaintiff sat should only be used for the printing of such portraits as she might order or authorize."[33]

A number of similar cases were also being heard in Europe, as the *American Journal of Photography* noted in an article entitled "Photographic Jurisprudence in Germany."[34] The question of the "ownership of the photographic negative" was hotly disputed. At a recent meeting of photographers in Berlin a letter was received from a Hamburg photographer who wrote: "I exhibited the portrait of a young lady whom I had photographed without first obtaining her permission to exhibit a duplicate. Shortly afterwards I received a communication from an advocate to remove the picture. This I did at once. I then received another communication demanding reimbursement of the expenses incurred by the young lady. The latter I refused to comply with. After a lapse of five months I am suddenly summoned to defend a suit. . . . Have I any chance to win? And how does my case stand? According to my views as a layman, I did not exhibit the lady, but merely my proficiency as a professional photographer."[35]

In this case all justices agreed that no photographer had the right to promiscuously exhibit his portraits, but because the Hamburg photographer had removed the picture on request, he was not liable. The court discussed the law in question (section 7 of the *Imperial Code of January 1876*), which stated that without prior contract, all rights of ownership in a likeness or portrait photographically reproduced vested with the original sitter. In this example and the others noted by the court, the photographic subject pressing for rights in her image was a "lady" and the picture taker a "gentleman."

There were very few cases, if any, in the nineteenth century of attractive men being used to sell goods and services. Where male plaintiffs did seek redress for "appropriated name and likeness," it was usually their name or face as a symbol of their professional standing and status that was the basis of their claim.[36] Such circumstances often allowed the men involved to successfully plead defamation, as their public reputation had been brought into disrepute. This outcome can be contrasted with cases concerning the use of likeness alone, because if the photograph of an unnamed woman was a "good" one, she was not considered defamed and therefore largely left without remedy (prior to the enactment or common law recognition of privacy laws). When legal scholarship combines both types of case into one category, that of appropriated name or likeness, it obscures the distinct and different kinds of harm suffered. Only when a name (with or without a likeness) was connected with a product or service could it be said that an "identity" was being "appropriated" or "borrowed." If a nameless "pretty" face was used in an advertisement, an individual's identity was not appropriated but obliterated. She became generic—an anonymous object to be consumed by the gaze of others.

The *Pollard* case demonstrated the burgeoning distinction in reasoning between the United States and the United Kingdom on these matters. Privacy was not raised in *Pollard* although the facts strongly resembled those privacy cases that would dominate court dockets in the United States, especially New York, during the following decades. The fact that privacy was not mentioned might highlight the difficulty of framing such a wrong as an invasion of privacy. In order to pose for Box, Pollard must have walked down the same public street in which her face was subsequently exhibited and willingly entered his studio. It begins to become clear that maintaining privacy by avoiding public exposure was less women's concern than the ways in which their images were used and their sense of self diminished.

When Warren and Brandeis brought the issue of the unauthorized circulation of private portraits to the attention of legal scholars and used it to argue for a common law right to privacy, they didn't refer to earlier newspaper discussion of the issue but chose instead to cite the recent case of *Manola v. Stevens*,[37] reported by the *New York Times* in June 1890. "The alleged facts of a somewhat notorious case brought before an inferior tribunal in New York a few months ago, directly involved the consideration of the right of circulating portraits; and the question whether our law will recognize and protect the right to privacy in this and in other respects must soon come before our courts for consideration."[38] As their footnote explained, this case concerned the actress Marion Manola, who, while performing on a Broadway stage in a costume with tights, was photographed surreptitiously from one of the theater boxes by the manager and defendant, Benjamin Stevens, and the photographer, Meyers. At the time, twenty-four-year-old Manola was a famous stage star in New York and was playing the role of Bul-Bul in the comic opera *Castle in the Sky*, staged by the De Wolf Hopper Opera Company.

It is curious that Warren and Brandeis chose this case to argue the need for a right to privacy. Perhaps this was due to the sensationalizing account in the *New York Times,* which in the first of a series of articles reported that Manola "refused to be photographed in tights owing to her modesty."[39] Other newspaper reports, however, queried "modesty" as her primary motive and suggested rather that she disliked the idea of becoming a tradable sexual object. She did not want her picture to become "common property, circulated from hand to hand, and treasured by every fellow who can raise the price demanded by the photographer for a copy of the picture."[40] In another interview Manola explained: "Well, I am not prudish and I should not like to be made to appear so. I have no objection to wearing tights on the stage—that is part of the business of my profession. But I object to being photographed in such a costume. My chief objection is that I have a daughter, only 10 years old, and I don't want her to see pictures of her mother in shop windows in such costumes as I am now wearing."[41]

The dispute highlighted the novel problems posed for public performers by the medium of photography. Suddenly, their appearance, skill, and appeal were divorced from the command of their actual presence and fractured into potentially infinite images for anonymous greedy consumption by common fellows. An analysis by the *Atlanta Constitution* made an insightful observation about the difference between a live performance and circulating photographs: "Miss Manola's tights, with their contents, belong to her. She has a right to exhibit them, but there is a difference between bewildering the spectators in the theatre for a few moments with a glimpse of something gorgeous and the cold matter-of-fact reality of a photograph to be hawked about and critically examined."[42]

The extensive newspaper discussion of Marion Manola's case was, as Dorothy Glancy has noted, primarily oriented to property rights, that is, who "owned" her pleasing figure: the gentlemen of the public, the photographer, or Manola herself?[43] It is significant that the foundational cases concerning privacy in relation to images, both in the United States and elsewhere, concerned the use and distribution of photographs of attractive young women. The press consistently described Manola as "pretty," "shapely and attractive," "beautiful," and "appealing."[44] Her photograph was snapped because of its ability to attract the attention of admiring and desiring crowds. The court granted Manola an interim injunction restraining Stevens and Myers from using her photograph on an ex parte basis, as they failed to appear in court or lodge a defense. Ten years after Manola's case another "pretty" young woman from New York would quote Warren and Brandeis to claim new rights for individuals in relation to their photographic portraits.

Roberson v. Rochester Folding Box Co.

In 1900, when young Abigail Roberson suffered "nervous shock" as a consequence of recognizing her likeness on a bag of flour, she instigated a case that would change legal history in the United States. Under the authority of her guardian, her aunt, Margaret E. Bell, Roberson sought legal advice and brought an action in the Supreme Court of New York, Monroe County, against Rochester Folding Box Company and

Franklin Mills Flour seeking damages of $15,000, a permanent injunction against the defendants using her image, and the destruction of all existing advertising material featuring her face. The complaint alleged "that without her knowledge or consent, the defendants had within the last three years, knowing they had no right or authority to do so, obtained, made, printed, sold and circulated about 25,000 lithographic prints, photographs and likenesses of the plaintiff for the purpose of profit and gain to themselves; . . . that the lithographic photograph or likeness of the plaintiff . . . is made upon white, rough paper, which is about 22 inches wide and about 30 inches long. The likeness of the plaintiff is a large profile view, being on the central portion of said paper . . . above the likeness are the words, in large, plain letters, 'Flour of the Family.' "[45] It was further elaborated that these posters of the plaintiff were conspicuously displayed in "stores, warehouses, saloons, and other public places throughout the United States and other countries, and particularly in the vicinity where the plaintiff resided."[46]

At first instance, Justice Davy heard a demurer by the defendants to dismiss the complaint on the basis that it did not state facts sufficient to constitute a cause of action. The defendants' argument was understandable, for the complaint articulated no claim known to common law, equity, or statute. Within submissions, however, Milton E. Gibbs, the plaintiff's lawyer and future champion of women's suffrage in Monroe County,[47] constructed an innovative argument based upon the twin claims of privacy and property. Gibbs argued that the plaintiff had a "right to privacy," which a Court of Equity should protect, and she had a "property right in her own features and beauty, which is absolute until voluntarily surrendered by her." On the point of an equitable right to privacy, he submitted: "Notice the acts of the defendants. They obtain, without [the] plaintiff's consent, her picture, and enlarge it; make thousands of them and circulate them for the purpose of making money and for that only. Do the defendants intend to *honor* the plaintiff by these acts? Is it showing *respect* to a beautiful young woman to hang her picture as an advertisement in restaurants and saloons? Is it to teach mankind lessons in philanthropy and morality? To ask these questions is to answer them."[48]

Roberson's supporters made much of her femininity and modesty. Justice Davy continually described Abigail as "modest and refined," a "modest and retiring" young woman, for whom such publicity was "extremely disagreeable and offensive," causing "great mental distress and injury."[49] Some feminist scholars have critiqued the outmoded assumptions about female modesty and seclusion that informed the legal discourse on privacy in the late nineteenth century.[50] Anita Allen and Erin Mack highlight the ways in which traditional norms required that "women, much more than men, exhibit speech, dress, and behaviour calculated to deflect attention from their bodies, views or desires."[51] Women, they argue, suffered from a surfeit of "the wrong kind of privacy" related to modesty, seclusion, and reserve and too little when it came to privacy within the home and autonomous choice.[52] Mack and Allen rightly conclude that there has been little gender-conscious discussion of privacy, as "legal scholars seldom focus squarely on the possibility that gender may have a role in explaining the shape of precedent."[53]

It is the case that the language of modesty, propriety, and honor pervaded the privacy arguments put forward by Gibbs and the various judgments in *Roberson*. Mack and Allen fail to recognize, however, that although privacy debates employed a traditional, conservative discourse, they were responding to wrongs and harms that were far from traditional, and rapid social and cultural change meant women were experiencing new types of harm. Women formed the majority of privacy plaintiffs, I suggest, not because the privacy doctrine espoused conventional norms of femininity but because this doctrine as it developed in response to action by women related specifically to the circulation of women's pictures. It was women who formed the majority of commercially exploited subjects and primarily women whose images were circulated for the gratification and profit of men. While women used the legal language available to them and shaped its meaning, we can never assume such discourse adequately reflected or represented their experiences or the redress they sought.

The potentially more radical property claim advanced by Gibbs took the following form: "The defendants are estopped from denying that the lithographic likenesses of [the] plaintiff are not of value and are not property. . . . Is it reasonable to suppose that the defendant corporations have sold 25,000 of these lithographs if they are not of value? *The value is not in the paper; it is in the picture.* . . . If the plaintiff has such a beautiful countenance that her photographic likeness is saleable in the markets, who is entitled to the proceeds of such sales? Is [it] any person who first steals the likeness, or obtains it in any manner without permission of the original owner? If that is so, then a new and strange theory of property must be read into the law."[54]

Gibbs's radical proposition that the court should recognize a woman's property right in her own face accorded with his suffragist sympathies. In his *New York Times* obituary, Gibbs was described as a "progressive" force in the Democratic Party, and after bringing the foundational privacy case in U.S. legal history, he went on to lead the Democratic campaign for women's suffrage in Monroe County in 1915. He also became district attorney, deputy attorney general, and a judge on the New York Court of Claims.[55] Unlike the Bill to Protect Ladies, Gibbs's proposed property right contested, rather than supported, the doctrine of coverture, and unlike a right to privacy, it did so on terms of equality rather than entrenching the gendered segregation of public and private spheres.

At the time of Gibbs's argument, the authority of the doctrine of coverture was being challenged and the position of women in the United States was in a state of rapid transition. A succession of state-based Married Women's Property Acts had changed the law since 1848 to allow women to hold property and sue in their own names.[56] By 1900 the divorce rate had risen to one in twelve couples, with two-thirds of divorces sought by women. By 1910 one couple in nine was divorcing. The proportion of women choosing never to marry at all had risen from 6 percent throughout the nineteenth century to 10 percent by the 1890s. Only 47 percent of twenty- to twenty-four-year-olds were married.

The decision to remain single or seek a divorce was enabled in part by women's increased participation in formal education and the paid workforce. In 1870 the percentage of college-age American women who enrolled in higher education was 0.7 percent; the rate had increased by 1900 to just under 3 percent, and by 1920 to just under 8 percent. These numbers were proportionally small but indicated significant social change. Between 1900 and 1930, women's enrolment at colleges and universities tripled. Although women made up only 35 percent of the college population in 1890, by 1920 their participation had leapt to constitute just more than 47 percent of college enrolment.

At the same time, women entered the paid workforce in increasing numbers, a matter of necessity as well as desire. In 1890, 40 percent of all single white women, 60 percent of single nonwhite women, and 70 percent of foreign-born women were employed outside the home.[57] By 1900 an estimated five million women, or one in every five, were employed in industries, including textile manufacturing, secretarial work, sales, housekeeping, primary education, nursing, agriculture, and domestic service. Approximately 10 percent of working women occupied professional positions as teachers and clerks. These figures highlight the rapid change in women's aspirations, circumstances, and legal status. As Karen Manners-Smith has argued, these shifts reflected in part the emergence of a "new eager and purposeful generation of women" who demanded greater rights and responsibilities.[58] At seventeen years old in 1900, Abigail Roberson was one of this new generation.

So profound was the social impact of the change in women's lives and ideas of womanhood at the turn of the last century that a new term emerged to describe the modern feminine ideal: the New Woman. This new figure, who rejected traditional womanly traits and roles, became a subject of much debate. In 1894 Sarah Grand published her influential essay "New Aspects of the Woman in Question" in the *North American Review.* Grand wrote that the New Woman had pondered women's position "until at last she solved the problem and proclaimed for herself what was wrong with Home-is-the-Woman's-Sphere, and prescribed the remedy."[59] The New Woman recognized that she was part of a worldwide phenomenon: the "sudden and violent upheaval of the suffering sex." "Women were awaking from their long apathy," Grand wrote, "and, as they awoke, like healthy hungry children unable to articulate, they began to whimper for they knew not what."[60] For many women the whimper became a loud demand.

Clearly connected to suffragist politics, the ideal of the New Woman also resonated with all those fleeing the bondage of marriage and a life sentence of self-sacrifice; with those pursuing achievement through career and work outside the home; and those embracing greater sexual freedom. Grand's championing of New Womanhood as the reexamination of "the whole social system," which had been "managed or mismanaged" by men for "all these ages" did not go uncontested, however. Another woman writer, Ouida, wrote in reply that the New Woman was a "menace to humankind" with "her fierce vanity, her undigested knowledge, her over-weening estimate of her own value and her fatal want of all sense of the ridiculous."[61] Ouida defended the virtue of traditional womanly traits, such as modesty, commending its distinctive charm: "Modesty is no doubt a thing of education and prejudice, a conventionality artificially stimulated; but it is exquisite grace, and womanhood without it loses its most subtle charm. Nothing tends so to destroy modesty as the publicity and promiscuity of schools, of hotels, of railway trains and sea voyages. True modesty shrinks from the curious gaze of other women as from the coarser gaze of man."[62]

Such public discussions of women's modern aspirations at the end of the nineteenth century provide a crucial context for the emergence of the legal doctrine of privacy. At a time when gender roles were in flux, the assertion of a right to privacy appeared to reinforce traditional conceptions of womanhood by emphasising the importance of modesty for women wanting to retreat from the public gaze. But women took heart from the ideal of New Womanhood by conceptualizing a quasi-property right in their images and asserting the right to control when and how one's image could be used and by whom. The doctrine of privacy had ambiguous implications for women, as it invoked a conservative discourse to potentially radical effect.

When Milton Gibbs proposed in support of Roberson that she had tradable rights in her own image and that she had property rights in her own "likeness," the trial judge, Justice Davy, was moved to reflect at length on the implications of this argument. He began his judgment with this conservative observation: "Every woman has a right to keep her face concealed from the observation of the public."[63] But then he added: "Her face is her own private property, and no photographer would have a right to take advantage of the privilege of taking her photograph for her own use, to make copies from the negative and sell them to the public."[64] He referred to *Pollard*[65] and took issue with the English ruling that no one had property rights in his or her own features: "If her lithographic likeness, owing to its beauty, is of great value as a trade-mark or an advertising medium, it is a property right which belongs to her."[66] He also cited the judgment of Justice Colt in the Massachusetts decision of *Corliss v. E. W. Walker Co.*:[67] "Independently of the question of contract, I believe the law to be that a private individual has a right to be protected in the representation of his portrait in any form; that this is a property as well as a personal right."[68] At this point, the doctrine of privacy seemed capable of awarding property rights in one's appearance.

When Chief Justice Parker of the New York Court of Appeals finally dashed Roberson's hopes in a controversial four-to-three decision, he confined consideration of the arguments to the right of privacy. He did not entertain the possibility that individuals might have property in their likeness. Treading a judicially cautious path, he was clearly concerned about the "vast field of litigation" that could result as a consequence of ruling that individuals had enforceable privacy rights in their images.[69] Wary about the court entering the novel legal territory of a right to privacy, he tempted the New York legislature to do so: "[T]he legislative body could very well interfere and arbitrarily provide that no one should be permitted for his own selfish purpose to use the picture or the name of another for advertising purposes without his consent."[70]

Following this unpopular decision against Roberson, the New York legislature heeded Parker's advice and in 1903 almost copied word for word the cause of action suggested by the chief justice. Section 1 of chapter 132 of the New York Laws of 1903 stated: "A person, firm or corporation that uses for advertising purposes, or for the purposes of trade, the name, portrait or picture of any living person without having first obtained the written consent of such person, or if a minor of his or her parent or guardian, is guilty of a misdemeanor."[71] Section 2 of chapter 132 provided an individual whose name, portrait, or picture was used as proscribed under the above provision with the ability to seek an injunction prohibiting further misconduct by the offending party and/or to recover damages.[72]

Chief Justice Parker was careful not to appear insensitive to Roberson's claims and distress, but he also observed that some people would find such publicity "agreeable" and that some others "would have appreciated the compliment to their beauty implied by the selection of the picture for such purposes."[73] His remarks are interesting because he was clearly thinking of women when he referred to "others"—it was unlikely that he would ever envisage, let alone welcome, his own image being used to sell flour in the United States and abroad.

But only a year after *Roberson,* the chief justice's judgment would return to haunt him. In 1904, he became a Democratic candidate for president and attracted much unwanted publicity. He warned the press publicly that he and his family would no longer tolerate being the subjects of "ubiquitous photography" and being "everlastingly afraid [of being] snapped by some fellow with a camera."[74]

Parker's objections to being photographed by a fellow with a camera were reported in local newspapers, provoking the particular anger of one young reader. Abigail Roberson wrote an open letter to the former chief justice, published in the *New York Times,* in which she quoted his words back to him: "I take this opportunity to remind you," wrote Roberson, "that you have no such right as that which you assert. I have very high authority for my statement, being nothing less than a decision of the Court of Appeals of this State wherein you wrote the prevailing opinion. . . . You referred to my cause of action as a 'so-called' right of privacy, and admitted that such publicity, 'which some find agreeable,' is to the plaintiff very distasteful, and that I suffered mental distress, 'when others would have appreciated the compliment to their beauty,' and in an opinion sixteen pages long you arrived at the conclusion that I had no rights that could be protected by your tribunal. . . . I am forced to the conclusion that this incident well illustrates the truth of the old saying that it makes a lot of difference whose ox is gored."[75]

Roberson's eloquent and fiery riposte challenges the characterization of "privacy" plaintiffs such as herself as "modest and retiring" ladies. Here was a twenty-two-year-old woman challenging the former chief justice of New York and possible future president by advancing a basic premise of twentieth-century feminist legal theory, that gender identification defines the structure of law. Roberson could see that Chief Justice Parker's inability to identify with her meant he could not understand or empathize with her plight, which led to his unwillingness to provide her with a remedy. Her argument supports the proposition that the law privileges the interests of those who create and enforce it. As feminist legal scholar Regina Graycar has noted in "The Gender of Judgments": "Because of the long-standing exclusion of women from law, the substantive legal doctrines we use on a day-to-day basis were developed by men, with their problems and concerns in mind, and reflect men's perspectives on the world."[76] Roberson lost her case due to the inability of the common law to recognize her gendered grievance as legitimate. But as a result of the action taken by Roberson and others who came after her, the legal doctrine of privacy was shaped by women to address their distinctive problems and concerns.

By the end of the nineteenth century, the suffragists had the common law, that ancient and unyielding tradition responsible for their disenfranchisement, clearly in their sights. As Kathleen Sullivan explains in *Constitutional Context:* "In the women suffragists' capture of the narrative of progress the common law fell into disrepute. It had long been associated with and accommodated by liberalism, but now the two doctrines were wrestled apart and juxtaposed."[77] Liberalism, the individual-rights-based approach to law, became associated with ameliorative, civilized reform, the common law with a dark and oppressive barbarism. Perhaps, in part, it was this shift toward a rights-based method of jurisprudence that contributed to the recognition of the right to privacy (and later the "right of publicity") in the United States almost a hundred years before other common law jurisdictions such as the United Kingdom and Australia followed suit.

Despite *Roberson*'s enduring legacy within the canon of privacy law, commentary that followed the decision demonstrated the extent to which a woman's property rights in her face, and not her privacy, was *the* issue of interest. "Has a beautiful girl the right to her own face?" the *Boston Globe* inquired.[78] "Her beauty is the peculiar personal property of a woman," one reader wrote to the editor of the *New York Times.*[79] As with Marion Manola, references to Roberson's attractive appearance abounded, the *New York Tribune* describing her as "the pretty plaintiff,"[80] and the *Evening Times* in Little Falls, New York, terming her "a handsome young woman."[81] *The Sun* called her "a good looking girl,"[82] and the *Saint Paul Globe* "a beautiful girl."[83] Female beauty was thought to be at the heart of the issue, and the question was whether it should be accorded legal protection.

In an editorial on the decision by the New York Court of Appeals, the *Salt Lake Herald* mused: "The young woman who said her face was her fortune had never heard of the decision recently handed down by the court of appeals of the State of New York. The pretty maid's face may be somebody else's fortune but it is not hers according to the learned judges. . . . Average citizens will consider this mighty poor law. It lets down the bar, in New York, at least, to all kinds of liberties, in the advertising line with women's pictures. Under this decision it will be possible to steal a photograph, put her head over any kind of picture, for instance a corset advertisement, and there is no recourse for the injured woman."[84]

At the time *Roberson* was decided, product advertisements mainly used illustrations rather than photographs. Sharing the newspaper and magazine pages with reports of the case were advertisements for soap, shampoo, clothing, apparel, and medicinal tonics, all displaying illustrations of (seemingly) fictional persons. Even early advertisements for photographic cameras most often used hand-drawn pictures. But in the world of print, a shift from drawings to photographs was slowly occurring and would accelerate in the early twentieth century.[85] Not only was the use of women's photographs within advertisements enabled by developments in the art of photography, it proliferated with the rise of the periodical press. The turn of the century witnessed an exponential rise in the number, variety, and circulation of magazines—the first mass medium in the United States. In 1865 there were nearly seven hundred titles, with a total circulation of about four million; forty years later, in 1905, there were approximately six thousand magazines, with a total audience of sixty-four million, or about four magazines per household. In the same year, the *Ladies' Home Journal* and the *Saturday Evening Post* both surpassed readerships of one million. The superfluity of pages in these periodicals beckoned the inclusion of more and more photographic portraits within advertising and features.

The enactment of privacy laws following *Roberson* assisted numerous female plaintiffs in New York to control the use and abuse of their images.[86] Most important, the cases that followed began to illuminate the changing character of the claims. No longer solely concentrated on maintaining privacy, the claims would center more and more on the proprietary investment in the right to control one's likeness, as both women and men sought professional and personal agency and advancement in the public world.

Privacy on the Public Record

Following the decision of *Roberson* in New York, it quickly became clear that the American judiciary was staunchly divided on the issue of whether to recognize a right to privacy in the common law and on the related issue of an individual's property in his or her own image. In 1905 the Supreme Court of Georgia handed down the decision of *Pavesich v. New England Life Insurance Co.*,[87] heralding the beginning of a widely varying state-by-state approach to privacy law. The case was exceptional, not simply for its status as the first state Supreme Court decision in the United States to recognize a right to privacy, but also because the plaintiff was a man. His photograph was used (unnamed) to sell insurance, not because he was well known professionally. It is one of very few cases at this time in which a man's image was used purely because it was pleasing to the eye.[88] A right to privacy's feminine origins and its association with the protection of traditional womanly virtues meant, however, that the court was pushed to momentarily reconfigure the doctrine in masculine terms.

Paolo Pavesich, an artist by profession, brought an action for libel and breach of his right to privacy against the New England Life Insurance Company, its general agent, Thomas Lumpkin, and photographer, J. Q. Adams, in relation to an advertisement published in the *Atlanta Constitution*. It showed a photograph of Pavesich looking handsome, healthy, and successful alongside a photograph of a sickly and miserable looking man. Above the plaintiff was the caption "Do it now. The man who did" and above the poor man: "Do it while you can. The man who didn't." Underneath the photographs were apparent testimonials from each man—the plaintiff allegedly stating: "In my healthy and productive period of life I bought insurance in the New England Life Insurance Co., of Boston, Mass., and today my family is protected and I am drawing an annual dividend on my paid-up policies" and the other man lamenting: "When I had health, vigor and strength I felt the time would never come when I would need insurance. But I see my mistake. If I could recall my life I would buy one of the New England Mutual's 18-Pay Annual Dividend-Policies." The photograph of the plaintiff was produced from a negative held by the defendant photographer, without the plaintiff's knowledge or consent. Pavesich claimed the advertisement was malicious and false, as he never made such a statement and never held a policy with the defendant's insurance company.

In many ways the plaintiff's privacy claim was similar to Roberson's. Both claimed to have suffered ridicule by virtue of being recognized in the advertisement by friends and acquaintances. The court in *Pavesich*, however, interpreted and framed a right to privacy in terms strikingly different from those invoked by the New York Court of Appeals and the lower courts in *Roberson*. Moving away from a conception of privacy as a protection of feminine modesty, Justice Cobb in *Pavesich* propounded that the foundation of a right to privacy was natural law and was protected by the Constitutions of Georgia and the United States in their declarations of the protection of individual liberty. Justice Cobb expertly wove a right to privacy together with the fundamental (white, masculine) American ideal of liberty: "The term 'liberty' is not to be so dwarfed, but is deemed to embrace the right of man to be free in the enjoyment of his faculties with which he has been endowed by his Creator, subject only to such restraints as are necessary for the common welfare. . . . Each is entitled to a liberty of choice as to his manner of life, and neither an individual nor the public has a right to arbitrarily take away from him this liberty. . . . The right of one to exhibit himself to the public at all proper times, in all proper places, and in a proper manner is embraced within the right of personal liberty."[89]

In fact, Justice Cobb went so far as to refer to the right of privacy as "the liberty of privacy."[90] Susan Gallagher argues that the Georgia Supreme Court differentiated between *Roberson* and *Pavesich* by depicting a woman's claim to privacy as a prayer for protection and a man's claim as an expression of his natural authority to control his personal affairs.[91] While Justice Cobb did attempt to rebrand a right to privacy as masculine, he also endorsed the minority judgment of Justice Gray on property rights, choosing to quote from it at length. Of particular note is Justice Cobb's approving adoption of Justice Gray's analogy between copyright and privacy: "I think the plaintiff has the same property in the right to be protected in the use of her face for the defendant's commercial purposes as she would have if they were publishing her literary compositions. . . . It would be, in my opinion, an extraordinary view, which, while conceding the right of a person to be protected against the unauthorized circulation of an unpublished lecture, letter, drawing, or other ideal property, yet would deny the same protection to a person whose portrait was unauthorizedly obtained and made use of for commercial purposes."[92]

Milton Gibbs's property argument in *Roberson* appears to have convinced Justice Gray in that decision and subsequently the majority in *Pavesich*. The language of property was, however, still couched within the right to privacy, not in any separate proprietary interest. Justice Cobb declared that "the form and features of the plaintiff are his own."[93] For if they were not his own, "one's picture may . . . be reproduced and exhibited anywhere. If it may be used in a newspaper, it may be used in a poster or placard. It may be posted upon the walls of private dwellings or upon the streets. It may ornament the bar of the saloon keeper or decorate the walls of a brothel. By becoming a member of society, neither man nor woman can be presumed to have consented to such uses of the impression of their faces and features upon paper."[94]

Clearly, when the judge referred to "ornamenting" a saloon bar or "decorating" the walls of a brothel, he had in mind pictures of women, not of Paolo Pavesich. This passage in fact provides real insight into the issue in question. Women's claim to privacy entailed a refusal to become the object of voyeurism—circulated from hand to hand, as Marion Manola had put it, and gazed at by anonymous men. It also illustrates an understanding of the inherent contextual instability of photographs, their meaning determined as much by context and the circumstances of display as by their actual content.

The court in *Pavesich* concluded its discussion of a right to privacy by submitting in dramatic terms that the unauthorized use of another's photograph was tantamount to colluding in that institution most antithetical to liberty—slavery: "The knowledge that one's features and form are being used for such a purpose, and displayed in such places as advertisements brings not only the person of an extremely sensitive nature, but even the individual of ordinary sensibility, to a realization that his liberty has been taken away from him; and as long as the advertiser uses him for these purposes, he cannot be otherwise than conscious of the fact that he is for the time being under control of another, that he is no longer free, and that he is in reality a slave, without hope or freedom, held to service by a merciless master."[95]

This speech located the right to privacy within the historical narrative of American freedom, drawing an analogy between the individual whose photograph was used by another without consent or reward and the individual whose labor was thus appropriated.[96] To Justice Cobb, the right to control one's own photographic image was essential to enjoying the full rights of citizenship. The association of privacy with citizenship shows the right to privacy's potential compatibility with, rather than opposition to, women's struggle for suffrage. Lacking fundamental liberties in the early twentieth century, such as the right to vote, American women brought claims asserting their right to privacy to control the use and abuse of images of their faces and bodies. In an area of law dominated by female plaintiffs, however, it is notable that the first successful privacy case in the United States, at Supreme Court level, was brought by a man.[97]

After *Pavesich* and the enactment of privacy laws by New York State in 1903 prohibiting the use of an individual's name or likeness for trade or advertising purposes,[98] the number of cases for breach of privacy in relation to photographic images increased rapidly, and the majority involved female plaintiffs. The relatively few cases brought by men were markedly different in their content and arguments and referred to the use of a man's name or likeness as a symbol of his public reputation and standing. In 1907, for example, the inventor Thomas Edison obtained an injunction against the Edison Polyform Manufacturing Company to restrain its breach of his right to privacy by using his name and likeness in connection with its corporate name and medicinal preparations.[99] In 1909 J. P. Chinn brought a case in Kentucky against the Foster-Milburn Company for using a false testimonial (alongside his picture) within an advertisement for its kidney pills. Confirming the plaintiff's right to recover damages in such circumstances, Justice Hodgson of the Kentucky Court of Appeals stated in *Foster-Milburn Co. v. Chinn:* "It is a fraud on the public to publish indorsements [*sic*] of public men in publications of this character which are not genuine. A man has the right to complain when he is published in a directory having a circulation of 8,000,000 copies, as indorsing [*sic*] a patent medicine he has never seen."[100]

The reference to "public men" in *Foster-Milburn Co. v. Chinn* was telling. At this time a small number of notable public men were able to appropriate the doctrine of a right to privacy to prevent the use of their famous identities to advertise goods. But these cases were not representative of the majority of plaintiffs or actions. In its infancy, "a right to privacy" was forged and shaped by a majority of women who brought actions protesting the use and circulation of unidentified images of their faces or bodies by others. Their images were not used in conjunction with testimonials or endorsements and didn't highlight or invoke their individual expertise or public achievements. In fact, their professional skills (as singers, actresses, or even divers) were ignored. They were reduced to anonymous attractive images.

In 1906 the New York Supreme Court heard the case of *Riddle v. MacFadden*.[101] The plaintiff, Felicity Riddle, was a young woman who brought an action under New York's new statutory privacy laws[102] against Bernarr MacFadden and Luther White for publishing a photograph of her in the book *MacFadden's New Hair Culture*.[103] Bernarr MacFadden owned and operated the Physical Culture Publishing Company, responsible for publishing popular titles on health, beauty, and fitness, including the magazines *Beauty and Health* and *Physical Culture*. Luther White was a professional photographer in New York City. According to the complaint, in December 1904 Riddle attended White's studio with a female friend and paid him to take her photographic portrait in eighteen different poses, with the understanding that all copies and negatives were for her exclusive use and subject to her orders and direction.[104] White disputed this evidence, claiming that as she was an actress he gave her "special rates" for the photographs in consideration for her relinquishing and giving to him the right to make copies and sell or give away any of the photographs as he saw fit. He stated in his answer to the complaint that this was customary in the theatrical photography business and benefited the performers in question by making them more well known to the theatergoing and non-theatergoing public.[105] The belief that the publicity would be welcomed by Riddle seems to have been shared by Bernarr MacFadden. One of his employees testified: "I told him [MacFadden] that I had no permission from the photographer nor from the girl to use that picture, and he said, 'Oh, that will be all right, the girl is probably an artist's model or an actress and will be very glad of the advertising, and we will use it anyhow,' and that is the last I saw of the picture until it appeared in print."[106]

At the time, Riddle was an actress and member of the chorus of the Comic Opera Company, and she had previously posed for professional photographs. But her dispute with these particular photographs was the context of their publication, the fact they were displayed in "magazines and publications which contained many sparsely clad and even nude pictures of men and women, both in the body of the reading matter thereof and in the advertising matter."[107] It was this lewd context that, according to Riddle, subjected her to taunts, gibes and the disdain of others, particularly her soon-to-be parents-in-law. She said in evidence: "He [her fiancé at the time] told me his folks were very much opposed, very much upset and opposed to the photograph, told me how angry they were with him, that he was disgracing his family, and that I was not any fit wife for him, and of course he said there was different language used in regard to my character. . . . He said his father said that I must be a *public character,* that no woman would allow herself to be photographed in a magazine of that sort unless she was some *public character.*"[108]

A "public character" had connotations very different from the designation "public man." Riddle's evidence demonstrates that maintaining privacy was still regarded in the early twentieth century as necessary for a woman's reputation and social value. As the public debate between Sarah Grand and Ouida had demonstrated only a decade earlier, contests continued between the assertions of freedom that characterized New Womanhood and the necessity of modesty for "true womanhood." To become a "public character" (as her fiancé's father put it) was to lose one's modesty, virtue, and marriageability. Women often had to walk a fragile line between pursuing their careers and satisfying their familial and matrimonial duties. As Elizabeth Otto and Vanessa Rocco have observed, photographic and film images and their accompanying contexts of display were crucial in this negotiation.[109] As Riddle explained to the court, neither her fiancé nor his parents objected to her performing on stage or being photographed in theatrical costumes: "I don't think my husband's folks objected to me because of my connection with the stage before this publication of the photograph had ever taken place, as they had relatives of their own on the stage. . . . I had some pictures taken at that time in costume. In the costume that I wore in the Baroness Fiddlesticks Company . . . I ordered a hundred of the various photographs in all. I sent them to my husband. . . . My husband was living in Detroit at that time, with his parents. He did not say anything about his parents objecting to that costume."[110]

It was the type of publication, *MacFadden's New Hair Culture,* that made the otherwise innocent photographs offensive. As Cass Riddle (the plaintiff's fiancé, later husband) testified: "My father said that any one that had any respect for themselves would not have their picture in *such a book*."[111] The photographs of Riddle were not private in nature, and they seem to have been taken for the purpose of gaining further employment upon the stage. In many ways, this case is similar to *Manola v. Stevens*,[112] where the plaintiff's chief concern was the transformation of her theatrical performance into a sexualized postcard to be passed between men. A right to privacy was not utilized in *Riddle v. MacFadden* to maintain or protect privacy so much as to resist objectification and wrestle back control over the terms of display. A single image in a salacious context had the power to overwhelm careers and reputations built upon talents and skills, to silence Riddle's voice in the opera, and to reduce her worth to her visual appeal alone. Riddle used a right to privacy in court to protest against her objectification and visual exploitation, and she won her case.

Another young woman, twenty-six-year-old Mary Almind, brought an action under the New York privacy laws[113] just a few years later, when her image was used in a poster illustrating how to board and disembark safely from a trolley car.[114] She was not, however, the primary subject of the photograph. The advertisement, produced by the defendant, the Sea Beach Company, who operated trolley cars in Brooklyn, New York, stated:

> DO YOU KNOW NINE out of TEN ACCIDENTS Could Be
> Avoided BY PASSENGERS?
> Carefully Compiled Statistics Show from 90 to 95%
> of Boarding and Alighting Accidents are Caused
> by BOARDING MOVING CARS
> ALIGHTING FROM MOVING CARS

ALIGHTING IMPROPERLY FROM STANDING CARS.
We Deplore Injury to Our Passengers.
WILL YOU HELP IN REMOVING THE CAUSES?
BROOKLYN RAPID TRANSIT SYSTEM[115]

The poster included a photograph of a man being dragged along the ground by a trolley car as a result of trying to board or disembark improperly and another photograph of a woman behaving in the correct manner. In each photograph, the plaintiff was seated as a passenger inside the trolley car. The complaint alleged that she had not consented to such use of her image in writing or otherwise.[116] In its answer, the defendant took issue with the complaint on two main grounds: first, that the plaintiff had been informed of the purpose of the photographs and had requested to be included, and second, that the posters were not advertising but part of an informative campaign to protect public safety.[117]

In relation to the first ground, the plaintiff recounted that on 18 March 1912 she was taking a stroll with her baby, her sister-in-law, and her six-year-old niece on Tenth Avenue in Brooklyn when they happened upon a stationary, empty, trolley car. A group of people, approximately nine men and one woman, were surrounding the trolley car, including a man with a folded camera. The plaintiff and her sister-in-law watched the group of people, including the woman, who was having her picture taken in various poses by the man with the camera. Then a man from the group came up and asked them if they wanted to have their pictures taken, to which they agreed. Two men then escorted Almind and her sister-in-law to the trolley car and told them where to sit for the photographs.

During the trial the plaintiff was cross-examined at length by the defendant’s attorney, George D. Yeomans, as to what then happened. The following is an extract from the record of testimony:

> Q: Did this man who came up to you and asked you if you wanted your picture taken say anything else to you?
>
> A: That was all.
>
> Q: Did you ask him any questions?
>
> A: No.
>
> Q: Did you ask him what was going to be done with your picture after it was taken?
>
> A: No, sir.
>
> Q: Did you make any agreement with him that the plate was to be turned over to you?
>
> A: No, sir.
>
> Q: Never said anything to him about it?
>
> A: No.
>
> Q: Never requested him not to use your picture, or any thing, did you?
>
> A: I did not know anything about it at the time.
>
> Q: Well, you knew you were going to have your picture taken?
>
> A: Yes.
>
> Q: And at the time you never made any request, to him not to use your picture, did you?
>
> A: No.[118]

At this point, the defendant's attorney rested his cross-examination, and the plaintiff's attorney asked her why she did not ask what he was going to do with her picture. She replied that she thought it was a bridal party and the bride and groom were about to depart on their honeymoon. When asked what she thought of the man in the "falling" pose, she stated: "I thought it was a bridal party. We thought it was funny when we saw this gentleman being taken down here, in the lower picture, but we did not know what it was. I absolutely mean to tell this Court that I did not know what this picture was being taken for. I did not have any conversation with anybody about my later getting a copy of this picture, and where I could get it. I did not make any remark to anybody about what fun it would be to have my picture taken in the car. I thought this was a bridal party. . . . This lady appeared to be dressed as a bride, to me. She had a large bunch of violets and an evening dress and a large hat when her picture was taken."[119]

George Pierce, employed by the defendant, then testified against Almind, stating he had explained the purpose of the photographs to her at the time and she had consented.[120] Four men, also employed by the defendant, testified to support his version of events, stating they had overheard this conversation.[121] This evidence seems to have weighed heavily on the trial judge, Justice Kapper, who dismissed Almind's version of events and found that "the plaintiff fully knew the use to which it was to be put by the defendant, and that she willingly and quite eagerly agreed to sit in the car for that very object."[122] For this reason, he held, Almind was unworthy of equitable relief. This conclusion is surprising given the clear and direct testimony by Almind that she thought she was being photographed as part of a bridal party, an observation so specific and curious it was unlikely to be fabricated.

The New York Supreme Court (Appellate Division) agreed with Justice Kapper, finding Almind's version of events "incredible."[123] Nonetheless, the court made the important clarification that oral consent or acquiescence was not sufficient for the purposes of respecting the right of privacy tort enacted by the New York legislature.[124] Written consent was necessary in order to prevent "any person making a picture of one willingly sitting" and then using it within advertising. It was necessary to prove that "*he* disclosed the purpose and that *she* either consented or did not demur."[125] The choice of gendered pronouns here to expound a universal principle is notable: *he* is the picture maker, *she* the pictured subject. Women, the court concluded, have the right to determine when, in what context, and by whom their pictures will be displayed.

The Supreme Court then turned to the second issue within the trial: whether the use of Almind's picture was for "advertising" purposes. In argument, Almind's attorney, Louis Weinberger, conceded that the posters were not being used by the defendant to increase profit but being used for altruistic motives concerning safety. Weinberger, however, contended that this still fell within the definition of "advertising": "The common meaning of the word 'advertise' is strictly in accordance with its etymological meaning: 'to advertise' is 'to cause others to turn towards, to attract attention to.' "[126]

This definition touches on the motivation behind using women's pictures (more than men's) within advertising material. Traditionally objects of the voyeuristic gaze, women's pictures were regarded as being able to turn heads, both male and female. Justice Thomas appeared convinced by this broad definition: "[T]he right of privacy under the statute cannot be invaded for purposes purely informative or redemptive, whether the altruist be entirely a charitable envoy or a railway company. No cause is so exalted that it may allure by exposing the portrait of a person to the public gaze.”[127] The Court of Appeal reversed the judgment and granted Almind an injunction restraining the use of her picture by the Sea Beach Company.

Two other New York cases in the early twentieth century involving the unauthorized use of young women’s pictures also turned upon the definition of “advertising” within the statutory protections of right to privacy.[128] In 1913 Joanna Colyer brought a case against Richard K. Fox Publishing Company on behalf of her sixteen-year-old daughter, Mabel Colyer.[129] The complaint alleged that on Saturday, 18 January 1913, the *National Police Gazette* published five pictures of women, including one of the plaintiff, with the following caption: “Five of a Kind on This Page. Most of them Adorn the Burlesque Stage. All of Them Are Favorites With the Bald Headed Boys.”[130] The plaintiff sought an injunction restraining the use of her photograph by the *Police Gazette* and $25,000 for suffering “in her body and mind” and for damage to her “good name, reputation and her profession.”[131]

Mabel Colyer was a professional high diver, having learnt the art at Dreamland Park, Coney Island, when she was fifteen years old. When testifying in court, she described her talent as “diving from a height into a shallow tank of water” and said that at the time the photograph in question was taken, she was performing in Canada as part of the Diving Girls Show, owned by a Mr. Harry Fox, in a costume “appropriate to her public performances.”[132] Colyer, like Manola and Riddle, appeared as a New Woman, embracing a career in public performance and entertainment, rather than retiring to the domestic hearth. The *National Police Gazette* was known as a fierce critic of modern women and regularly pilloried them in its pages by featuring them in bloomers or tights, smoking, drinking, boxing, or committing crimes.

The primary issue for the court in this case was, as in the *Almind* case, whether the photograph of the plaintiff was being used for advertising purposes as stipulated by the relevant New York privacy statute. The defendant's attorney, Louis Vorhaus, argued that the *National Police Gazette* was a weekly "sporting journal . . . suited and intended to be suited to the wants and desires of the sporting fraternity."[133] Its intended audience was people who desired information pertaining to "boxers, actors and actresses, wrestlers, fencers, expert swimmers etc."[134] A journal or newspaper directed at such an audience, he submitted, should not be treated any differently from one focused upon matters of politics or science.

The plaintiff's attorney, Frank Davis, resisted such a neutral (or flattering) characterization of the magazine. At first glance, he stated, the name of the publication suggested it presented information concerning "policemen, police management, police control or police government in any community, and especially in the City of New York."[135] A brief review, however, revealed "not one word of news within the pages."[136] He contended that it was not a "newspaper" or journal of any kind but rather a "money making sheet" of the type often circulated in "barber shops," consisting of "pictures of men and women in a semi-nude state, and of nasty and filthy advertisements."[137] Its intended audience, Davis asserted, was "an abnormal class of persons interested in immorality and crime."[138]

Davis's denigration of the defendant's publication may have helped engender sympathy for Colyer, but it did not suffice to demonstrate that her picture was being used for "trade" or "advertising" purposes. This was a trickier task. Davis put forward that if the seminude pictures of women, such as Colyer, were dropped from the publication, its demand and circulation would immediately cease, as "no one would pay ten cents a copy for a publication containing a few filthy and sordid advertisements without any other *attractions*."[139] He concluded that the defendants were using pictures, such as that of the young plaintiff "semi-nude" in her professional diving costume, to attract attention to their publication in order to sell other wares and commodities.

The trial judge was not particularly taken by this argument. He concurred with Davis's unflattering description of the *National Police Gazette* and explained that this would be relevant in a suit for libel, if the plaintiff could show her "reputation" had been harmed by the inclusion of her picture in such a periodical.[140] Given that the case was based on the New York right of privacy statute, however, the question of whether use of the image fell within the statutory definition of "advertising" or "trade" was crucial. The judge concluded that the argument advanced by the plaintiff on this point was erroneous, as it would apply equally "to a picture of President Wilson, printed in the *New York Times*, the *New York Tribune* or any of the great newspapers, except as to the character of the sheet itself."[141] For as a newspaper was managed for the purposes of profit and pictures (as well as stories) were used to attract the attention of readers in order to induce sales, all use of such pictures and names by newspapers would be a potential invasion of privacy, according to the plaintiff's reasoning. In examining the origins of the privacy statute, he proffered that "it was known to be the habit of some persons to advertise commodities for sale and to take the picture of some *attractive young lady* and print it as a kind of trade-mark in connection with the advertisement of that article for sale."[142] His account clearly recognized the gendered nature of the harms recognized in the privacy statutes.

Mabel Colyer appealed, but the Appeal Court concurred with the trial judge, Justice Carr holding: "So far this statute has not been so far extended as to prohibit, under penalty of exemplary damages, a publication, in a daily, weekly, or periodical paper or magazine, of the portrait of an individual. When the statute was enacted originally in 1903, the custom of publishing in papers the portraits of individuals who were distinguished in their activities of life was very general. If the Legislature had intended to wipe out this custom, it could have said so easily in positive language. It did not so say in terms, and the courts have proceeded to give the statute full enforcement, within the meaning of its express provisions, considered in the light of its history."[143]

On one hand, the judgment seems fair, as Colyer's picture was not being used within an actual advertisement (as the New York right to privacy statute requires). On the other hand, the parallel drawn between the use of the president's image within the *New York Times* and the use of this image of Colyer within the *National Police Gazette* was misleading. Colyer was not being used to advertise a commodity, she was being used as a commodity herself. Her image was provided to attract a certain kind of attention, whereas an image of President Wilson would likely be used to illustrate a news story. Colyer's legal team struggled to appropriately describe her plight. The court endorsed the incongruous analogy of the U.S. president on the front page of a daily newspaper with the picture of a half-naked sixteen-year-old girl in a men's magazine. Based on the statutory New York right of privacy laws,[144] this 1913 case is a direct descendent from *Roberson,* but it also introduces the theme of my next chapter, which examines in detail privacy cases that involved the violation of women's bodies.

Writing in 1944, legal academic Louis Nizer stated that "the right to privacy, in essence, is anti-social. . . . It presupposes a desire to withdraw from the public gaze, and to be free from the insatiable interest of the great mass of men in one who has risen above—or fallen below—the mean."[145] It is easy to suppose that early privacy cases in the United States demonstrated a desire on behalf of plaintiffs to retire from the public domain, to remain known only to those within their immediate circle, and to avoid notice by society at large. In fact, however, by bringing court actions for breach of privacy, these women plaintiffs lost their anonymity. As the *Washington Post* noted sarcastically of Roberson's criticism of Parker: "Miss Abigail Roberson, whose picture was used on an advertisement, is so indignant that Justice Parker and his three associates could not allow her damages that she keeps alive the publicity by writing a letter to Parker and publishing it before it reaches him. She suffers from an acute stage of privacy apparently."[146]

Radical changes in visual representation brought about by the invention and development of photography in the mid to late nineteenth century proved particularly hazardous for women. Their "pretty portraits" might be taken and circulated among common fellows without the women's knowledge, consent, or access to a viable legal remedy. The paternalistic congressman John Robert Thomas proposed to answer this problem in 1888 with legislative intervention to "protect" "ladies" (the wives, daughters, and mothers of American citizens) from the use of their portraits in advertising. Media debate surrounding the bill first connected this issue with a right to privacy. Warren and Brandeis's seminal 1890 article catapulted a right to privacy into serious contemplation within the legal fraternity and provided a platform from which women could begin asserting ownership over images of their faces and bodies in courts.

A right to privacy employed the language of conservative gender stereotypes, seeming to espouse the feminine virtues of "modesty" and "reserve," but, as I have shown, it was also a vehicle enabling modern women to bring claims asserting their autonomy, self-ownership, and individuality. Far from being a shrinking violet, Abigail Roberson and her attorney, suffragist champion Milton E. Gibbs, should be remembered as part of a broader struggle for equal rights and full citizenship for women in the United States at the turn of the twentieth century. By awarding rights to those in front of the camera, a right to privacy posed a direct challenge to the masculine prerogative of copyright law, as seen by the numerous objections voiced by professional (male) photographers in 1888. Roberson's claim changed the law in New York and led increasingly to common law or statutory recognition of a right to privacy in other states, which led in turn to numerous claims by women who wanted to control the use and abuse of their images. Their claims were not always successful, but the *privacy* discourse they adopted and refashioned allowed them, at the very least, to begin registering protest on the *public* record.

3

Medical Men and Peeping Toms

Spectacles of Monstrosity and the Camera's Corporeal Violations

Prior to the advent of the camera, physical architecture—walls, windows, and fences—effectively shielded an individual's face and body from public view. Legal doctrines such as trespass and nuisance worked to reinforce material barriers by patrolling the boundaries of private property. The law "protected" bodies (of women particularly) from optic violation by locating them within private places and spaces. When bodies were examined for pleasure, profit, entertainment, or as a result of professional practice, the physical proximity between the observer and the observed, together with established professional codes, worked to define the types of gazes appropriate to a scenario and to regulate the conduct of participants.

Performers danced or acted on stage for an appreciative and curious theater audience, and physicians probed and prodded the bodies of patients with the seemingly dispassionate eye of medical science. These established codes and practices were radically disrupted, however, by the new visual technologies of modernity—photography, cinema, and X-rays—which dis-located the image *seen* from the *scene* of its production. In place of an exchange of looks, the camera rendered the pictured subject blind to those who might view her or him. Laws governing private property and private relations were no longer effective in preventing breaches of privacy. The camera could view the body directly and expose its contours and secrets to the hungry eyes of others.

In the previous chapter I showed that a right to privacy emerged in the United States as a way for women to protest against their reduction to anonymous objects of consumption. In this chapter I trace the transition from the common law's protection of privacy through the masculine institution of private property to women's own attempts to protect their bodies from visual violation by invoking a right to privacy.

I begin with an account of laws that protected the body from the looks of others that centered on the idea of private property before considering the changes introduced by the use of the photographic and cinematic camera. I consider a series of medical cases that invoked the language of privacy, beginning with the first case in the United States to expressly name "a right to privacy" (though it did not recognize it as a separate tort)—the 1881 Michigan case of *DeMay v. Roberts.*[1] The facts of this case are intriguing in the way they represent the medical treatment of a woman's maternal body in terms of the discourse of privacy and also highlight issues of the gaze and its regulation prior to arrival of the camera. The case signals a transition between the traditional "protection" of women's bodies as an extension of male private property and the introduction of the concept of privacy as part of a woman's claim for bodily autonomy. I then compare *DeMay v. Roberts* with later medical privacy cases that involved cameras, such as *Feeney v. Young*,[2] a 1920 New York case that followed the filming of a caesarean section operation. Finally, I focus on the invocation of the concept of a right to privacy in relation to the products of women's wombs by examining two cases involving photographs of dead deformed newborn babies. Here I suggest that women also used a right to privacy in the late nineteenth and early twentieth centuries to protest against the transformation of their bodies (and those of their dead children) into spectacles of monstrosity.

Private Property and Peeping Toms

In the previous chapter I discussed cases that forged a right to privacy in the United States resulting from the unauthorized publication of women's photographic portraits. Alongside this history, there is a parallel one of privacy law grounded in the idea of private property. This account of privacy law places the sanctity of the home—preventing access by the state or strangers—at its center. Legally, it did not lead directly toward the recognition of a right of privacy (as a tort), but it did inform the conditions of conception of this right. One case in particular, *DeMay v. Roberts*,[3] can be studied as a conjuncture of privacy law as a defense of private property (and women's place within it) and a right to privacy asserted as women's bid to prevent violation of their bodies. This case did not involve photography or cinema, but it was concerned with the wrongs of looking and is therefore a useful case to compare and contrast with later medical cases relating to the use of a camera. It represents a transition between masculine notions of privacy grounded in physical property and a feminine framing of privacy as a way of shielding the body from the unwanted looks of others.

The case resulted from the distressing experience of Alvira Roberts, who lived in a poor rural area of Michigan. In January 1880, she was expecting the birth of her fourth child. She had a medical history of "fits" and sent her husband to ask the neighbor's son to fetch a "professional man," a doctor, for help. The son found young Dr. John DeMay, who went with him to inspect Roberts. Finding no signs of imminent labor, DeMay left and said he would return later. The Roberts's house was a one-room log cabin with one area loosely partitioned off as a collective bedroom, in which Alvira Roberts awaited the birth of her child.

After DeMay left the cabin, he rode all day making house calls and in the evening went on a social visit to a neighboring town with a friend, a jeweler named Alfred Scattergood. When they returned at midnight, DeMay found a note urging him to go to the Roberts house. He was reluctant to venture out so late and persuaded Scattergood to go with him, to help carry his things and provide company. The young men arrived, knocked, and entered the cabin. There was evidence given at trial as to the confusion regarding Scattergood's identity—the midwife, Roberts, and her husband all assumed he was another physician. Roberts was now lying on a couch in the central part of the cabin. Scattergood took a seat by the stove, facing away from her. When DeMay requested Scattergood's assistance he moved to sit by Roberts and held one of the hands of the woman in labor to prevent her throwing her arms about in pain. Roberts testified at the trial that her body was "exposed" during childbirth and she saw Scattergood looking at her and "noticed a smile on [his] face."[4]

The baby was born alive and healthy that night, but two weeks later, Roberts's husband came upon DeMay in the street and in conversation DeMay revealed that Scattergood was neither doctor nor medical student. Outraged by this news, Alvira Roberts took DeMay and Scattergood to court for fraud, assault, and battery. In a strange moment of judicial creativity, however, the Michigan Supreme Court formulated the grounds of complaint as follows: "It would be shocking to our sense of right, justice and propriety to doubt even but that for such an act the law would afford an ample remedy. To the plaintiff the occasion was a most sacred one and no one had a right to intrude unless invited or because of some real and pressing necessity which is not pretended existed in this case. The plaintiff had a legal *right to privacy* of her apartment at such a time, and the law secures to her this right by requiring others to observe it, and to abstain from its violation."[5]

The court found that Scattergood's presence had breached that right, and Roberts was awarded $5,000 in compensation. This was the first recorded instance in United States legal history in which a court enunciated and based its judgment on a right to privacy.[6] The Michigan Supreme Court did not recognize a right to privacy as a separate tort, unlike the state courts in the cases (starting with *Pavesich v. New England Life Insurance Co.)*[7] discussed in the previous chapter. But they were moved to use the phrase "a right to privacy" in a context in which a woman's bodily integrity and her right not to have her laboring body exposed to the eyes of others was breached. Once again a right to privacy was articulated in relation to unlawful looking at women.

Clearly this case presents a conception of privacy different from that elaborated in Warren and Brandeis's article, one grounded in the "very tangible affronted female body," as Caroline Danielson has argued, rather than an intrusion for the purpose of broadcasting information or circulating photographs.[8] Conceived alongside battery and assault, rather than breach of confidence or copyright, the case had a "corporeal referent" rather than a proprietary one. There was no evidence that Scattergood told others what he had seen or relayed his experience. He was simply there, looking. Roberts's testimony reveals that it was the fact that he "smiled" when looking at her that most distressed her. Whereas DeMay's professional medical gaze was never questioned, Scattergood's presence invaded Roberts's privacy because his look at her body, accompanied by a smile, was of a different nature. Danielson argues that Roberts's success was due, in part, to the operation of traditional notions of femininity; the case represented a "duty of modesty" as much as a "right to privacy."[9] She does note that the case was a victory for Roberts, albeit in her view an ambiguous one. I wish to suggest that the dynamics at work in the case were rather more complex than Danielson allows.

DeMay v. Roberts was the first of many cases in which women invoked privacy as a discourse of resistance against the voyeuristic eyes of others. It provides evidence of the distress that could be caused by being subject to a certain kind of look. Much of the court's time was taken with establishing Scattergood's identity and who the Robertses thought he was when they let him into their home. The court proceeded on the assumption that determining his identity would answer the question of whether his touch and gaze were, as Danielson puts it, "knowledgeable or lascivious."[10] The fact that Scattergood was not a medical man and was unmarried seemed enough to raise the possibility that he was looking at Alvira Roberts for improper reasons. The case suggests that prior to the presence of a camera, identity, relationship, and spatial relations were crucial to determining the types of looks that could be conferred. Women, rightly or wrongly, did not feel their sexuality was being violated when gazed upon by a member of the medical profession. The Michigan Supreme Court used the concept of a right to privacy to assert that Roberts had a right to determine who and how others looked on her exposed body. In this way, it can be read as a progressive judgment that recognized women's right to bodily autonomy.

DeMay v. Roberts was the first case in which a woman summoned the language of privacy to protest against the optical violation of her body. But it also called on a history of privacy law grounded in physical barriers between the public and the private, created for example by "apartments." Until the advent of photography opened up new debates, "privacy" was synonymous with "private property." The paramount privacy of the domestic residence was encapsulated by the English legal maxim and proverb "a man's home is his castle."[11] This principle informed and shaped a large body of legal doctrine, including criminal law, the law of trespass, and the Fourth Amendment to the U.S. Constitution.[12] In the 1905 decision of *Pavesich v. New England Life Insurance Co.*, discussed earlier, Justice Cobb stated: "It is conceded that prior to 1890 every adjudicated case, both in this country and in England, which might be said to have involved a right to privacy, was not based upon the existence of such right, but was founded upon a supposed right of property."[13] William Prosser identified *DeMay v. Roberts* as the first case that involved the type of privacy tort he named "intrusion into the plaintiff's seclusion or solitude."[14]

At the time of *DeMay v. Roberts*, no specific offence existed at common law to restrain unwelcome eyes. Peeping Toms were punished under state or city laws relating to disorderly or immoral conduct.[15] In 1897 in Michigan, a man was convicted under a city ordinance for "indecent, insulting or immoral conduct" for "peeking" at women through the window of a domestic residence late at night.[16]

It was clearly problematic to employ the law patrolling the borders of men's private property to protect the integrity of women's bodies. Anglo-American laws protecting private property may have shielded women from the lascivious eyes of strangers, but they also worked to contain, constrain, and control women. As many feminist legal scholars have argued, the principle of a man's home is his castle allowed domestic violence and marital rape to flourish unhindered.[17] This "protection" was complemented by the common law doctrine of coverture that treated women as the property of their male family members, whether fathers, brothers, or husbands. When crimes in the home occurred against women and children, the eyes of the state were most often blind.

Beyond the home, changes in cityscapes and increased population densities expanded fields of vision and opened up new vistas. Elevated structures such as bridges, railroads, and high-rise dwellings generated new viewing platforms, which allowed looking to become a regular urban pastime. As Elizabeth Arens has pointed out, cases involving elevated railroads swamped court dockets at the turn of the century as conflicts emerged about incursions into private property.[18] In the case of *Moore v. New York Elevated Railroad*,[19] a landlord was awarded substantial compensation for loss of privacy as his female tenants were being looked at through their windows by passengers and employees of the adjacent rail company. Such a scenario brings to mind the menacing culture of voyeurism depicted by the artist Edward Hopper in such pictures as *Eleven A.M.* (1926), *Night-Windows* (1928), and *Room in New York* (1932). The architecture of the modern metropolis enabled novel viewing situations, and so too did cameras that could also penetrate the privacy of physical places. The implications for the visual assault and violation of women's bodies were profound.

In the medical context, the use of the camera meant that the distinction between the "safe" gaze of a doctor and the menace of the voyeuristic stranger began to blur, and with projections on big screens violations might be magnified. A woman's reproductive body might become not just an object of fascination and manipulation by medical men but an object of mass entertainment for city audiences. The maternal body could be rendered a monstrous spectacle.

The Cinematic Caesarean

In April 1920, forty years after *DeMay v. Roberts,* the New York Supreme Court heard the strikingly similar case of *Feeney v. Young,*[20] but this time a camera was involved. In 1916 Katherine Feeney was due to give birth via a caesarean section operation. Just prior to the procedure, she gave oral consent to her doctor, John Van Doren Young, for the birth to be filmed so that the operation could be exhibited for "medical societies or assemblies, composed solely of medical men."[21] Some time earlier, unbeknownst to Feeney, Dr. Young had been approached by Alfred Warman, a budding filmmaker, who testified at the trial: "I said to Dr. Young that I would like to bring out a picture; it would be a very interesting picture; showing the care of babies, and in order to make the picture more striking, I should like to put in that picture to be prepared, a part of the Caesarean section."[22]

The film, called *Birth,* was exhibited publicly and commercially in leading moving picture theaters across the country, including in New York City. Under their agreement, Warman paid Dr. Young 25 percent of the box office net profits. According to evidence in the case, friends and acquaintances of Katherine Feeney attended a theater screening the film and by chance saw the birth and recognized her likeness. Feeney sued her doctor for breaching New York's statutory privacy laws.[23]

Feeney's case failed due to a technical argument about "best evidence."[24] Feeney refused to allow the film to be projected for members of the jury, and instead she, her husband, and friends testified that they had gone to the moving picture theater and recognized her "likeness" on screen. The defense argued that the "best evidence," and therefore the only admissible evidence, for proving that the film depicted "portions of the plaintiff's body" was the film itself.[25] On appeal to the New York Supreme Court, Feeney's attorney argued that to uphold the ruling of the lower court that exhibition of the picture was necessary "would require that she would herself have to submit to a new invasion and a new humiliation by a new exhibition of the photograph of her private person in travail, before a jury, and the miscellaneous spectators of the public court room before she could recover her damages."[26] He went on to submit "that the law will not compel a party whose right to privacy has been violated to submit to a new violation before she is redressed. She may not be called upon to sacrifice her decency in this way."[27]

The defense argued that the plaintiff failed to answer vital questions of fact, namely, whether the film *Birth* "exposed a *recognizable* part of the plaintiff's body to public view" and whether "the portrait or picture of the plaintiff which the defendant exhibited was a *distinguishable likeness* of the plaintiff."[28] The case for the defense seemed to rest on the assumption that as the images of the plaintiff's body did not identify her there could be no invasion of her privacy. It stated: '[T]he plaintiff, while the picture of the Caesarean operation was being taken was flat on an operating table, covered from neck to toes under an antiseptic sheet, the top of her head, including her hair, was concealed by a cap, which even covered her ears and an ether cone was suspended over her face. The operation was performed through a small slit in the sheet, which covered her body, and the only part of her body shown in direct focus was the local area of the operation. From such a picture no one could determine the identity of the *object* upon which the operation was performed."[29]

The evidence presented in the case made it clear that whether or not the moving picture showed Katherine Feeney's face in enough detail to make her publicly recognizable was irrelevant to her distress. The complaint asserted that the film showed "portions of [her] body to the public for profit and for trade."[30] Feeney clearly felt violated, humiliated, and exploited by the picture, which transformed her into an *object* for mass entertainment. In fact, so distressed did she feel that she chose to lose her Supreme Court case rather than consent to the projection of the film in court for new audiences.

The requirement that a person be able to be recognized was not central to the privacy cases discussed in the previous chapter, as they all concerned portraits. Equally, while Scattergood's identity was a cause for debate in *DeMay v. Roberts,* Roberts's identity was not. Roberts's form was not fragmented, and her face was as visible to Scattergood as was her exposed body. Recognition only became an issue when a case concerned a part of an individual's body and not the individual's face. But why was it necessary for a plaintiff to be recognizable for the offence to be accepted as an invasion of her privacy? This proposition, put by the defense in *Feeney v. Young* and agreed to by the court, assumed that the distress experienced by Feeney was socially centered, as in the tort of defamation.

Defamation provides redress for harm caused or potentially caused to an individual's reputation. In order to prove a defamation claim, plaintiffs must show they were identified in a publication or, at least, were identifiable. Privacy, however, could be understood by a woman as embodied and psychic. The integrity of women's bodies can be violated without the world knowing. The photographic or cinematic camera might record parts of an individual's body and broadcast these images to others while only the subject may recognize herself or himself on film. Nonetheless, she or he might still feel violated or exploited.

The similarities and differences between *DeMay* and *Feeney* raise a number of interesting issues, primarily concerning what difference is made, if any, by the substitution of the camera for Scattergood? Is it more or less of a violation to have the eyes of a strange man watching or the eye of a camera? Is the offence the presence of the mechanical or masculine eye or the subsequent disclosure of information—its projection—after the event? The answers to these questions are related. The significance of Scattergood's presence in the cabin centered upon his identity, for in defining this the appropriateness of his gaze might be determined. The Robertses allowed Scattergood to enter on the basis that his eyes would look for professional purposes only. Whether or not the pure, unsullied medical gaze was or is a figment of fiction is irrelevant, as the doctor's (that is, DeMay's) presence did not disturb Roberts.

Feeney's concern was also that her body should only be looked at for professional purposes—by "medical societies, in the interests of medical science"—but by her submitting herself to the camera lens, the consequences of her exposure were substantially more serious. The camera's presence as witness to the birth assumed the possibility of subsequent disclosure. It was a recording technology; its raison d'être was playback. The question thus became not if but to whom and in what circumstances the images could be disclosed. Thousands, if not millions, of eyes may have run over the body of Feeney in commercial movie theaters. In addition, further playbacks of the film probably took place in following years. Even now, as the film languishes in an archive, it is possible the same offence Feeney attempted to guard against during the court hearing may be committed by researchers. For Alvira Roberts, on the other hand, once Scattergood left the premises, the offence ceased. In the case of Feeney, the pictured "object" was rendered blind to her future viewers. The identity of those watching could not be interrogated (as had been the case with Scattergood), as they were eclipsed within the anonymity of an audience.

It is likely that other women had experiences similar to Feeney's. Cinema and medical archives contain numerous early movies of surgical procedures, as the technology of film allowed new possibilities for instruction and entertainment. One eight-minute film held by Prelinger Archives in San Francisco depicts the delivery of a baby via caesarean section in a hospital during the 1920s. It states by intertitles at the beginning that it is intended for showing to "Professional, Adult Audiences only." Whether sufficient consent was obtained from the mother and whether the limits placed on its viewing audiences were strictly observed we do not know. Now, however, the film of this anonymous young woman being spliced and sutured on the hospital table and the emergence of her bloodied and bewildered newborn can be studied by everyone with access to the Internet.

The camera multiplied the kinds of gaze that might greet a photograph or film. As we have seen in earlier cases, a film or photograph taken in one context was easily transported and exhibited in another. The intersection of medicine and visual technologies led to a number of privacy cases in the early twentieth century. The body and its ailments, its anatomy and diseases all attracted voyeuristic curiosity.[31] The majority of these cases concerned photographs or films of women or their newborn infants. In *Screening the Body,* Lisa Cartwright examines the extent to which the history of visual culture is tied to the history of medical science.[32] Her work approaches film through the discourse of medicine and by doing so uncovers aspects of film often forgotten in histories of visual technologies. Cartwright argues that film historians tend to regard the scientific experiments conducted with cinema, such as those by Étienne-Jules Marey and Eadweard Muybridge, as a prehistory that disappeared at the turn of the century and as distinct from the popular cinema that emerged in its wake.[33] But, as she points out, scientific cinema thrived well into the twentieth century. The case of *Feeney v. Young* demonstrates the extent to which scientific film was also popular cinema. It can be regarded as a precursor to the medical "exploitation" cinema of the 1940s, which elided female subjectivity through silencing a woman's voice, fragmenting her body, and encouraging the spectator to adopt a medicalized, distanced gaze.[34] These films worked to consolidate the authority of the medical profession over the birthing process and cast women as "fleshy spectacles."[35] The film historian Felicia Feaster has suggested that "some of the intrusive culpability of science or the audience is removed when the subject participates or allows the look," but *Feeney v. Young* demonstrates that consent to be filmed did not equate to consent to be displayed before a public audience.[36]

The case of *Feeney v. Young* also points to a common theme in the majority of medical cases involving claims to a right to privacy between 1880 and 1950: the woman's "monstrous" body constructed as voyeuristic spectacle. Different cases focus on her pregnant or birthing body,[37] the dark insides of her pelvis,[38] her insatiable appetite,[39] or the deformed products of her womb.[40] I use the term "monstrous" as defined by the film scholar Barbara Creed, who argues in her book the *Monstrous-Feminine: Film, Feminism and Psychoanalysis* that images of the "monstrous feminine," that is, the female reproductive body as monstrosity, saturate classical and contemporary art, particularly popular horror cinema.[41] Invoking psychoanalytic theory, Creed points to the numerous ways in which the monstrous feminine is treated as an object of terrifying and horrifying curiosity: as archaic mother, womb, vampire, witch, and castrator.

In *Managing the Monstrous Feminine: Regulating the Reproductive Body,* written in response to Creed's work, Jane Ussher has examined the ways in which a woman's fecund body conceptualized as "abject monstrosity" has been subject to continual legal and medical surveillance in attempts to contain and control its unsettling excesses.[42] The cases discussed in this chapter connect the treatment of women's bodies by "medical men" with popular curiosity about the internal and external working of women's bodies. Evidence given in *Feeney* demonstrated how the plaintiff's body became simultaneously an object of regulation and of voyeurism. Medical men transformed her birthing body into a medicalized passive object and extricated the child from her womb as if from a machine. The camera saw a live bloody child pulled from the flesh of a scientific monster, not a mother. With a cap over her hair and an ether cone over her face and covered by a sheet from head to toe, the woman had disappeared. Evidently, filmmaker Alfred Warman thought such an image would appeal to the audience of his popular film. The film's subject, Katherine Feeney, attempted to use the doctrine of a right to privacy to reassert her human dignity and protest against her representation as a monstrous spectacle.

In *Banks v. King Features Syndicate,* more than a decade later, a woman's body was treated as an object of mass curiosity when the insides of her womb were pictured in the pages of a popular news publication.[43] Following extended illness, the plaintiff, Ina Banks, had consulted physicians and surgeons in Tulsa, Oklahoma, who in the course of treatment took and developed an X-ray picture of her pelvic region that disclosed a six-inch steel medical tool, a surgical clamp, lodged in her abdomen. After removing the foreign object and without consulting her, the doctors gave the X-ray photograph to a newspaper reporter, who in turn gave it to the defendant, who wrote up the plaintiff's case alongside the X-ray image and caused it to be published in the *New York Evening Journal.* The plaintiff claimed to have suffered "humiliation and agony" as a result, and she won her case.

In the cases I have been discussing in this chapter, the presence of the camera enabled bodily images to become infinitely accessible to the eyes of the viewing public. X-rays, in particular, turned the dark insides of the body into a fascinating spectacle. The first publicized X-ray photograph of a human body showed the hand of the inventor Wilhelm Conrad Roentgen's wife in 1895. Soon after, X-rays of women's hands became popular items, traded and given as gifts, suggesting, as Lisa Cartwright has written, "that the female body, like the fetish object, is ownable."[44] X-rays, while exposing and invading the female body to an unprecedented extent in the early decades of the twentieth century, could also obliterate sexual difference and identity, obscuring defining organs and the unique features of individuals. It is likely that if the *New York Evening Journal* article had not named Ina Banks alongside the X-ray image, her right of privacy would not have been upheld. This case, alongside *Feeney,* suggests that even the most intimate and invasive pictures of a woman's reproductive body would not be protected unless the woman was somehow recognizable.

Another privacy case involving the practice of medicine and constructions of the monstrous feminine was *Barber v. Time, Inc.*[45] Here, photographs were taken against the plaintiff's will, as she lay ill in hospital. She suffered from a rare condition characterized by an inability to stop eating. An article entitled "Starving Glutton" was published in *Time* magazine in March 1939, which said: "One night last week pretty Mrs. Dorothy Barber of Kansas City grabbed a candy bar, packed some clothes and walked to General Hospital. 'I want to stay here,' she said between bites. 'I want to eat all the time. I can finish a normal meal and be back in the kitchen in ten minutes eating again.'"[46]

Her picture was published with the captions "Insatiable-Eater Barber" and "She eats for ten." According to the evidence, Barber had refused publicity, but the photograph was taken against her will, while she was confined to her bed. It was a close-up picture showing her face, head, and arms, with the bedclothes pulled up to cover her chest. The Supreme Court of Missouri unanimously found for the plaintiff, Commissioner Hyde stating: "Certainly, if there is any right to privacy at all, it should include the right to obtain medical treatment at home or in hospital for an individual personal condition without personal publicity. . . . The representative of the defendant's medical department testified that so far as interest from a medical standpoint is concerned it wasn't necessary to have her picture or her name and address at all but that 'an attractive picture of a young lady will attract reader's interest.' "[47]

As the court suggested, it is likely Barber's photograph was taken and published by the newspaper because she was an "attractive" woman, but the story also appealed to the morbid curiosity of readers about grotesque conditions. Barber was characterized by the article as a "pretty" girl with a monstrous appetite, insatiably consuming everything in her path. It was this clichéd juxtaposition between Barber's beauty and her beastly nature that provoked the defendants to intrude upon her privacy and take a photograph of her in hospital. It is unlikely that in the absence of these circumstances *Time* would have run the story. The consequence of the photograph for Barber was not simply the publication of her condition but the exposure of her body to readers of the magazine as if they were all crowded around her hospital bed.

In his 1960 survey of cases concerning privacy, William Prosser characterized the cases of *Feeney* and *Banks* as ones involving the "unauthorized appropriation of an individual's name or likeness" and *DeMay* and *Barber* as ones concerning "intrusion upon an individual's seclusion or solitude."[48] Such categories—and categorization—tell us little, however, about the nature of the distress and harms suffered by women in these cases. *Feeney* and *Banks* sit uneasily with the majority of the early "appropriation of name and likeness" cases I discussed in chapter 2, which originated from protests by women against their reduction to anonymous pretty objects of consumption, as in *Roberson v. Rochester Folding Box Co.*[49] The cases in the present chapter derive not from women's beauty and its exploitation within advertising but from the constitution of women's bodies as grotesque sights.

Medical practice enabled access to the bodies of Alvira Roberts, Katherine Feeney, Ina Banks, and Dorothy Barber, but the fecund bodies also became objects of voyeuristic fascination. The distress caused to Roberts when she was "exposed" to the strange eyes of Alfred Scattergood and the harm she suffered were confined to the four walls of the log cabin. They ceased once his unwelcome eyes left the premises. The visual technologies of photography, cinema, or X-rays, on the other hand, transformed Feeney, Banks, and Barber into spectacles of monstrosity: as birthing bodies, darkened wombs, or insatiable monsters. The camera collapsed traditional distinctions between the dispassionate eye of medical science and the avid appetites of popular entertainment. In these circumstances women invoked a right to privacy to protest against personal violation and to protect the integrity and dignity of their bodies. I will now turn from the living to the dead, to a consideration of the employment of a right to privacy in cases where images of women's dead newborn infants were the subject of contestation.

Privacy and the Dead Body

There is a subset of privacy cases concerning medicine and the body that involved claims over images of dead bodies and in some cases images of dead deformed newborn babies. Since the 1895 case of *Schuyler v. Curtis*[50] and the 1899 case of *Atkinson v. Doherty*,[51] it has been held in the United States that the common law right of privacy does not survive death.[52] In *Schuyler*, Judge Peckham of the New York Court of Appeals stated: "Whatever right of privacy Mrs. Schuyler had, died with her. Death deprives us all of rights in the legal sense of that term, and when Mrs. Schuyler died her own individual right of privacy, whatever it may have been, expired at the same time. The right which survived (however extensive or limited) was a right pertaining to the living alone."[53]

Schuyler, *Atkinson*, and other cases upholding this decision[54] concerned attempts to protect the privacy of the dead or their living relatives, where the deceased received publicity for their deeds or character while living. In many ways, these cases can still be regarded as pertaining to the "living," even though the subject of the publicity had passed away. In some cases, however, the court recognized a right of privacy attaching to the dead. They involved images of dead babies, mostly images of dead, deformed newborns represented as medical curiosities. The following two cases concern the employment of the right to privacy in cases where the dead bodies of infants who had just been born. Julia Kristeva's theory of abjection helps us to comprehend the courts' rationale for protection offered in these cases. Kristeva defined "abject" as that which elicited feelings of horror and disgust by being neither "subject nor object," neither "self nor other," that exists in a liminal space where meaning collapses.[55] Barbara Creed has suggested that Kristeva's theory of the "abject" can be used to explain the feelings of disgust and terror elicited by the female reproductive body.[56] Here I look at cases that concern not the mother's body but the products of her womb: her dead, deformed offspring. Kristeva proffered the corpse as a prime example of the abject. As ideas of privacy are based upon a sense of self, the abject human body posed a particular challenge to the right to privacy.

In 1908 in Kentucky, G. W. Stokes's "wife" gave birth to twin boys described by the court as being "together from the shoulders down to the end of their bodies."[57] They had one bowel and one breastbone, or sternum, but were "otherwise twins, and not one baby."[58] The conjoined twin babies died, and the parents employed a professional photographer, S. S. Douglas, to "take a photograph of the corpse in a nude condition" as a keepsake for the family.[59] They agreed he would take no more than twelve photographs and deliver them all to the parents. Without their knowledge, however, Douglas developed further photographs from the negatives and attempted to register them with the U.S. copyright office, with the likely intention of exploiting them commercially. According to the complaint, upon learning of the registration, the parents suffered "humiliation" and had their "feelings and sensibilities wounded." They brought an action against Douglas for violation of their right to privacy and sought $10,000 in damages.[60]

At trial, the jury found in favor of the Stokes family and awarded them damages of $2,500. Douglas appealed, however, claiming that there was no cause of action to support the decision and that a professional photographer had the right to copyright his photographs, as they represented the skill in his art. In its judgment, the Court of Appeals of Kentucky quoted at length from the British decision of *Pollard v. Photographic Co.* that found "the bargain between the customer and the photographer includes, by implication, an agreement that the prints taken from the negative are to be appropriated to the use of the customer only."[61] This principle of law, Chief Justice Hobson stated, had been approved unanimously by courts in the United States. Nonetheless, the Court of Appeals did not conclude its judgment and rest its decision on this sound principle of copyright and contract law.

Chief Justice Hobson chose rather to base his decision upon the wrong done to the bodies of the dead twins: "The most tender affections of the human heart cluster about the body of one's dead child. A man may recover for any injury or indignity done to the body, and it would be a reproach to the law if physical injuries might be recovered for, and not those incorporeal injuries which would cause much greater suffering and humiliation."[62] The Court of Appeals held that Douglas had violated the Stokes' right of privacy by trying to register the unauthorized photograph of their children's bodies, even though the photograph was never published to anyone other than those in the copyright office, and the Stokes family was not identified by the photograph. The court considered the harm occasioned to the parents as akin to physical interference with a corpse, rather than as unwelcomed notoriety through the broadcasting of information. Chief Justice Hobson concluded: "If the defendant had wrongfully taken possession of the nude body of the plaintiff's dead children and exposed it to public view in an effort to make money out of it, it would not be doubted that an injury had been done them to recover for which an action might be maintained. When he wrongfully used the photograph of it, a like wrong was done; the injury differing from that supposed in degree, but not in kind."[63] We see here a right of privacy used as a means to protect the body from optical violation, akin to doctrines of assault and battery (wrongs to the body) rather than to copyright or breach of confidence. The judgment provides evidence in support of Danielson's reading of the embodied concept of privacy in *DeMay v. Roberts,* as the recognized harm was violation of the integrity or dignity of the babies' bodies caused by unauthorized display.

In 1961 an anonymous author in the *Ohio State Law Journal* noted that in the few cases where a relative had been able to successfully make a claim for breach of privacy in relation to a deceased person, the courts had equated the taking of a photograph of a dead body with its physical mutilation.[64] The right of privacy in these instances was perceived by the courts as deriving from laws vesting next of kin with property in a dead body and criminalizing theft or physical interference with the corpse. This principle can be observed at work in another case on the rights of a relative to sue to protect the privacy of a deceased individual: *Bazemore v. Savannah Hospital.*[65]

On 29 May 1928, Slatie Merl Bazemore gave birth to a baby boy in Glenville, Georgia. The infant was deformed, its heart located on the outside of its body. The family physician carried the infant to Savannah Hospital for an urgent operation, but it was unsuccessful, and the baby died. Neither of the parents attended the hospital at the time of the operation. Without the knowledge or consent of the Bazemores, Savannah Hospital permitted a photographer, Foltz, to photograph the dead body of the child "in a nude condition" and gave details of the case to the local Savannah press. Foltz "commercialized" the photographs, selling one to a local newspaper, which published it, as well as to other parties.

The Bazemores filed a petition with the Superior Court of Chatham County alleging that the hospital, the newspaper, and Foltz had violated their "rights of privacy" by exposing "the *monstrosity* and nude condition" of their child; they sought an injunction prohibiting Foltz from continuing to sell his photographs of their dead infant, and an order that the newspaper deliver up any photographs and pay damages in the sum of $20,000.[66] They claimed the acts caused them "pain and distress"; the petition stated: "[T]hey have been greatly shocked, humiliated, and made sick, and have been obliged to employ a physician for their treatment, incurring expense thereby; and [their] health has been impaired by the acts of the defendants, being in a highly nervous state and on the verge of collapse."[67] The defendants brought a demurrer to the petition, arguing that it set out no cause of action and that the alleged damage suffered by the Bazemores was too remote (not the natural and proximate result of the defendants' acts). They won, and the claim was dismissed. The Bazemores then appealed to the Supreme Court of Georgia.

The court was divided on the issue of whether the Bazemores could claim breach of privacy in relation to wrongs committed after the death of their child. The majority upheld the Bazemores' claim, holding that their right of privacy was invaded through publication of their dead child's photograph. It considered the leading Georgian privacy authority of *Pavesich v. New England Life Insurance Co.* and Chief Justice Cobb's words: "If damages for wounded feelings can be recovered in such a case for the wanton removal of the bleaching bones of the deceased relative, it would seem, for a stronger reason, that such damages ought to be allowed to be recovered when those matters which the deceased had jealously guarded from the public during his lifetime, and his portrait, which was likewise protected from the public gaze, are made public property after his death."[68] Here, again we see a parallel being drawn between publishing photographs of the deceased and physical interference with the corpse (the theft of bones from a grave site).

The defendants in *Bazemore* pointed out that Chief Justice Cobb also cited with approval the New York case of *Murray v. Lithographic Co.*,[69] where it was held that a parent could not recover damages for the invasion of their child's right to privacy. To this, the majority in *Bazemore* stated that Chief Justice Cobb's reference to *Murray* could only be treated as *obiter dictum* (not a binding principle of law), as *Pavesich* did not concern the right to claim breach of privacy with regard to the publication of a dead relative's portrait. Further, the majority asserted: '[T]here is a wide difference between the *Murray* Case, decided by the New York court, and the present case. In the *Murray* Case the parent sought to recover damages for the unauthorized publication of the portrait of his living infant child, and the court held that the right of action was in the living child. In this case the child was dead when the unauthorized acts were committed, and the right of action could not be in the child, but in the parents."[70]

The majority concluded that the Bazemores could sue for breach of privacy for the taking and publication of a photograph of their deformed baby's dead body. However, Justices Hill and Beck of the Supreme Court of Georgia delivered a strongly dissenting judgment. Justice Hill, quoting at length from both *Pavesich* and *Murray,* declared that the right to privacy was a strictly personal right: '[T]here are no cases mentioned where the right to recover is not in the person sustaining the injury. . . . The child, if living, would have a right to sue and recover for a violation of the right of privacy, but the cause of action would not be in its parents."[71] For Justices Hill and Beck, the dead child's right to privacy did not survive its death and transfer to its parents.

The Georgia Supreme Court's disagreement on this issue highlights the uneasy and ambiguous position occupied by the corpse of a baby. In deciding the question of whether a right to privacy was infringed in *Douglas v. Stokes* and *Bazemore v. Savannah Hospital,* the courts were confronted by a multitude of ultimately unanswerable questions. Were dead newborn babies persons in their own right or the property of the parents? Were these the photographs of individuals or photographs of things? Was the injury done to the child to the dignity and integrity of their bodies or to the reputation and feelings of the parents? Kristeva's theory of abjection suggests an explanation as to why such questions confront and disturb us. On the place of the corpse, she writes: "There, I am at the border of my condition as a living being. My body extricates itself, as being alive, from that border. Such wastes drop so that I might live, until, from loss to loss, nothing remains in me and my entire body falls beyond the limit—*cadere,* cadaver. If dung signifies the other side of the border, the place where I am not and which permits me to be, the corpse, the most sickening of wastes, is a border that has encroached upon everything."[72] The corpse cannot be located or defined, escaping the limits of language, of self and other, subject and object, human and inhuman. The newborn infant's corpse is acutely abject—only just fallen from the mother's birthing body in an abrupt moment of individuation.

The law is predicated on clear-cut categories and cannot tolerate liminal spaces. And so the courts in *Douglas* and *Bazemore* were forced to an artificial conclusion. In *Douglas,* as with the majority in *Bazemore,* the courts chose to construct the dead newborn infant as an object, an other, whose body belonged to its parents. Therefore, an indignity done to it was conceived as a trespass on the property of the parents. The minority in *Bazemore,* however, chose to treat the newborn corpse as an expired self, a deceased, individual, rights-bearing subject, who could not be owned or characterized as the property of another. To Justices Hill and Beck in *Bazemore,* the newborn baby had a right of privacy during its fleeting moments of life that was extinguished upon its death. Photographic abuses of its dead body were not harms against the personal property of another but rather, against a non-other (not anymore a subject, but not quite an object).

It is significant that these two privacy cases involving images of dead bodies involved photographs of deformed newborn babies. The Bazemores stated that the photographs published by the defendants exposed the "monstrosity" of their child. Here, it was the abnormal products of women's wombs that were positioned as grotesque spectacles for mass voyeuristic curiosity. It is highly unlikely that the body of a "normal" dead infant would attract such interest or controversy. The "monstrosity" of particular bodies, the fecund female body or the deformed newborn, marked them out as objects of fascination that transformed them into "monsters" for public entertainment. Katherine Feeney, Ina Banks, Dorothy Barber, Mrs. G. W. Stokes, and Slatie Merl Bazemore invoked a right to privacy to protect the dignity and integrity of human bodies and to assert their own status or the status of their offspring as rights-bearing individuals deserving respect.

I opened this chapter with *DeMay v. Roberts,* the first court case in the United States to expressly name a right to privacy in the context of a case concerned with medical attendance at childbirth. It thus offers an alternative beginning to the history of this right to that provided by Warren and Brandeis in their article on the subject of unauthorized use of photographs. *DeMay* can be seen as a turning point in United States privacy law, illustrating a shift in thinking about how women's bodies were best "protected." It highlights a move away from the expectation that women should be protected from the eyes of strangers through confinement to the "four walls of a man's home" toward the new idea that women might themselves assert a right to privacy in court.

Prior to the advent of the camera, laws patrolling the tangible boundaries of private property, such as trespass and nuisance, could effectively guard against unwelcomed looking. But the invention of photographic and cinematic cameras rendered the protection of privacy through the erection of physical barriers inadequate. Private places and spaces could be penetrated by camera lenses and the recorded images of faces and bodies be taken away and projected to mass audiences. The camera transformed women undergoing medical treatment and the deformed products of their wombs into monstrous spectacles and by doing so elided their subjectivity and individual identity. A right to privacy was invoked by women to protect the integrity and dignity of their bodies and those of their newborn babies.

In this chapter I have considered the cases in which a right to privacy was asserted by women to object to the optical violation of their exposed bodies (and those of their dead babies) in private spaces and places. In the next chapter I look at those cases in which women used a right to privacy to register their protest at being filmed in public and subjected to the ridicule of cinema audiences.

4

Privacy, the Celluloid City, and the Cinematic Eye

"The range of the moving picture camera is becoming so vastly extended that it seems as if there would soon be neither secrets, privacy nor mysteries left in the world. For there are few things, from the construction of a bridge down to the habits of the humble fly, that now escape its penetrating eye."[1] Thus began an article in the *New York Tribune* in 1910 about the troubling potential of motion pictures to penetrate the privacy of the city. The invention of cinema transformed visual representation, releasing it from the limits of the here and now. With their bodies fixed upon seats, cinema spectators could scan different and far removed worlds, witnessing historic battles and landscapes of mountain and sea, but they could also peer into the uncanny familiarity of their own neighborhoods. No longer did viewers simply glance at an image, however. The cinematic camera demanded a new type of optic attention, eliciting a more concentrated and embodied gaze.

Unlike photography, cinema was an intensely urban medium. It required a means of projection available only in city centers, and it developed an interest in reflecting back to city crowds the changing nature of their metropolitan environment. As scholars of cinema history have highlighted, the invention of moving pictures dramatically altered the perception, experience, and architecture of urban landscapes.[2] It created new lines of vision and moved mass audiences through celluloid portals, where they collided with the forms and faces of multiple strangers—and sometimes acquaintances. The city was experienced not only as a structure of glass and concrete but also as a manifestation of the imagination. Those who documented, recorded, and presented the city to itself played a key role in fashioning the modern city and people's place in it.

There is much scholarship examining the relationship between urban life and cinema at the beginning of the twentieth century, investigating the ways in which the modern city absorbed, reflected, and was reflected by the increasingly pervasive technology of motion pictures.[3] But these examinations of visual history are overwhelmingly shaped by the accounts of those who sought an active role within the film industry as creators and audiences. There has been little, if any, attempt to investigate the impact of the proliferation of cinematic lenses on the lives of the subjects who fell under their gaze.[4]

Privacy cases during the first decades of the twentieth century point to the determined resistance on the part of some individuals (especially women) to the representation of their filmed bodies in the public domain. In chapter 2 I looked at the protests of women at the use of their photographs by others in a way that undermined their dignity and status, reducing them to anonymous objects of consumption. In chapter 3 I examined a number of medical privacy cases to show how the photographic and cinematic camera challenged the nineteenth-century tradition of protection of privacy via property laws, by penetrating private spaces and transforming women's bodies (or the bodies of their newborn babies) into monstrous spectacles.

In this chapter, I investigate women's protests at being filmed in public for the delectation of cinema audiences, women's sense of being mocked and ridiculed when projected upon the big screen in newsreels, documentary cinema, and advertisements. Here I focus on nonnarrative and nondramatic motion picture films subjected to privacy litigation in the early years of the twentieth century and the competing claims of "public interest" advanced by filmmakers. By giving voice to the protests of these otherwise silenced filmed subjects, my examination of legal cases contributes to a more complete understanding of early film history. It is also important to our understanding of legal history that we place these court cases within the context of cinema history, as they were not discrete events but rather arose in the context of and in response to a burgeoning modern culture of filmmaking and cinema going.

The cases I discuss in this chapter begin to illustrate the difficulty of framing women's demands for greater rights (to determine how and when their images were used by others) within the discourse of a right to privacy. Feminist legal theorists have long demonstrated how the public/private dichotomy, so ingrained in the Western liberal tradition and legal thinking, has worked to subordinate the unregulated sanctuary of the home and family in relation to the state and domain of "public" life, through association of these spheres with women and men, respectively. In the previous chapters I discussed ways in which this dichotomy (played out within nineteenth-century doctrines of coverture and property law—"a man's home is his castle") has worked to inhibit women's participation as citizens and as legal subjects by presuming to "protect" them within the home as male property. In this chapter I explain how and why women appealed, somewhat incongruously, to the language of *privacy* as a way of resisting the use of film images taken in *public* spaces. I also show how the power asymmetry of the public/private dichotomy worked to privilege "public interest" above "privacy rights." Women's claims, cast as personal grievances, were framed as jeopardizing the common good of information and education.

Kunz v. Allen and the Cinematic Gaze

At its most basic level cinema distinguished itself from photography through its capacity to depict and display movement. As the film theorist and historian Giuliana Bruno points out, the term "cinema" is derived from the Greek *kinema,* which connotes both motion and emotion.[5] Bruno's work draws strongly on the work of an early film theorist, Hugo Munsterberg, whose book *Photoplay: A Psychological Study* was first published in 1916. There he discussed cinema's unique ability, as a new aesthetic art, to animate the external world and the self within.[6] Munsterberg argued that cinema's impression of movement created an intensity of experience for the spectator beyond that enabled by the photograph: "Whatever in nature or in social life interests the human understanding or human curiosity comes to the mind of the spectator with an incomparable intensity when not a lifeless photograph, but a moving picture brings it to the screen."[7]

Here we see the traditional alignment of photography with the stillness of death, and of cinema with the kinetic energy of life.

Technically, to present persons within a moving picture was merely to take and publish, in quick succession, numerous photographs of them. It is therefore not surprising that until 1912 U.S. copyright law protected motion pictures under the category of photographs: a moving picture designated as a single photograph for the purposes of registration.[8] The effect of numerous photographs in a motion picture was radically different, however, from a collection of a series of still images, for both the viewer and the pictured subject. It was not simply "likeness" that was being appropriated in the case of a motion picture but an uncanny replication of a person's expressions, mannerisms, and behavior. Through this imprint of individual personality, cinema offered much greater and more penetrating information about an individual to a viewer. Outside the context of motion pictures, such information about another could only be acquired through a prolonged stare, or "gaze," the term used by film theorists Laura Mulvey and Christian Metz to describe the distinctive position of the cinematic spectator.[9] This can be contrasted with photography, which offered the information available at a glance. Of course, the photographic information was caught, frozen, locked in time for infinite investigation, but nevertheless, there was less of it to apprehend and less need to continue looking.

The invention of cinema transformed the experience of being "caught" on camera. Whereas the photograph created the sense of being an object for others to handle and view, cinema created the potentially more uneasy feeling of being "watched." The Lumière Brothers' 1895 *La sortie des usines Lumière* (*Workers Leaving the Lumière Factory*) ran for one minute and depicted employees (seemingly uninformed of the camera's presence) leaving the Lumière factory at the end of a working day, from a fixed, slightly elevated point near the factory exit. One could be mistaken for reading this moving image as surveillance footage, were it not for our knowledge of its status as the first commercial film and the first to be exhibited to paying customers as entertainment.[10] As Thomas Levin put it, "No matter what else it is, Louis Lumière's *La Sortie des Usines Lumière* is also the gaze of the boss/owner observing his workers as they leave the factory."[11] The aesthetics of early cinema foreshadowed closed-circuit television (CCTV) almost a century before its establishment as a separate technology for both public and private surveillance.

This association between surveillance footage and early cinema is also apparent in the first privacy case in the United States concerning a nonnarrative motion picture, *Kunz v. Allen,* heard by the Supreme Court of Kansas in 1918.[12] It is perhaps not surprising, given the development of privacy law that I have outlined, that this case concerned the use of a woman's image for the purpose of advertising. On 20 September 1915, Stella Kunz visited the "dry goods store" of the defendants, W. H. Allen and Charles H. Bayne, in Kansas City. According to the amended petition,[13] she was greeted in the store by the proprietor Wilfred Allen, who engaged her in conversation while she waited to be served by one of the female shop assistants. Allen directed the plaintiff to sit and wait on a revolving stool located at the shop counter. During the conversation, Allen moved positions a number of times, causing Kunz to swivel on the stool in order to remain facing him. At this time, unbeknown to the plaintiff, she was being filmed by a motion picture company contracted by the defendants to take moving pictures of the shop interior and its customers for advertising purposes. At trial, Kunz testified that the camera and its operators were located in an obscure corner of the store, some fifteen or twenty feet away from her, and she was not aware of their existence until the end of her conversation with Allen.[14] A week or so later, Kunz was informed by friends and neighbors that her picture was being shown on the screen at a local moving picture theater.[15] The footage was part of an advertisement for the Allen and Bayne Store. Kunz brought an action against Allen and Bayne on 18 December 1915.[16]

The trial began on 9 April 1917, and the plaintiff lost.[17] The court discharged the twelve male jurors and returned a verdict for the defendants on the basis of their demurrer to the plaintiff's petition (claim) and other evidence.[18] The defendants' ground of objection was common in early privacy cases: they argued the plaintiff's pleadings disclosed "no cause of action."[19] She did not plead libel, nor could she, since there was no evidence of malice on the part of the defendants (required at the time by statute in the state of Kansas).

The defendants submitted that in relation to their no cause of action claim that the plaintiff failed to demonstrate requisite damage. The evidence submitted by the plaintiff "not only failed to show any damage sustained, pecuniary or otherwise, but it went farther, and affirmatively showed that no damages had been sustained, by the plaintiff, either by her character, reputation or social standing."[20] In fact numerous friends and acquaintances called by the plaintiff to give evidence had testified that although they felt sorry for Kunz, who showed signs of distress and anxiety as a result of the incident, they did not respect her less after her picture was shown on screen. The defendants' reliance on this evidence was questionable, however, because the court testimony revealed that each of the witnesses upon first learning of or seeing the moving picture advertisement did question Kunz's character, until they were reassured that she had not authorized the use of her image. One witness, Pearl Armstrong, testified that she spoke to another woman who had seen the advertisement, and the woman had asserted that "Mrs. Kunz looked very much like a great, big, fat colored woman."[21] This is a striking comment, and it is not clear from any of the court documents whether Stella Kunz identified as a woman of color. But if she did, she may have been particularly sensitive to slights on her respectability in Kansas in 1915.

The plaintiff appealed the lower court's judgment, arguing it erred in sustaining the defendants' demurrer, by excluding certain testimony from the plaintiff and by not submitting the case to the jury for consideration.[22] It was upon the issues of cause of action and evidence of damage that the case reached the Supreme Court of Kansas in 1918. Citing the Supreme Court of Georgia's 1905 decision in *Pavesich v. New England Life Insurance Co.*[23] as authority, the court in *Kunz* stated the proper cause of action was invasion of the plaintiff's common law right to privacy, and it held that she was entitled to general damages in consequence of the tort and was not required to prove any actual loss.[24] The court also commented that the evidence provided by the plaintiff's witnesses concerning their continued esteem for her spoke only of the sincerity and warmth of their friendship, rather than providing evidence that Kunz had not been harmed. It found in favor of the plaintiff and reversed the lower court's judgment.

This case is notable for a number of reasons. First, it was the first case in Kansas to recognize the common law tort of privacy. In 1919 the *Yale Law Journal* reported that with the judgment of *Kunz v. Allen,* "another State has recently been added to the lengthening list of jurisdictions that recognize the existence of a 'right to privacy.'"[25] The author was critical of the Supreme Court of Kansas's judgment for avoiding any engagement with the precise limits of what was in his view an increasingly nebulous cause of action. Did the right to privacy, in preventing the use of one's portrait for advertising purposes without consent, protect interests of inviolate personality, property, or reputation? The first interest, it was argued, concerned wounded feelings, and so proof of actual damage did not seem necessary. A proprietary interest, on the other hand, was quantifiable, and so perhaps proof of special damage (financial loss) was desirable in such cases. With regard to the third interest, that of reputation, it was contended that a right to privacy did not apply, for the laws of defamation were best designed to respond to loss of reputation.

The second notable feature of *Kunz v. Allen* was, of course, its subject matter. In 1917 very few privacy cases had concerned motion pictures. The first was *Binns v. Vitagraph Company of America* in 1911 concerning a dramatic motion picture *Saved by Wireless,* based upon the plaintiff's heroic acts in rescuing hundreds of passengers during the collision of the steamships *Republic* and *Florida* in 1909.[26] I discuss this case in chapter 6, as it primarily constructed a claim to privacy in terms of the right to control the narrative of one's own life.

Kunz v. Allen was the first time a nondramatic film was subject to a privacy claim. Its similarity to the many cases involving the unauthorized use of women's photographic portraits in advertising raises the question of the difference, if any, between the position of an unconsenting subject of a motion picture used for advertising compared to the position of the subject of a still photograph. During the trial, Kunz and witnesses who testified in her support repeatedly stressed the extent to which the moving picture humiliatingly captured so much, too much, of a person's very being. The roaming omniscience of the motion picture camera captured "everything" of Kunz's face and form at all angles, her gestures, the detail of her clothing, her physical movements. The amended petition described the images projected on the screen in which "a central figure greatly enlarged was the said pictures of the plaintiff showing her face, form, expression of countenance, side and back views, garments and every motion and movement of her body taken while she occupied said revolving stool."[27]

In testimony, Kunz described seeing herself in the theater: "It was a life-sized picture of me, and it showed me from the time I came up to the counter. . . . I never had seen anything like it before; the other [advertising] pictures I have seen just a slide, just an advertisement, but never seen just a regular movie act, and it showed just everything I did from the time I came up to that counter, and then he walked down to the counter with me and placed me on this stool. . . . Everything [showed]; my clothing showed, the kind of waist I had on, the buttons I had on."[28] Kunz's husband, Jacob Kunz, also testified: "Well, I saw the picture of my wife shown on the screen there; a life-sized picture, sitting in Allen & Bayne's store . . . it would give almost all views of her; side view, front view and back view . . . every little move or motion, or anything, it would show in the picture, you could see they were talking just by the movement of their lips."[29]

In reviewing the record of testimony and pleading documents, it is clear there was a substantial difference between being snapped in a photograph and being watched and recorded by a moving picture camera. The emphasis (in the claim and the testimony) placed on the film showing "everything" about Stella Kunz—the details of her waist, dress, buttons, countenance, "side and back views," "every motion and movement of her body"—revealed the extent of bodily exposure she experienced. Kunz evidently felt she was put on public exhibition by the store advertisement. The size of the image was also significant. It was "life-sized"—or even "greatly enlarged"—so large and vivid that details such as buttons were easily seen on the screen.

The startled observation by Kunz's husband reminds us of the significant difference in size between a photograph and a motion picture at the beginning of the twentieth century. Photographs were generally printed on small pieces of paper or card—postcards—whereas the cinematic image was magnified on a big screen. The way in which witnesses, particularly her husband, described seeing Kunz on film as akin to seeing her in person ("just like any person sitting here on the chair"; "the parties that were in the picture were just the same as though you would see me sitting here")[30] also suggest a certain uncanny element to recognizing people on the screen. This experience was no doubt even more troubling for those who recognized themselves.

In his book *Body Shots,* Jonathan Auerbach argues that the early cinematic camera compelled people to self-consciously imitate themselves.[31] In early films such as Lumière's 1895 *La partie de cartes* (*The Card Game*), we witness the gestures and mannerisms of people posing and presenting themselves in a particular way—a process of corporeal self-articulation.[32] But the films in Auerbach's study include only subjects who were aware of the camera's presence at the time of filming. When filmed surreptitiously, as Kunz was, an individual was robbed of the chance to articulate herself—compose herself—for the viewing audience. She was, in effect, unknowingly exposed to the scrutiny of hundreds, if not thousands, of viewers.

Needless to say, it was not a happy experience for Stella Kunz. On the night of 1 October 1915, when she attended the Gene Gauntier Theatre with her husband to view the advertisement, there were hundreds of people in attendance, and she and her husband were forced to sit in the front row. After seeing the advertisement that preceded the featured entertainment, Kunz was so traumatized that she left straight away: "I wanted to get out of there—I couldn't get out of there fast enough."[33]

Unlike in the cases discussed in the previous chapter, the invasion of Kunz's privacy did not take place within a private space, and so it might be difficult to understand her objections. When being filmed, Kunz was sitting in a store that, while technically private property, was freely accessible to the public. She was in a quasi-public space and willingly placed herself within the purview of other shoppers. It was the moving picture camera that produced the harm in creating the possibility of Kunz being subjected to criticism and ridicule in a large movie theater. It had the capacity to infringe the privacy of individuals to a greater extent than still photography by recording and reproducing in enlarged images more information about personal appearance and behavior for an infinite number of viewers. The moving film put the plaintiff on prolonged view to a substantial audience of staring eyes for the profit and gain of others.

Kunz v. Allen provides a rare insight into a woman's experience of being surreptitiously caught on film at a time when "the movies" were still a relatively recent phenomenon. As the plaintiff's lawyers submitted: "The moving picture craze is a modern invention, but the well-established rule of the right to be left alone and not photographed without permission remains."[34] The case complicates traditional legal categorization of these cases as simply concerning the appropriation of "likeness," whereas, unlike a photograph, the moving film appropriated more than the static imprint of one's face, form, and features. Reading the actual court documents highlights the ways in which, for the pictured woman, becoming a cinematic subject unknowingly entailed becoming a larger-than-life but uncannily lifelike exhibit under the gaze of multiple audiences.

Truth or Fiction: The Status of Privacy in Newsreels

At the beginning of the twentieth century, motion pictures offered an exciting new way of presenting news and current events. Newspapers were only just beginning to employ photographs to illustrate their stories, and rates of adult literacy in the United States were low.[35] As a genre of cinema, the "newsreel" became one type of "actuality" or "documentary" filmmaking. The newsreel could transport viewers straight to the events, to see the news of the week animated in lifelike size and motion. It could also manufacture or reconstruct events, particularly wars and battles abroad, where the contingencies of contemporary cinematic equipment made filming almost impossible. Newsreels quickly became popular, and a number of motion picture production companies emerged to corner this lucrative new media market.

Through exhibiting the faces and forms of numerous (often unknowing) individuals on the screen, newsreels also had the capacity to routinely compromise individual privacy.[36] The question of how the emerging privacy laws would deal with newsreel footage came before the courts in 1917 in the case of *Humiston v. Universal Film Manufacturing Co.*[37] Grace

Humiston, a lawyer and private detective in New York City, had been engaged to investigate the disappearance of a young girl, Ruth Cruger. For some time the police had been diligently, though unsuccessfully, conducting a search for Cruger, but it was only when Humiston intervened in the case and insisted on searching the shop of "an Italian"—as it was reported—that her body was found buried beneath the floorboards. The story of Cruger's disappearance and the discovery of her body attracted substantial attention and publicity in New York and was featured in all the daily papers.[38]

When Cruger's body was discovered, the defendants compiled a motion picture news story for inclusion in their newsreel *The Universal Animated Weekly.* A picture of Grace Humiston in a car with the captain of police, taken while she was engaged in the investigation, featured both in the newsreel story of the event and in a poster advertising the story. Humiston protested and sought an injunction, under New York's statutory privacy laws, prohibiting Universal Film Manufacturing Company from including her image in its newsreel and the accompanying poster.[39] The defendants argued that their newsreels were akin to newspapers and were not covered by the New York privacy laws, which concerned use of an individual's name or likeness for trade or advertising purposes. They also submitted that to subject them to such laws would "seriously interfere with, if not destroy, their business, which [provided] information as to current events and innocent amusement to thousands."[40]

Justice Ordway of the Supreme Court of New York disagreed with the defendants and granted the injunction, stating that the exception to privacy laws applying to newspapers in New York[41] did not extend to newsreels. Relying on a recent decision of the Supreme Court of the United States concerning censorship,[42] he held that newsreels (as motion pictures) were not part of the press and were commercial enterprises operating purely for the purpose of profit.[43] The defendants appealed and found a more sympathetic ear in the Appellate Division of the Supreme Court of New York.

Justice Smith of the Appellate Court began his judgment by describing the business of the defendants in some detail. He explained that Universal Film Manufacturing was one of five companies engaged in the business of producing motion picture films of current events and news. Each week it produced two films, entitled *Universal Animated Weekly* and *Universal Current Events,* with each featuring ten to fifteen newsworthy subjects. The stories were compiled and edited in New York from motion picture footage sent from correspondents across the state and the country and from abroad. These weekly films were shown in "motion picture theatres, schools, churches, cantonments, vessels of the navy and wherever there are motion picture machines."[44] The newsreels were made for public entertainment and education as well as for municipal governments and the government of the United States for the purpose of public good. It is clear from the judgment that Justice Smith approved of the type of business undertaken by the defendants.

The Appellate Court conceded that the defendants' publication of motion pictures was a trade, but it made a crucial distinction between different genres of motion pictures, holding that whereas a "photoplay" was subject to privacy laws, a newsreel was not. "A photoplay," it asserted, is "inherently a work of fiction," whereas "a newsreel contains no fiction, but shows only actual photographs of current events of public interest."[45] Justice Smith described further differences that inhered in the distinction between "truth" and "fiction": "The newsreel is taken on the spot, at the very moment of the occurrence depicted, and is an actual photograph of the event itself. The photoplay, as the result of fiction retains its interest, irrespective of the length of time which has elapsed since its first production; whereas the newsreel, to be of any value in large cities, must be published almost simultaneously with the occurrence of the events which it portrays. This news service, as far as it goes, is a truthful, accurate purveyor of news, quite as strictly so as a newspaper."[46]

The court held that the legislature of 1903 could not have intended the New York privacy laws to apply in cases such as *Humiston,* as "at that time the moving picture industry had not yet developed."[47] To make the producers of newsreels subject to the privacy laws, it asserted, would mean that every time a motion picture of a street parade or baseball game was played, the producers would be required to acquire written consent of all involved or risk being guilty of a misdemeanor. Such a proposition, it concluded, was untenable, as it would make practically impossible "the exhibition of films representing current events . . . whether of interesting, instructive or elevating content."[48] Unlike Justice Ordway, Justice Smith saw no "practical difference between the presentation of these current events in a motion picture film and in a newspaper," and thus the Appellate Court held that the public interest in the unrestricted publication of newsreels outweighed an individual's right to privacy.[49] The facts of the case at hand, it concluded, were fundamentally different from those of *Roberson v. Rochester Folding Box Co.,* which had inspired the statute.

The Appellate Court further held that to say that the use of the plaintiff's image in the poster was for the purposes of advertising and thus subject to privacy laws would mean the producers of newsreels could no longer advertise their content. Such use did not fall within the "spirit" of the New York privacy laws, the court argued, as it was merely "incidental" to the publication of the motion picture. The statute, it held, "only prohibits advertising with respect to a trade falling within the scope of the statute."[50] The judgment was practical in orientation rather than strictly based in law, and it limited the application of the right to privacy to motion picture actualities or early documentaries. In a later discussion of the case, legal scholar Carl Zollman commented approvingly in 1937 that with the *Humiston* decision "a considerable degree of protection [was] afforded to newsreel agencies in their quest for interesting pictures."[51]

The decision in *Humiston,* that the use of a woman's image within a newsreel should not be subject to New York's privacy laws, set up an arbitrary but ambiguous distinction between fictitious and nonfictitious content in motion pictures. By equating newsreels with newspapers, the court in *Humiston* ignored the complexities of creating a motion picture story and the unique relationship between the screen and the viewing subject. Newsreels did not simply present reality to the audience, they created that reality. The camera transformed self-determining subjects into objects, whose movements and meaning were created not only by the motion picture creators but by every viewer who watched them. Court judgments of the early twentieth century, however, demonstrated little awareness of the fragile and unstable connection between real-life events and their subjective cinematic representation. Nor did they express much sympathy with the anguish experienced by women who saw themselves projected without their permission on the big screen.

Three years prior to the *Humiston* judgment, the film theorist Munsterberg had provided a key insight that would shape much of cinema theory for the twentieth century: that cinema audiences were active spectators.[52] As a psychologist, Munsterberg was intensely interested in the ways in which motion pictures seemed to "move" audiences. He argued that they did not present "reality" but rather played upon our capacities for perception to create intense "impressions" of the real world. Cinema's power could only be understood by exploring the intricate relationship of exchange between the viewer and the screen. Cinema told "a human story by overcoming the forms of the outer world, namely space, time and causality, and by adjusting the events to the forms of the inner world, namely attention, memory, imagination and emotion."[53] Munsterberg's work displayed an acute awareness of crucial distinctions not only between cinema and photography but also between cinematic representation and "reality" that were little heeded by the courts deliberating on the harms caused (especially to women) by breaches of privacy.

The relevance of privacy law to newsreel film was also tested in the New York case of *Sweenek v. Pathe News, Inc.*[54] The plaintiff, Gertrude Sweenek, brought an action for breach of privacy under the New York statutory privacy laws[55] against Pathe News, Inc., for the inclusion of her image in a newsreel as part of a group of overweight women exercising with "novel and unique apparatus." The footage contained a number of "amusing" captions that arguably subjected the women to ridicule. Judge Moscowitz found for the defendant, stating: "While it may be difficult in some instances to find the point at which public interest ends, it seems reasonably clear that pictures of a group of corpulent women attempting to reduce with the aid of some novel and unique apparatus do not cross the borderline, at least so long as a large proportion of the female sex continues its present concern about any increase in poundage. The amusing captions which accompanied the pictures did not detract from their news value."[56]

The plaintiff apparently gave oral consent to the filming, causing the judge to comment unsympathetically that her legal action seemed to be "an afterthought."[57] But as I have suggested in relation to a number of cases, the vast majority of actions involving breach of privacy through the circulation of women's images were of necessity afterthoughts. At a time in the evolution of the cinematic process, when the extent of editing, lighting, music, captions, and context (in fact all elements of postproduction) could hardly have been known, filmed subjects, even if they gave permission to be filmed, could have no idea how they would subsequently be represented. In *Sweenek*, given the nature of the film content it is likely that its intended spectators were more interested in laughing at corpulent female bodies grappling with "novel and unique apparatus" than in being informed about the latest news about cures for "increased poundage." This case demonstrates a recurring feature in many cases relating to privacy and the pictures: that the bodies of others (the aberrant bodies of women, and of the sick, corpulent, deformed, or dead) were more often presented as objects of fascination in themselves, regardless of their professed educational or scientific value.

New York's statutory right to privacy, enacted in response to *Roberson v. Rochester Folding Box Co.*, enabled Grace Humiston and Gertrude Sweenek to protest against the presentation of their images on the cinematic screen even when such images were filmed in quasi-public places: inside a car on a city street and in a gymnasium. But these cases also demonstrated some of the challenges entailed in attempting to access rights through the discourse of privacy. The asymmetry of power institutionalized by the gendered public/private dichotomy that informed law meant that feminine privacy claims could easily be trumped by opposing masculine arguments of public interest. Newsreel operators were able to present their own commercial interests as furthering a collective good and to characterize the plaintiffs' protests as personal and trivial grievances. The general capacity of newsreels to inform citizens alongside other instruments of the press was privileged by the courts above the evidence of the humiliation and anguish they caused women plaintiffs. Rather than confining their judgments to an assessment of the facts of each case, the courts chose to afford a wide protection to the genre of nonfiction filmmaking. The rights afforded to individuals, primarily women, to control the use of their images via the doctrine of privacy began to be eroded. The public's right to attend the cinema and watch news stories, whether about grisly murders or methods of losing weight, was prioritized over women's right to be protected from personal violation.

Privacy, the Celluloid City, and the Travelogue

Just as the advent of the cinema transformed our ways of seeing and being seen, so the concurrent modernization of cities, with new bridges, railways, electric subway trains, powered flight, skyscrapers, department stores, and exhibition halls, provided new perspectives, vantage points, and lines of vision.[58] The emerging medium of cinema became fascinated by modern urbanization and preoccupied with recording it. Early films demonstrated an intense interest in documenting the changing built forms of the city as well as in exploring the range of perspectives made possible by its transformation, looking for new ways to see the city and its residents. Cinema began to shape metropolitan vision: "The machine of modernity that fabricated the city [was] also the fabric of film."[59]

A number of early films point to the intimate connection between the modern city and the motion picture. In *At the Foot of the Flatiron Building* (American Mutoscope and Biograph Company, 1903) a stationary street-level camera recorded pedestrians coming and going at the base of the Flatiron Building in the Lower East Side of Manhattan. This corner of the city was notorious for providing loiterers with a glimpse of passing women's legs as strong gusts of wind—or drafts from the subway—lifted their ankle-length skirts. The camera shared and participated in the male voyeur's delight at such city spectacles. Nearly all of those captured on this film would have been identifiable to those who knew them. In *Panorama from Times Building, New York* (American Mutoscope and Biograph Company, 1905) a fixed and watchful camera stationed at the top of a twenty-five-story skyscraper at Forty-second Street and Broadway in Times Square pans to the north over the tops of smaller buildings, from Bryant Park, south of Forty-second Street, up Sixth Avenue to the Hippodrome Theatre, toward Forty-fourth and Forty-fifth streets between Sixth and Seventh avenues, until coming to rest looking directly north from Times Square to Forty-sixth Street. When it was built, the Times Square skyscraper was the second-tallest building in the world and seemed to command the skyline of Manhattan with ease. From this perspective, people's washing hung on rooftops was visible, as were pedestrians on sidewalks, residents in enclosed courtyards, and vehicles on the streets.

Cinema's fascination with documenting the city and its citizens intensified in the 1920s, evident in such films as

Manhattan (Paul Strand and Charles Sheeler, 1921), *Metropolis* (Fritz Lang, 1926) and King Vidor's *The Crowd* (1928). And importantly, these films began to integrate fiction and nonfiction elements in their attempts to move and entertain audiences. *The Crowd* presented a montage of the metropolitan masses of Manhattan in motion unaware of their status as timeless celluloid objects. During production, Vidor apparently hid his camera, allowing it to peer through a peephole on the back of a truck or sit camouflaged within a stack of crates on a street corner. Peter Conrad has written of this film: "Like all other individuals in the Manhattan streets, Vidor's camera had been effaced by the mass. Yet every image it caught served as a testimonial, witnessing the existence of some nameless, unregarded person."[60] After documenting the city crowds, the camera scaled the sides of a city skyscraper to enter one of its windows to display a grid of (seemingly identical) workers undertaking the same mechanical movement of labor. The camera then focused on one individual and zoomed toward his face in a close-up. Jean-Paul Sartre wrote of this acrobatic movement as "the sport of a god," with a view from nowhere and everywhere.[61] The cinematic camera allowed an omniscient command over the seemingly impermeable concrete landscape of the city and its citizens. As Conrad wrote, whereas "men in simpler days fancied that they were under observation by God, who looked down from a point of vantage above the clouds," men and women in modern times came under the observation of the camera.[62]

Histories of documentary film and street cinema during this period rarely interrogate the experience of the camera for those silently captured within its frame, perhaps assuming acquiescence or ignorance. Privacy cases from this period are valuable in providing rare evidence of the feelings of some individuals and protests by unwilling cinematic subjects. In 1932, Miriam Blumenthal, a poverty-stricken widow from the Lower East Side in Manhattan, brought an action for breach of privacy (under New York's statutory privacy laws)[63] against the production company Picture Classics and its general manager Max Weisfeldt to prohibit them from using her moving image in their seventeen-minute film *Sight-Seeing in New York with Nick and Tony.*[64] Following *Humiston,* the case was fundamentally important to the film industry in New York, because of its likelihood of setting a legal precedent in relation to films documenting the city and its inhabitants.

In an affidavit Blumenthal filed in support of her initial application for an injunction, she described being a widow who sold bread and rolls on the streets of New York for a livelihood. During November and December 1931, Blumenthal was advised by friends and family that "her picture was being shown on the screens of several neighborhood motion picture theatres."[65] She stated that she was never aware of having her picture taken and never consented to or authorized its use. The plaintiff believed the film presented her in a "foolish, unnatural and undignified manner" and held her up to the "public ridicule and contempt of her neighbors and friends."[66] She sought not only an injunction but also $10,000 in damages for "great anxiety of mind, humiliation and mortification."[67]

Adele Blumenthal, the plaintiff's twenty-one-year-old daughter, also filed an affidavit in support of her mother's claim.[68] She stated that on 11 January 1932 she attended with friends a motion picture performance entitled *Sight-Seeing in New York with Nick and Tony* at the Hollywood Theatre, located on Avenue A between Sixth and Seventh streets in the borough of Manhattan. During the screening of the picture a full-sized picture or photographic likeness of her mother, Miriam Blumenthal, was displayed.

In opposing the plaintiff's motion, Weisfeldt filed an affidavit defending himself and Picture Classics.[69] Weisfeldt deposed that he had produced and distributed motion pictures for twenty-seven years and that Picture Classics was organized primarily to produce films "of travels and of educational and scientific subjects."[70] Some of its recent successes, he stated, included *Simba, Hunting Tigers in India, Trip to the South Seas, I Am from Siam, Out West Where the North Begins,* and *Seeing the United States by States.* He explained that these pictures involved photographing "actual scenes, incidents and events" and "actual peoples, animals and places."[71] The emphasis placed on the term "actual" throughout the defendants' material was most likely an attempt to align Picture Classics with the language of the court in *Humiston.*

In July 1931 Picture Classics had decided to produce a short motion picture of "historical points, views and life in various quarters of the Borough of Manhattan."[72] In order to "add interest," Picture Classics hired two professional actors, Nick Basil and Henry Armetta, to play the role of guides to two out-of-town schoolteachers wishing to take a tour of New York. In the summer of 1931 Weisfeldt, with the actors and one cameraman, began filming, "taking general views from the public highways of the streets, buildings and, incidentally, the people who were passing, walking, or at rest upon the public streets at the time when the photographing was actually taking place. The views so taken were normal, natural and actual occurrences in the everyday life of New York City; there was no preliminary posing, selection, action or direction with respect to any of the people who were included. . . . All of the views which were photographed were those of life and scenes in and from the public streets, and no scenes or views of the interior of any store, shop or home were taken."[73]

Miriam Blumenthal succeeded in obtaining an injunction, the defendant appealed, and the lower court's judgment was upheld by a three-to-two majority of the Appellate Division of the New York Supreme Court. Justice McAvoy, presenting the brief majority judgment, stated that the defendant, Picture Classics, was in the business of producing and distributing motion pictures and without the knowledge or consent of the plaintiff sold, distributed, and displayed moving pictures of her selling bread rolls in Orchard Street, New York. He stated that the New York privacy laws gave the plaintiff "an absolute right to have the defendants enjoined from using her picture for trade purposes even though her trade [brought] her into public view."[74]

Justices Finch and O'Malley disagreed, the latter providing a rigorous dissenting judgment. He argued that New York's privacy laws must be strictly construed and that, as held in *Humiston,* the legislature did not intend to prohibit the use of an individual's name or likeness in an "actual photograph of current events of public interest."[75] The dissenting opinion made clear that the primary issue of the case was whether the film at stake was a record of actual events, peoples, and places (such as the newsreel in *Humiston*) or whether the importation of fictional elements "to add interest" barred it from claiming the newsreel exemption from privacy laws established in *Humiston.* Justice O'Malley distinguished the earlier case of *Binns v. Vitagraph Company of America*[76] on the basis that it was a dramatic reenactment of past happenings and not a record of current events. He agreed with Weisfeldt's affidavit that stressed that the purpose of the film was not entertainment but rather to inform and educate the public.

In an affidavit replying to Weisfeldt, Harry Roter, the plaintiff's attorney, stated that the film was advertised not as news but rather as an entertaining comedy.[77] He submitted as evidence the program of the Hollywood Theatre, which read "Nick and Tony, Ace Funsters on Same Bill in Sight Seeing in New York," and he added that *Webster's Imperial Dictionary of the English Language* defines "fun" as "to make fun of, to make the object of ridicule."[78] He disputed the defendant's claims that the plaintiff was merely the accidental and unintended victim of the camera's range and asserted that given the angles required to make the shot and acquire the close-range footage, "there [could] be no doubt that it was the intention of the photographer to take her picture and show [her] as one of the unusual characters . . . [who] might be of interest and tend to amuse the general public, and primarily net returns or profits to the exhibitors and the defendants."[79]

The arguments in *Blumenthal* make clear the difficulties created by the distinction between truth and fiction drawn by the *Humiston* judgment. The minority of the court was convinced by the defendant's position that despite the fictional framework of *Nick and Tony,* the motion picture was informative and depicted current events and happenings, and thus should not be subject to the same laws as those pictures clearly made for "entertainment." This was in some ways a credible argument. Nonfiction pictures (documentaries), like newspapers and serious periodicals, were regarded at the time as playing a key role in educating the public about social issues, scientific discoveries, and political events. Distinguishing between the genres of motion pictures made by commercial producers for profit was, however, arbitrary and questionable. There was no evidence that Picture Classics (and other filmmakers) was motivated to produce educational or informative pictures by a sense of altruism or social responsibility. Whether a film contained a fictional narrative or not, it needed to entertain and amuse in order to attract crowds to the box office.

Blumenthal was a significant case for the film industry, as it tested the limits of the *Humiston* decision and seemed as if it would set a precedent regarding privacy laws and documentary filmmaking in the United States, especially in the state of New York. If film producers required the consent of all pictured subjects before a film could be exhibited, it would radically change the means and methods of shooting street and other urban scenes. Both the affidavits and the submissions filed in the case engaged directly with the question of who, if anyone, should have rights to one's own image in this context.

The affidavit of Weisfeldt set out that Picture Classics, like other film companies, commonly produced "travelogue" films of foreign peoples and places. These pictures, like ones of street life in New York, relied upon the participation of people who were either unaware of the camera's presence, uneducated as to the consequences of being caught on film, or unfazed by the thought of being projected on a big screen. The suggestion that all filmed subjects should have a right to actively decide whether or not they wished to have their image featured within a commercial motion picture was framed in the defendant's submissions as both ridiculous and untenable: "If the ruling below should be upheld, it would make impossible the exhibition of a travelogue showing the Dutch on the Island of Marken, the native quarter of Shanghai or the life of an African tribe. Every Hollander, Chinaman and

Negro whose features were distinguishable could insist that his rights were invaded and bring suit for damages for every public showing of the picture."[80]

In the respondent's submission, Harry Roter, the plaintiff's lawyer, responded to the obvious racism of such an assertion: "If the reference be to Hollanders, Chinamen and Negroes who seek vindication here, then we know no rule which excludes Hollanders, Chinamen and Negroes from the protection of the Civil Rights Law. The aegis of that statute is not withdrawn from those who do not qualify racially. The sole test is the use made of their portraits, which—the Legislature of this state has said—is as important to them as it is to others of different nationality or more fortunate lot in life."[81]

In recent decades, scholars working in a postcolonial analytical frame have pointed to the problematic rendering of foreign peoples in early documentary (or "ethnographic") cinema. At the beginning of the twentieth century, the travelogue, or travel picture, was one of the most popular and pervasive genres of motion picture. It promised to take the viewer on a journey to see strange peoples, unusual animals, and scenes of everyday life in exotic, faraway places. On one level, such pictures were educational, exposing audiences to cultures, languages, and landscapes they could rarely hope to visit. These pictures, however, commonly relied upon packaging others as curious objects of fascination and entertainment. As the cinema historian Lauren Rabinovitz has noted, these filmmakers were complicit with colonialism in "making faraway cultures into commodities that could be enjoyed for the price of admission."[82] They were closely aligned with the live exhibits of foreigners, as occurred at the 1904 St. Louis World's Fair, where passengers were ferried on a miniature railroad through reconstructed "native" villages of exotic peoples.[83] Granting privacy (or image) rights to those pictured in travelogues would radically challenge the assumptions underpinning such motion pictures, by transforming *objects* of amusement into rights-possessing *subjects*. That is precisely what Blumenthal's lawyer suggested.

Sight-Seeing in New York with Nick and Tony was not a travelogue featuring the sights and sounds of an exotic land, but it did take viewers on a tour of the "foreign" parts of their own city. As the defendants described in the submissions: "The foreign quarters of our large cities have always attracted the traveler. The local color, the juxtaposition of old and new-world life and customs, the curious makeshifts and adaptations of an old life to a new world are a matter of public interest."[84]

The plaintiff's lawyer, Harry Roter, stressed in his affidavit and submissions that the camera's lens transformed the plaintiff into a subject of morbid curiosity and ridicule. Clearly the plaintiff would not have been featured in the defendants' moving picture unless she were regarded as an unusual subject worthy of particular scrutiny. Roter suggested to the defendant that if Blumenthal were "incidental" and not a vital element of its film that it should simply delete her image.[85] To this proposition the defendants replied that "to comply with such a request [was] to extend an invitation to a hundred others to make similar complaint" and that "to picture streets uninhabited, to depict the buildings and not the people is [to produce] the play without Hamlet."[86] It was indeed unlikely that Blumenthal was the only individual in New York or elsewhere to make such a complaint.

The defendants' final submissions stressed the importance of the court's decision for the future of nonfiction filmmaking in the United States: "At first blush it may be thought that no great hardship would be imposed upon the picture industry by adopting the ruling of the Court below. It may seem that picture producers can without too much difficulty first obtain written consents from those who are photographed in these travel and educational scenes. Such a procedure is obviously impractical to the point of being prohibitive. . . . All the genuineness, all the life-like characteristics would be lost from the picture. It is current life in its vivid reality that is the subject of that public interest and concern which takes the news reel and should take the travel and educational subject out of the realm of privacy set up by the statute. . . . This case at bar is of novel impression and of importance to the picture industry."[87]

The plaintiff argued that *Sight-Seeing in New York with Nick and Tony* was not an educational or informative film made for the purpose of furthering public knowledge but rather a (fictional) comedy made for the purposes of entertainment and profit that transformed a private person into public property. "The poverty-stricken plaintiff, who was selling her wares on Orchard Street, New York," submitted her lawyer, "was not an incident of any public event. Nothing had occurred to attract or deserve the pitiless light of publicity. She was not seeking publicity in any shape, manner or form. The public was not interested in her by reason of any current event. . . . Can one—without his tongue in his cheek—assert that this photoplay was a 'news service'—a truthful accurate purveyor of news, quite as strictly so as a newspaper?"[88]

The defendants lost the case. The New York Court of Appeals confirmed the lower court's judgment and held that Picture Classics had breached Blumenthal's right to privacy. The importation of dramatic elements into the film by Picture Classics barred it from claiming the newsreel or documentary exemption declared in *Humiston*. Documentary, ethnographic, and travelogue pictures could continue to be made without producers obtaining the consent of pictured subjects so long as they did not import fictitious narratives into the production. In effect, the judgments of *Humiston* and *Blumenthal* liberated the burgeoning film industry from privacy laws by constructing new conditions for their filmmaking and strictly delineating the distinction between fiction and nonfiction. Fictional films used actors who signed contracts and (mostly) waived their privacy rights, while nonfiction films could continue to use subjects who were unaware or unwilling, as privacy laws no longer applied to them if the films were purely documentary in character.

The courts found that the public interest in making and distributing nonfiction films such as documentaries, actualities, and newsreels outweighed an individual's right to privacy. Fiction films, on the other hand, made merely for entertainment, were not seen to involve sufficient public interest to tip the scales, and thus an individual's privacy should be protected. The language of "public" and "private" that permeated the arguments and judgments in the decisions of *Humiston, Sweenek,* and *Blumenthal* underscores the importance of this dichotomy in structuring the law.

In recent decades, the public/private dichotomy has been extensively interrogated and critiqued, especially by feminist legal and political theorists, with scholars pointing to the ways in which this construct has worked to subordinate women by relegating them to the unregulated private sphere, unable to access the rights, privileges, and protection offered by law within the public domain.[89] In this chapter I have shown that women's attempts to access rights through the discourse of privacy left them vulnerable to the prioritization of public interests, such as the educational value of newsreels. I have shown that they appealed to privacy in cases involving the public display of their pictures taken while they participated in public activities (such as shopping or paid work) within public spaces (a retail store or a street) because of the embarrassment, humiliation, mortification, and shame they felt as a result of their public exposure. Some feminist legal scholars, such as Nicole Lacey, have cautioned against a "total rejection of the notion that privacy can be valuable" for women.[90] Clearly the value of privacy is contextual. In the context of the unauthorized circulation of their photographic and cinematic images by others, women invoked privacy at the beginning of the twentieth century in an attempt to achieve some limited degree of control. In the next chapter I show that privacy increasingly became a discourse used by professional women to control and profit from what Liz Conor has called their "techniques of appearing."[91]

The cases examined in this chapter were significant to the development of privacy law in the United States. *Kunz v. Allen* was the first privacy case concerning a nonfiction film. *Humiston* stated that privacy laws were not applicable to newsreels. *Blumenthal* established if and when those captured within a (partly fictional) documentary had enforceable rights to privacy. But these cases should be seen as more than steps in the evolution of a legal doctrine. The court records also offer valuable insight into the emergence of the nonfiction or documentary film industry at the beginning of the twentieth century and its impact on some of those unwittingly subjected to the gaze of the camera. The voices of the women plaintiffs challenge our assumptions about the acquiescence, ignorance, or complicity of silent screen presences in early documentary films. Plaintiffs told of being humiliated, distressed, and mortified at being exposed in public in telling detail, their mannerisms and movements watched by mass audiences.

Their vivid stories illuminate the differences in the experience of being frozen in a photograph used in an advertisement or passed from hand to hand—distressing as that might be—and being gazed at by thousands in an urban cinema at a time when privacy law still treated these experiences as one and the same. These cases confirm furthermore that it was primarily women who negotiated the privacy rights of screen subjects in the face of competing, primarily masculine, claims of public interest.

5
Privacy for Profit and a Right of Publicity

On 18 April 1936 Pauline Myers, an accomplished professional model and dancer from New York, suffered "great mortification" and "shame" when photographs of her famous "tribal" dances were published by the Baltimore *Afro-American* magazine in a way that emphasized and highlighted "her nude breasts and torso." Justice Noonan of the New York Supreme Court held that her "right to privacy" had been breached, as the photographs were her "exclusive property" and "she had the right to prevent their exhibition in her profession as a dancer."[1] A right to privacy was gradually assuming the status of a property right, asserted by women (and some men) to control the circumstances in which their images were shown in the interests of their careers. By the 1930s a right to privacy was becoming a means and mechanism to protect one's professional earnings.

Some scholars have professed confusion over how "a right to privacy" became "a right of publicity." In *The Rights of Publicity and Privacy* Thomas McCarthy has suggested, for example, that because of semantic confusions a "legal czar" should have "decreed a new label altogether, throwing overboard the whole cumbersome baggage of misleading words like 'privacy' and 'publicity.'" Then the decks would have been cleared for a straight-forward debate as to the contours of the new concept, "whether labelled 'property' or 'tort' or both."[2] I suggest, however, that the seeming confusion can be clarified and better understood once the historical and cultural dynamics of the development of privacy law in the United States are better understood. A gendered analysis of these changes proves useful in this regard.

From its beginning, a right to privacy was a doctrine used by individuals (primarily women) to assert control over photographic or cinematic images of their faces and bodies. And as I have shown, the key individuals who established the rights of pictured subjects to their images were women. In the late nineteenth and very early twentieth centuries, the problem of the unauthorized circulation of portraits was framed in "conservative" terms as a matter of privacy. In order to prevent the use and exploitation of their images by others, female plaintiffs appealed to the courts' willingness to protect and reinforce traditional feminine virtues of modesty and reserve and shield them from the prying eyes of others. Nonetheless, imminent in the new personal right of privacy was an assertion of property rights. The Court of Appeals in *Roberson v. Rochester Folding Box Co.* might have decided to discuss the case solely in terms of a right to privacy, but it is clear from the primary case documents that the plaintiff also argued that she had property rights in her portrait.[3] Similarly, in *Manola v. Stevens*[4] (upon which much of Warren and Brandeis's original argument was based) the actress had also asserted a property right in her own professional image. From the beginning, a right to privacy was summoned by individuals (primarily women) as a way of wresting control over still and moving images of their faces and bodies. The reasons they wished to do this, however, began to change.

By the 1930s the right to privacy had increasingly begun to be asserted by professional women like Myers—working as models, dancers, and actresses—for pecuniary purposes as the number of women engaged in paid employment increased. As feminist historians have noted, the first few decades of the twentieth century witnessed dramatic changes in the social and cultural conditions in which young women forged their lives. Women looked forward to greater independence. By 1920 a quarter of the industrial workforce was female, and in recognition of this change the U.S. government created a new division, the Women's Bureau, within the Department of Labor.[5] Black women of necessity entered the workforce in especially large numbers. Many were the main breadwinners. More than a third of married African American women worked for wages, double the proportion of white women.[6]

The creative industries of film and advertising employed growing numbers of young women, who projected back images to female spectators of modern beauty, glamour, and fashion. The American film industry "offered women opportunities that existed in no other workplace," as the film historian Karen Ward Mahar has noted. Film stars such as Mary Pickford, Mabel Norman, and Gloria Swanson earned some of the highest salaries in the world.[7] Women's images, in photographs or on the screen, were no longer simply signifiers of demure prettiness or sexual availability but became central to the promotion of professional careers.

The evolution of a right of publicity from a right to privacy, evident in the cases I discuss in this chapter, corresponds, then, with changes in the construction of femininity during the early twentieth century, away from ideals of modesty and refinement toward incitements to display, denoting a move away from the imperative of self-effacement to the demand for self-articulation. The traditional association between womanliness and modesty was disrupted as new feminine ideals emerged, based upon the presentation and publicity of the female face and form. Pictures provided the medium for defining and negotiating these new styles of femininity. The camera did not simply capture the physical features of its subjects, it also operated as a means of self-invention.

In *Spectacular Modern Woman,* Liz Conor has argued that the new conditions of feminine visibility shaped modern women's subjectivities as "appearing women."[8] Through their mode of "appearance," women could identify as New Women in the ocularcentric economy of modernity. In this context their "techniques of appearing" became their most valuable assets.[9] The right image published in the right context could give women access to financial security and thereby the kind of privileges traditionally acquired through the right kind of marriage. With changes in the visual economy consequent upon the advent of the camera, women's emotional and professional investment in their appearance in still and moving film became ever more intense. Thus the ability to control the circumstances and context of the use and publication of their images was vital. Paradoxically, the right to privacy came closest to realizing its most radical potential during this publicity-oriented era, when it was invoked as a doctrine that recognized women as the owners of themselves as spectacles. Such a legal right would necessarily occupy an uneasy relationship with copyright, because ownership rights in an image might be claimed simultaneously by the picture taker and the pictured subject.

Some women's efforts to control the circulation of their professional images in this period could go to extremes. In the 1920s Australian screen star Lotus Thompson traveled to Hollywood to pursue a career in cinema, but rather than attracting film roles, she became stuck in the frustrating position of being contracted only to "appear" as a leg model for other actresses. In a desperate and dramatic protest against her effective dismemberment, she poured nitric acid over her legs, disfiguring and thus withdrawing them from the gaze of the camera. Writing of this tragic incident, Conor suggested that it showed that "one's image could not be cast off like a shed skin, that it was not separate from and incidental to one's subjectivity."[10] Thompson sought control over the construction of her image rather than invisibility, and her radical strategy worked in that it briefly made her a celebrity. The incident was widely reported in the media and catapulted her into the type of screen roles she so desperately sought, such as *Desert Dust* (directed by William Wyler in 1927) and *Terry of the Times* (directed by Robert Hill in 1930).

Other women also expressed a desire to own the mode and manner of their appearance, to turn their visibility into an assertion of subjective identity rather than acquiesce in a process of objectification. Seeking less destructive strategies than Thompson's self-mutilation, they chose to go through the courts. The female plaintiffs whose cases I examine in this chapter certainly did not resist publicity. Rather they embraced it, but rejected the kind of display forced upon them by others. Here I discuss those potentially progressive cases that moved toward establishing a property right for individuals in their own images. I also examine some more privacy cases involving men and suggest that in the visual culture of modernity, men preserved their masculinity by constructing themselves as actively "performing," rather than passively "appearing." Finally, I examine the resulting doctrine of a right to publicity, first articulated in *Haelan Laboratories v. Topps Chewing Gum Inc.*,[11] which finally accorded women and men quasi-property rights in their images.

Making an Income from "Techniques of Appearing"

Prior to the late nineteenth century, prominent Americans were largely known for their words or deeds, such as those of the founding fathers. Presidents such as Washington and Jefferson saw their images as a kind of common republican property, public circulation of which benefited democracy and nation building.[12] As the United States moved to become an image-based as well as a word-based society, however, the attitudes of prominent Americans toward the promiscuous use of their images began to shift from active support to acquiescence to concern. They sought to control and contain the use of their images by others. This was due, in part, to the changing culture of advertising and the rise of the popular "yellow" press. The greatest push toward individuals claiming property rights in their own images came, however, with the changing status of women within a modern ocularcentric culture.

The young women who brought the first cases in the United States for property rights in their images were working women. The images contested were not depictions of status or achievement, but they were of professional and subjective value. In *Spectacular Modern Woman,* Conor coined the phrase "techniques of appearing" to describe the variety of practices women engaged in during the 1920s to display themselves as modern subjects—as beauty queens, mannequins or models, stage and cinema stars, and flappers.[13] In this chapter I show the ways in which women used the legal doctrine of a right to privacy to protect their techniques of appearing. In doing so they helped transform the right of privacy into the right of publicity.

In the summer of 1917, seventeen-year-old Gladys Loftus appeared as a Ziegfeld girl in the *Ziegfeld Follies,* a series of lavish theater productions on Broadway, conceived and created by Florenz Ziegfeld. They were modeled on the Folies Bergères of Paris, which specialized in exhibiting attractive young women, such as the famous black icon Josephine Baker. Loftus appeared in the show *Midnight Frolic* at the New Amsterdam Theatre wearing a red "rose costume," specially created for her by the leading fashion designer Lady Duff-Gordon, known professionally as Lucile. Publicity photographs were taken of Loftus in her costume by Alfred Cheney Johnston and used in publicity about the show.

In April 1918 Loftus brought an action against Greenwich Lithographic Company for using one of these photographs without her consent in marketing material for a "photoplay" entitled *Shame* (directed by John W. Noble, 1917).[14] The complaint alleged: "T]he defendants, on or about the first day of January, 1918, and without the written or other consent of the plaintiff, and in violation of her rights, produced, exhibited, leased and released, a certain photoplay entitled Shame, and for the purposes of advertising such photoplay and for the purposes of trade, designed and printed theatrical posters, circulars, and other advertising matter containing the picture of the plaintiff."[15]

The theatrical posters for *Shame* were published in *Harper's Bazaar* and *Town and Country* magazines in July 1917 and in *Metropolitan Magazine* in September 1917. The complaint alleged that this conduct by the defendants breached New York's statutory privacy laws,[16] but interestingly the complaint did not use the word "privacy." The plaintiff claimed $50,000 in damages and an injunction restraining the defendants from using her likeness in any of their marketing material. Unlike in many similar privacy actions discussed in earlier chapters, however, no reference was made to the emotional impact of the use of these images on the plaintiff. There were no reports of "mortification," "humiliation," "offended modesty," or "hurt feelings" as a result of the defendants' act. Loftus was using a right to privacy to protect her professional and business interests.

The primary issue in this case became whether the image used by the defendants was actually of the plaintiff. Evidence at trial revealed that the plaintiff was the only one to have worn the costume and that she would be well recognized as that particular character from *Midnight Frolic*. The respondents contended that the image was a sketch produced by an artist in their employ, Ira Cassidy, and that he was instructed simply to draw "a picture of any girl with downcast eyes."[17] Cassidy was not called as a witness, but the respondents contended that so far as they knew, he drew the sketch of a woman "of his own conception and imagination" and did not rely upon any photograph or model.[18] Johnston (the original photographer), however, testified for the plaintiff that as soon as he saw one of the posters for the motion picture *Shame* he instantly recognized it as a sketched copy of his photograph. There were only minor alterations—"changing slightly the tilt of the head and the outline of the nose, chin, and neck, and slightly lowering the position of the hair."[19]

The debate about whether the poster did or did not reproduce the photograph of Loftus echoed debates in copyright cases. In fact, Loftus's lawyer, Nathan Burkan, recognized the parallels, submitting: "The statute does not require an exact likeness true in every detail. That has never been required, even in cases involving copyright infringement, where it will be admitted, there must be 'copy-ing' and where the evidence must be conclusive on that point."[20] It is significant here that Loftus brought a privacy case over the photograph, rather than Johnston, the photographer, bringing a copyright case. Johnston had a legally recognized property right in the photograph, while Loftus was attempting to assert one. The court's response was comparable to a copyright decision. Justice Laughlin stated that he did not accept the respondents' view that Cassidy had created the image purely from his mind and that "the only reasonable inference is that the artist must have copied it from a copy of the plaintiff's photograph."[21] It is notable that he referred to the photograph in question as the *plaintiff's*. He concluded: "It is perfectly evident that he had and used a copy of the photograph and that he copied the features of the plaintiff; but in order to make the picture fit the subject, with the man pointing his hand in scorn at the woman and charging her with shame, it was necessary to tilt her head somewhat to put her in an appropriate attitude."[22]

Justice Laughlin held that the defendants had breached New York's statutory privacy laws by reproducing the photograph on the poster and that the plaintiff was entitled to an injunction and damages. Significantly, the court did not mention the term "privacy" in its decision. Justice Laughlin stated that the statute provided a cause of action to any person whose portrait was used without his or her consent for trade or advertising purposes, but he did not refer to the name of the provisions (Right of Privacy) or any of the cases under which the law originated (such as *Roberson v. Rochester Folding Box*

Co.).[23] It is curious that the defendants relied only on a denial that the image was of the plaintiff, rather than interrogating whether the plaintiff was actually trying to protect her privacy. Her image was used and circulated widely as publicity for the *Ziegfeld Follies*, so it may have been difficult for her to claim that use of the same image in advertising for a film was an invasion of her privacy and thus caused her personal distress. In any case, the essence and import of the privacy laws were absent from the arguments of the plaintiff, the defendants, and the court. This was presented as a commercial case (akin to copyright, trademark, or contract), brought by Loftus in order to assert ownership over her technique of appearance and to reap the pecuniary benefits flowing from that property. It was one of the first right to publicity cases, although not identified as such by legal scholars. The plaintiff was able to argue her case without mentioning the word "privacy." As the case entailed an action based on statute, the origin and context of the laws prohibiting the unauthorized use of an individual's image could be obscured because the provisions provided a quasi-property right amenable to commercial grievances. In jurisdictions where a right to privacy was not codified but based in common law, this posed a more difficult challenge.

Beatrice Lillie confronted this difficulty when she brought a suit against Warner Bros. Pictures in the state of California for the use of her image without her consent in motion picture "shorts."[24] Lillie had forged a successful career in both the United States and the United Kingdom as a stage and motion picture actress. The complaint stated that "she [was] an actress and public performer of great artistic ability and accomplishments" and received "high remuneration" for her appearances.[25] In May 1929 Lillie entered into a written contract with Warner Bros. Pictures to appear in certain scenes of an "All Star" talking picture called *The Show of Shows* (directed by John G. Adolfi, 1929). *The Show of Shows* was a lavish technicolor picture, featuring nearly all of Warner Bros.' contemporary film stars. It was styled in the same format as Metro-Goldwyn-Mayer's feature *The Hollywood Revue of 1929* (directed by Charles Reisner).

The contract between Lillie and Warner Bros. stipulated that Lillie would appear in two scenes—one of six or seven minutes and the other between two and three minutes—and that "the two scenes [would] only to be used in connection with this revue and [would] not be used in 'Shorts.'"[26] "Shorts" was a term used to refer to short motion pictures, as opposed to feature-length movies. Lillie's attorneys submitted that to include the plaintiff in a "short"—a "brief and minor production" of "inconsequential importance"—would present her to audiences and the theatrical world as a "cheap and inconsequential performer" and "would thereafter impair her ability to command as high a remuneration, or as important engagements . . . [as well as] impair and damage her prestige and reputation as a star or feature performer."[27] They alleged that in breach of her contractual rights and "in violation of the plaintiff's right of privacy," the scenes from *The Show of Shows* were subsequently separated by Warner Bros. Pictures and exhibited in various theaters and large public performances as shorts. They also claimed the plaintiff had been defamed by the rearrangement of the film material. Altogether they claimed actual (financial) damages of $50,000.[28]

It is difficult to conceive how such conduct by Warner Bros. Pictures could be considered an invasion of Lillie's privacy, unless we understand "a right to privacy" as a discourse invoked from the beginning to claim ownership over one's image. Its rationale is to be found in its gendered evolution, even though it began to be used to achieve quite different ends. In their submissions regarding a right to privacy, the plaintiff's attorneys referred to the 1931 decision of *Melvin v. Reid*[29] (discussed in detail in the next chapter) and its recognition of the "right to privacy" in California based upon the Californian constitutional right to "pursue and obtain happiness." They stated that: "By the publication here complained of, the defendants, for purely commercial purposes and without the consent of Beatrice Lillie, have published her picture acting in such a way as to interfere with her enjoyment of life and her acquisition of property."[30]

Privacy was here explicitly annexed to property. The plaintiff's attorneys noted the shift, noting that a right to privacy was limited in circumstances where a person has become "so prominent" that he or she can be said to be a "public figure."[31] They argued, however, that this exception was not absolute and that even public figures were entitled to privacy in certain circumstances. They used the example of President Hoover, noting that just because he was "a figure of national prominence [did] not forsooth give the right to a photographer to photograph him in his bathroom and to publish his picture in its unbecoming disarray."[32] They then compared Hoover's hypothetical exposure in "unbecoming disarray" to the situation of Beatrice Lillie, who, "having been photographed as associated in a play with actors of great distinction," was entitled to make complaint when "her picture and acted part is so displayed that she will appear to be acting in accompaniment to a negro troupe of vaudeville performers."[33] Here we are again reminded of the racist underpinnings of much argument about what constituted demeaning and damaging images. Their comparison between President

Hoover being photographed in his bathroom and Lillie appearing in a "short" alongside "negro" performers was flawed and illogical. In the former case, President Hoover's right to privacy would be imperiled by a photograph of him in a private space, whereas Lillie's representation, whether or not damaging to her reputation, would not impose on her privacy as such.

The defendants attacked Lillie's privacy claims, opening with an observation that the privacy argument was "advanced with considerable trepidation and lack of confidence" on the plaintiff's behalf, for reasons that are not difficult to discern.[34] They referred to *Melvin v. Reid* and contended that it was clearly not comparable to the immediate case: "These scenes, from all that is apparent from the pleadings or from the brief itself, made no disclosure of anything whatsoever in Miss Lillie's private life. They consisted of an act in which she appeared and in which she did not necessarily portray any incident of her own life, but presumably acted a part."[35]

The defendants also stated that on the evidence the picture in question did not contain anything "so offensive" as Lillie in the company of "a negro troupe" of actors. They concluded: "The appellant's final claim that a cause of action for invasion of privacy has been stated, is wholly unsupported by any authority, example or tenable argument. The bare facts, and even the appellant's own argument, show clearly that no actionable invasion of privacy has been pleaded."[36] The California Second District Court of Appeal agreed with the defendants, stating that by virtue of copyright laws, the defendants acquired full ownership of the picture and thus had the right to use and exhibit the picture in any way they pleased, except as limited by contract. Presiding Justice Conrey held: "It seems clearly to follow that the exhibition of the scene as a short would not be a tortious invasion of the plaintiff's right to privacy. If wrong at all, it necessarily was only a breach of the contract."[37] Lillie failed to articulate a cause of action for breach of contract because, according to the court, the complaint failed to show facts demonstrating any damage. The defendants' demurrer was therefore successful, and the plaintiff lost her case.

The court's reasons for dismissing Lillie's privacy claim seemed to be that recognition of a right to privacy in such circumstances would conflict with existing rights of contract and copyright. This rationale demonstrates judicial awareness of the tension developing between copyright and a right to privacy (or publicity). If a picture taker and a pictured subject were both vested with property rights in an image, then there was inherent conflict with regard to the use of the image. The threat posed to copyright holders by the assignment of rights to pictured subjects was recognized decades before, as we saw in chapter 2, by the professional photographers who publicly opposed the Bill to Protect Ladies introduced in the House of Representatives by Congressman John Robert Thomas in 1888.

The conflicting rights of copyright and contract were also evident in early right of privacy law. For instance, after the statutory right to privacy laws were passed in New York in 1903, a photographer could exploit his photograph for trade or advertising purposes only if he first acquired the written consent of the pictured subject. Equally, if a photographer and pictured subject contracted to use the photograph for certain purposes, the photographer was still required to obtain the written consent of the subject before using it for a different purpose (if that purpose were trade or advertising). The evolution of a right to privacy toward a right of publicity rendered the inherent conflict explicit and problematic. Instead of a property right (copyright) conflicting with a tort (privacy), there would potentially be two competing property rights in the same matter.

In *Lillie v. Warner Bros. Pictures,* the court failed to adduce the most obvious and valid reason for denying the plaintiff's privacy claim: that there was no evidence her privacy had been invaded. The case demonstrates the increasing uncertainty, on the part of both litigants and the courts, concerning the quasi-proprietary doctrine of privacy. From the beginning of the case law, the term "privacy" worked to obscure as much as illuminate the nature of this new cause of action. Intimately connected to visual representation, it seemed to confer image rights to individuals. But as the law developed in response to changing historical circumstances, the content and application of the action diverged to an ever-greater extent from its name. It is therefore not surprising Lillie argued that her privacy—the right synonymous with a right to one's own image—had been breached. If the true nature of this "right" had been recognized earlier (as when Milton E. Gibbs argued in *Roberson v. Rochester Folding Box Co.* that it was proprietary),[38] the "whole cumbersome baggage of misleading words like 'privacy' and 'publicity'" (as Thomas McCarthy put it)[39] might have been dispensed with. As it was, there was no clarification by any court, and "a right to privacy" continued to be used through the 1930s by those individuals with a professional investment in their appearance (mainly women) as a way of controlling the use of their image. It filled a vacuum, as no other doctrine seemed so well suited to protect the pictured subject from exploitation and abuse, whether or not that abuse involved a breach of privacy as such.

In the same decade, a New York model, Gloria Middleton, brought a suit against the News Syndicate Company for using her photograph in a daily news column entitled "The Inquiring Photographer."[40] She was erroneously described in the column as a "cigarette girl" employed by the Commodore Hotel. A cigarette girl was a young woman wearing a special short-skirted uniform, who sold cigarettes, cigars, and candy from a tray held by a strap around her neck. The court described the claim as brought under sections 50 and 51 of the Civil Rights Laws (New York's statutory privacy laws), but again, as in *Loftus*, the court did not mention the term "privacy." Middleton lost her case, as the court held that the use of her image by the defendant was not for trade or advertising purposes. She also sued for libel, but on that ground the court held that the article was not libelous of her but rather used her picture in error. Middleton clearly regarded the use of her picture by the newspaper as bringing her into disrepute and undermining her modeling career, but as New York's privacy laws were so narrow in scope, protecting pictured subjects only in circumstances of "trade and advertising," she was left without legal remedy.

A year later, in 1938, the City Court of New York heard another case that highlighted the tension between the professional right to control the use of one's image and the right to privacy.[41] In this instance, New York's privacy laws hindered rather than helped another model forge a career based on professional appearance. Marian Semler, under "legal age" and thus described as "an infant" by the court, was a professional model who consented to the use of her photograph taken while dressed in a "negligee," in the defendant's magazine entitled *Silk Stocking Stories*. The court stated: "It would appear from all the evidence that it was the pictures of partly draped women appearing in this magazine that sold the magazine as well as the stories. It would further appear that the magazine was intended to and did make an appeal to sex."[42]

Semler's parents objected to the use of their daughter's photograph in the magazine and brought an action alleging that her apparent agreement was irrelevant, as she was underage and they (as her guardians) had not provided the requisite written consent. In many ways, this case was similar to the 1914 *Colyer*[43] case (discussed in chapter 2), when a young professional diver's photo was published in a salacious context in the magazine called the *National Police Gazette*. In that case, the court held that New York's privacy laws did not apply to periodicals and newspapers, and thus the plaintiff lost. In the 1938 case of *Semler v. Ultem Publications*, however, the court held that the use of the photograph was unauthorized—because Semler was underage—and found for the plaintiff. Again, mention of privacy was noticeably absent from the judgment. This was possibly due to the fact that not only was Semler a professional model, she had consented to the use of her "risqué" photograph by the defendant, even though her parents still retained the right to restrain the use of her image rights under New York's privacy laws.

In the following year, 1939, yet another case was brought by a young woman seeking to protect the property value of her well-known face. Judy Lane was a singer who brought an action under New York's statutory privacy laws[44] against F. W. Woolworth Co. for the unauthorized use of her photograph in an advertisement for lockets.[45] The complaint alleged that for many years she had been "engaged in the entertainment world in the profession of singer on the stage, in motion pictures and on the radio and her photograph [was] known to thousands of people."[46] The defendant operated retail stores in New York

City known as “five and ten cent stores,” selling “novelties, cheap and inexpensive jewelry and other articles of personal property.”[47] The plaintiff alleged that by virtue of the defendant’s use of her photograph to advertise its jewelry, she had been injured in the sum of $50,000.[48]

The defendant’s primary argument was that Lane’s photograph was not being used to advertise its lockets but rather being used to demonstrate to prospective buyers how to use the locket. They explained that on the back of the plaintiff’s photograph was a designation that it could be replaced with the purchaser’s favorite photo. Justice Noonan of the Supreme Court found this argument completely unpersuasive: “This contention is without force. The photograph was obviously used to bring attention to the lockets on display, to make them more attractive. This is a use for ‘advertising’ and for ‘trade’ purposes.”[49] He also commented that the defendant’s suggestion to the purchaser that “he” could replace the plaintiff’s photograph with another also meant that “he” might prefer to retain the plaintiff’s smiling countenance. Justice Noonan thus struck this particular argument from the defendant’s “Answer to the Complaint.” He also dismissed another of the defendant’s submissions: that it had assumed that the wholesale vendor in Rhode Island had already obtained consent. He ordered it to amend its “Answer to the Complaint” within ten days. The case did not appear on the court record again, and so one assumes the matter was discontinued or settled out of court.

Privacy and the “Primitive” Woman

The individuals who first brought privacy actions at the end of the ninteenth century and the beginning of the twentieth were usually white women. The only case brought by an African American during this time, *Myers v. African American Publishing Co.*,[50] involved the claim of a young, attractive "tribal" dancer, who sought an injunction over professional photographs of her that had been doctored to emphasize her nudity. I discuss this case in detail below, but first we need to consider a right to privacy's racial dimension in the United States.

In the 1900 trial of *Roberson v. Rochester Folding Box Co.* Justice Davy stated: "Privacy is regarded as a product of civilization. It was unsought and unknown among the barbarous tribes. It implies an improved and progressive condition of the people in cultivated manners and customs with well-defined and respected domestic relations."[51] Davy's judgment reflected a common view in the United States at the turn of the twentieth century that gender roles and attributes were differentiated to the greatest degree in the most "civilized" societies. As Gail Bederman has argued, popular discourse on "civilization" considered "primitive" men and women as closely resembling each other in their behavior, dress, and other characteristics.[52] Primitive women were seen as aggressive, accustomed to hard labor and unused to covering their bodies with clothing. Only "civilized" (white) women were regarded as displaying the proper virtues of modesty, delicacy, and devotion to the home. Privacy, as a right, was attached to this discourse of civilization, as the courts and legislatures sought to "protect" the sanctity of civilized white women's bodies and faces from the scrutiny of the outside world.

Eden Osucha has argued that Warren and Brandeis's articulation of a right to privacy and its application in early cases such as *Roberson v. Rochester Folding Box Co.* not only rested on gender assumptions but also inscribed racial difference.[53]

Osucha argued that being subject to media publicity "racialized" white women by calling upon a history of image making associated with generic and grotesque racial stereotypes.[54] Their becoming an anonymous image seemed to strip women of their agency and individuality, lumping them together with photography's other objectified bodies, such as those of the criminal classes, the poor, the diseased, and nonwhites. The prejudicial slur of publicity was reflected in snippets from case records, such as testimony in *Kunz v. Allen* in which Stella Kunz's very presence on the motion picture screen as part of an advertisement made her seem to one viewer "very much like a great, big, fat colored woman."[55] Losing one's privacy could be perceived as losing one's claim on the respectability of (white) femininity.

Osucha compares the white, middle-class conceptions of privacy and the perils of publicity evident in Warren and Brandeis's article and *Roberson v. Rochester Folding Box Co.* with the most popular and widely recognized brand in the United States in the last decade of the nineteenth century: Aunt Jemima's instant pancake mix. Aunt Jemima traded upon the national appeal of the plantation mammy—"a nostalgic, mythical figuration of an antebellum black maternity."[56] The white male entrepreneur Chris Rutt launched his product at the 1893 World's Columbian Exposition in Chicago, insisting to consumers that Aunt Jemima was a real person and employing fifty-nine-year-old Nancy Green to make and serve pancakes from a "giant flour barrel" while singing songs and telling stories of life on "the old plantation." Green was a former slave, but before becoming the pancake "mammy" she had been employed as a housekeeper to a prominent Chicago family. Her face, form, and past life were buried beneath the Aunt Jemima brand. Details of her life were reconstructed with company fabrications to create the fictional persona sold as authentic. Osucha argues that the *Roberson v. Rochester Folding Box Co.* case (in which Abigail Roberson unwillingly became the face of a flour brand) highlights the injustice of Green's plight. The public reacted with outrage toward the injuries to individuality and autonomy experienced by Roberson but unthinkingly inflicted the same indignities upon Green.

Osucha makes an important point, but her analysis does not go far enough. Unlike Abigail Roberson, Nancy Green was not simply objectified by the Aunt Jemima image; her individuality was obliterated through the use of a racial stereotype. Nothing in the Aunt Jemima image represented or referred to Green as an individual: she became, or rather always was, Aunt Jemima in the eyes of white consumers. She was identified as an "old, black woman" or "plantation mammy" and thus was denied the requisite personality or individuality necessary for any possible claim to breach of privacy. Further, she could not have argued any proprietary claim over the image, as even though it apparently was her, it did not depict her actual "likeness."

Osucha's analysis of the racial dimensions of claims to privacy fails to note the 1938 case of classical dancer Pauline Myers, which seems to be the first case to involve a claim of breach of privacy by an African American.[57] Myers brought an action for libel and breach of New York's statutory privacy laws[58] against the African American Publishing Company for featuring a story about her with accompanying photographs that had been altered to emphasize her nudity. She was twenty-three years old, a resident of Harlem, and a minor participant in the Harlem Renaissance. The complaint described her as a "classic dancer," with "a high public and professional reputation for her dance interpretation of the mood and spirit of her people," and "a model for painters, sculptors and photographers who sought to render the mood and spirit of the negro race."[59] Myers clearly had a professional investment in her particular techniques of appearing.

In April 1936, the defendants approached and interviewed Myers for the purposes of publishing a story about her in their weekly newspaper, the *Afro-American*. They requested some photographs of her dancing, and Myers showed them her portfolio. They chose three photographs that had been taken of her as part of an "art exhibit," but Myers refused to hand them over, as the photographs depicted her in a semi-naked state. The defendants promised that they would "cause the breast and torso to be draped" and that if they could not cover up the photographs satisfactorily they would return them to her.[60]

The story and photographs were published on 18 April 1936. The newspaper not only failed to cover up Myer's nudity but even used various techniques (such as outlining) to enhance it. The story in *Afro-American* read as follows:

> Pauline Meyers[61] who rocked Broadway with her interpretations of African dances and now makes her livelihood posing for artists as a typical native belle, had never been any closer to the Congo than Seventh Avenue and 135th Street.
>
> She made her Broadway debut in 1933 in "Growing Pains" and also was in "Emperor Jones" with Lawrence Tibbett in 1933. Among some of the recent shows that she played in are: "Enchanted Figures," "Zoonga," "Drums of the Bayou," and "Kykonkor," the native African drama. She has

> recently returned from the Coast, where she worked at the Warner Brothers Studio in the film version of "The Green Pastures." At present she is an artist's model. . . .
>
> Mrs. Laura Bowman Antoine is her inspiration, and she has been guided in her career by this grand woman of the stage. Miss Meyers hopes to have a chance to join her in Haiti, sometime soon, so as to continue her study of the native Haitian dance.[62]

With the aspirations of a modern woman, Myers thought it normal for "marriage and a career" to "go along together." She was a successful professional, who had spent considerable time and effort building a career incorporating diverse techniques of appearing—as a model, dancer, and actress. Her public image, based both on her attractiveness and on her talent, was a vital asset. She brought a court case for breach of privacy to assert control over photographs of herself that were being exploited, denigrated, and misappropriated by others. She won her case, the New York Supreme Court holding that, under New York's statutory privacy laws, "The photographs delivered to the defendant were the exclusive property of the plaintiff. Therefore, the publication of them without her consent or in violation of the agreement made was an unauthorized act."[63] Like the majority of cases considered in this chapter, the court did not refer to privacy rights in its application of New York's privacy statute. By 1938 the court preferred to state that the plaintiff's photographs were her "exclusive property."

In *Spectacular Modern Woman,* Conor argued that "appearing" as a "modern" woman was a privilege reserved for white women. Nonwhites, notably Indigenous Australians,

Africans, and African Americans, categorized as "premodern" or "primitive," lacked capacity "to transcend the racially inflected space of mimicry."[64] The black woman succeeded only in appearing comic or abject. The case of *Myers v. African American Publishing Co.* complicates this analysis. Pauline Myers built a successful career from performing "tribal" dances and sporting "native" dress. Both the article in *Afro-American* and the Supreme Court judgment classified her activities as a studied performance, rather than an instinctive or comic act. The article referred to her "posing," "playing," and "studying" her roles. Her nudity, though exploited by *Afro-American* for voyeuristic purposes, was considered by the court an "indecent exposition" of a woman with a "well known reputation" within her profession.[65] Myers's case disrupted the assumed relationship between "a right to privacy" and "whiteness" in the United States by showing that a black woman could also claim ownership and control over her photographs and performance.

Protecting Masculine Professions of Performance

Men didn't usually need to prove they were professionals. It was taken for granted that their careers were important to them. Two cases in the 1930s, *Redmond v. Columbia Pictures Corporation*[66] and *Franklin v. Columbia Pictures Corporation*,[67] involved male plaintiffs who wished to protect what I call their "professions of performance." I use this phrase in juxtaposition to women's "techniques of appearing" to describe male careers built upon visual performances of physical skill or muscular strength. Cases concerning women's techniques of appearing commonly involved still photographs (in *Loftus, Middleton, Semler, Lane,* and *Myers*), as the value lay in the image. Cases involving men's professions of performance, on the other hand, derived from cinema, which specializes in depictions of movement. Men could appear on the big screen and yet remain masculine.

This was important. At the beginning of the twentieth century, long-established ideas of manhood and womanhood were shifting and being reconfigured within a vision-dominated world. How sex and gender roles might interact with the new media of still and moving film and how these visual identities connected to institutions of authority and power were being debated. Femininity embraced visual display, but women insisted on controlling the terms of their appearance. Young women were actively constructing their subjectivities through shaping their appearance. Masculinity, however, resisted becoming a static spectacle.

Rapid urbanization and industrialization increased immigration, and the challenges of colonialism in the late nineteenth century contributed to new insecurities about the superiority of the white male body. Remaking ideas of manhood and reinforcing masculinity became a national preoccupation. As many cultural historians have noted, images of white masculinity proliferated during this period, with men choosing to be represented while engaged in feats of strength, physical skill, and sporting prowess.[68] Like women, men might construct their subjectivities on film, but they usually did so through physical activity, even if that meant simply flexing their muscles. Kodak advertisements pictured men hunting and fishing, while motion picture cameras recorded the popular, and increasingly professional, pastime of boxing. Images of such figures as Eugene Sandow, Bernarr MacFadden, "White Hope" Jim Jeffries, Houdini, and President Theodore Roosevelt (on horseback, on safari, as frontiersman) worked to model the virility of masculinity. A right to privacy, as it moved toward a right to publicity, allowed some men to assert legal rights over the valuable images that depicted their professions of performance.

Jack Redmond was a professional golfer who specialized in making trick shots—he was described by the Court of Appeals of New York as "a trick shot exhibitionist."[69] He performed these trick shots in nearly every country in the world and made frequent appearances in theaters across the United States, including on Broadway. On 23 June 1935, Redmond exhibited his talents for Fox Movietone News at a country club. The performance was also watched by several caddies, the manager of the country club, and some employees. The defendant purchased the rights to the scenes of the plaintiff's trick-shot exhibition from Fox Movietone News and edited the scenes into a motion picture entitled *Golfing Rhythm*. The defendant released the film, and it was sold and distributed to a range of cinemas. On 13 June 1936, after becoming aware of the film, Redmond notified Columbia Pictures that the company was using his likeness without his consent. He then filed an action against the company under New York's statutory privacy laws.[70] The defendant argued that there was no evidence of any damage to the plaintiff, he had incurred no pecuniary loss, and had suffered no hurt feelings as a result of its conduct. The trial court in fact found in favor of Redmond but agreed with the defendant's assessment of minimal loss, awarding only six cents in damages. The plaintiff appealed, and the judgment was increased to an award of $1,500 damages. The defendant then appealed, and the New York Court of Appeal affirmed the Appellate Court's decision.

At first glance, it is not clear why the trial court and subsequent courts considered Redmond's right to privacy (enshrined in sections 50 and 51 of New York's Civil Rights Laws) to be infringed. There was no invasion of his privacy by exhibiting the very skills for which he had become famous. As in the other privacy cases discussed in this chapter, here New York's privacy laws, first enacted in 1903 in response to *Roberson v. Rochester Folding Box Co.*,[71] seem to have been applied for a purpose far removed from their original aim. If, however, the laws are construed as enshrining a quasi-property right in one's image, as I have suggested in relation to other cases, we can see the logical trajectory. Redmond considered his performance, of which the representation of his "likeness" was a key element, to be something owned and controlled by him. To use the language of Attorney Milton E. Gibbs in *Roberson*,[72] the commercial value of the footage was not in the film stock but in Redmond's performance. By surrendering his performance to a motion picture camera, Redmond lost the ability to control the profits from the replication and representation of that act, if not covered by specific contract.

At the same time, Columbia Pictures faced another similar lawsuit, brought by the bullfighter Sidney Franklin.[73] Born in New York City, Franklin trained as a matador in Mexico before exhibiting his bullfighting expertise in Spain, Portugal, Mexico, Colombia, and Panama. In his 1932 book on the art of bullfighting, entitled *Death in the Afternoon*, Ernest Hemingway described him in the following terms: "Franklin is brave with a cold, serene and intelligent valor, but instead of being awkward and ignorant, he is one of the most skillful, graceful and slow manipulators of a cape fighting today. His repertoire with the cape is enormous, but he does not attempt by a varied repertoire to escape from the performance of the veronica as the base of his cape work and his veronicas are classical, very emotional, and beautifully timed and executed.

You will find no Spaniard who ever saw him fight who will deny his artistry and excellence with the cape."[74]

The same year in which *Death in the Afternoon* was published, Columbia Pictures made a documentary film about Franklin entitled *Throwing the Bull.* Franklin did not consent to the film, and he objected to the way in which he was depicted. He brought an action against Columbia on three grounds. First, he asserted that the defendant used his name and likeness without his consent and therefore breached sections 50 and 51 of New York's Civil Rights Laws.[75] His second and third claims were for libel and slander, respectively. He argued the film was defamatory and exposed him to ridicule and contempt. He claimed $100,000 in damages under each cause of action.

In relation to his privacy claim, Franklin submitted: "Since the year 1932, the defendant knowingly and without the plaintiff's consent, written or otherwise, has been producing, manufacturing, leasing, licensing, selling, distributing, displaying, circulating and using in the State of New York and elsewhere, for advertising purposes and for the purposes of trade, photographic pictures and films of the plaintiff, a living person, for use in motion pictures projection machines."[76] As a result of his picture being used, the plaintiff claimed that he was "greatly damaged in his business, occupation and profession" and had suffered "humiliation and mortification."[77]

The primary reason for Franklin's complaint was evident in the defamation claims, which focused on the following commentary from the film: "Now folks, meet Sidney Franklin, one of the greatest bull-throwers, er er . . . I mean, bullfighters, born under the sunny skies of Brooklyn."[78] In the 1930s "bull-thrower" was a term used to describe someone who was a grandstander. The plaintiff stated that the commentary and depiction in the film charged him with being "an extravagant imposter, liar and falsifier and humbug" and that it thus lowered him in the estimation of the public and others in his profession.[79]

It's interesting that Franklin did not simply bring a defamation claim, given that the damage was largely reputational. In the section of the amended complaint detailing the defendant's breach of sections 50 and 51 of the Civil Rights Laws (New York's statutory privacy laws),[80] no mention was made of offended privacy. This was no doubt because an appeal to privacy would jar with the description given of Franklin in his defamation claims: "The plaintiff has achieved a world-wide reputation, prominence and fame, and had become known as a unique skillful, competent and outstanding artist, celebrity and performer, and has enhanced and legitimately exploited the reputation he has heretofore achieved."[81]

It seems incongruous that someone with such "prominence and fame" could claim any violation of privacy in a film that depicted the performance that generated that fame. At trial, however, the judge found for the plaintiff on all three grounds and awarded him damages of $2,500 for breach of privacy, $2,500 for libel, and $2,000 for slander. The defendant appealed, and the Appellate Division of the Supreme Court affirmed the trial decision but reduced the damages to a total of $5,000. The defendant and plaintiff both appealed, the defendant upon the judgment entered for the plaintiff, and the plaintiff in regard to the reduced award of damages, but the New York Court of Appeal affirmed the Appellate Court's decision.

The fact that no argument was put by the defendant attacking the legitimacy of the plaintiff's claim under sections 50 and 51 of the Civil Rights Laws (New York's statutory privacy laws)[82] and the term "privacy" was not used by the Court of

Appeal suggests the extent to which the application of the Civil Rights Laws had evolved by the late 1930s to refer to something quite distinct from—even opposite to—"a right to privacy." A professional person's name or likeness could be seen to be in need of protection, without proving any incursion into his or her private life.

The new direction in the application of these laws away from the cases I discussed in chapter 2 that led to their enactment would be formally recognized in 1953 by the case of *Haelan Laboratories, Inc. v. Topps Chewing Gum, Inc.*, which first coined the phrase "a right to publicity."[83] The plaintiff and defendant owned rival chewing gum companies. Haelan Laboratories entered contracts with prominent baseball players for the exclusive right to use the players' images to advertise their products. Topps Chewing Gum, however, then induced the players to authorize the company to use their images in its advertising. The plaintiff argued that the defendant invaded the plaintiff's exclusive rights and that the contracts between the defendant and the players were invalid. The defendant argued that there was no actionable wrong, as the initial contract between Haelan and the players, allowing Haelan to use the players' photographs in trade and advertising, was merely a release of liability under sections 50 and 51 of New York's Civil Rights Laws (New York's statutory privacy laws).[84] In other words, by entering a contract with Haelan, the players agreed not to bring a breach of privacy claim for the use of their photographs. The relevant right to privacy provisions, the defendant contended, created a personal, nonassignable right for individuals not to have their feelings hurt by publication of their likeness.

The majority of the U.S. Court of Appeal, Second Circuit, rejected this argument, Justice Frank stating: "We think that, in addition to and independent of that right of privacy (which in New York derives from statute), a man has a right in the publicity value of his photograph. . . . Whether it be labeled a 'property' right is immaterial; for here, as often elsewhere, the tag 'property' simply symbolizes the fact that courts enforce a claim which had pecuniary worth. This right might be called a '*right of publicity.*'"[85] The court went on to note that without a "right of publicity," "many prominent persons," such as actors and baseball players, would be sorely deprived if they could not make money from their images. It is significant that, as in *Franklin v. Columbia Pictures Corporation* and *Redmond v. Columbia Pictures Corporation,* those pictured in the *Haelan* case were sportsmen—professional baseball players—whose visual value rested on the display of masculine skill within their chosen profession of performance.

After *Haelan,* cases contesting and affirming a right of publicity proliferated in New York. But the legislative basis for the right did not change—sections 50 and 51 of the Civil Rights Laws, still named "a right to privacy," now harbored an additional doctrine. Other states followed and began to establish a right of publicity in common law, statute, or both. Currently, thirty-one American states recognize a right of publicity, and twenty states, including California,[86] recognize a "postmortem" right of publicity. There has been some disagreement as to whether the right covers only famous people, but Thomas McCarthy has noted that the majority of authorities in the United States support a right of publicity for everyone, regardless of one's public presence.[87]

In the first decades of the twentieth century, a "right to privacy" evolved and changed in meaning primarily in response to the changing status and position of women. First used by women to claim ownership and control over their images as a way of protecting themselves from voyeurism and exploitation, as women entered the workforce and started to build careers based on techniques of appearing, a "right of privacy" also became a professional tool for those who might be designated New Women. "A right to privacy" was used to question the contexts of their display, to challenge contractual obligations and assert authority over the public display of their images as dancers, actresses, and models. Men also invested in their professional image and sought to control the conditions of its use, but they tended to do so in professions of performance—as baseball players, boxers, and bullfighters.

From a historical vantage point, it becomes evident that the right of publicity resulting from the pressures placed upon the traditional right of privacy doctrine in the 1920s and 1930s—that evolved as a result of the changing needs of professional women and men in an ocularcentric culture—should be considered a victory for those pioneering advocates (such as Milton E. Gibbs in *Roberson v. Rochester Folding Box Co.*)[88] of a property right in one's own image.

6

Hollywood Heroes and Shameful Hookers

Privacy Moves West

In 1925 Gabrielle Melvin (née Darley), a polite society matron from California, was subjected to "ridicule, obloquy and contempt" and suffered greatly "in body and mind" when Mrs. Wallace Reid, a Hollywood producer, released *The Red Kimono,* a feature film exposing Melvin's past life as "a murderess and a prostitute." She brought a successful case against Reid and her motion picture studio for "breach of privacy."[1]

Melvin's inventive and eloquent lawyers painted a powerful picture to the court:

> Through the exigencies of life a girl is led into the depravity of prostitution. She was put on trial for murder, a vicious sin as well as the highest crime, and exculpated by twelve of her peers before a court of justice. She sees the error of her ways and re-

> forms. By right thinking and right living she assuages the sting of an ignominious life and transposes it into an exemplary life. Twelve years later and many years after she has risen above the quagmire of desolation, her past life linked with her own name is blazoned across the screen for the purpose of amusing the public and bringing profit to the despoiler of her buried secret. Her new friends, who knew nothing of her past, now look upon her with contempt and scorn. Where she once met smiles and nods she is taunted with scurrility and obloquy. It is inconceivable to even think that a wrong has not been done and it is just as inconceivable to think that anyone had a right to commit such a wrong.[2]

In winning her case Melvin established "a right to privacy" in Californian law.

Privacy cases involving pictures arose not only from situations where the image of an individual's form or features had been appropriated and used by another. As the moving picture industry expanded in the United States during the first few decades of the twentieth century, so too did the market for interesting and arresting film narratives. Fiction films began to dominate the box office from around 1910 after the initial awe and amazement of seeing "actual" moving images of people, animals, and events on the screen wore off. The traditional vehicles for narrative—plays, novels, and histories—were pillaged for suitable material. For instance, between 1907 and 1911 Vitagraph (one of the major early film studios and defendant in the first case discussed in this chapter) released more than fifty films based on literary, historical, and biblical sources, including works by Edgar Allen Poe, Charles Dickens, Émile Zola, Leo Tolstoy, Victor Hugo, and William Shakespeare.[3] But as demand for fiction films increased, producers began to look to other sources of marketable stories, including living people's life stories, such as the sorry saga of Gabrielle Melvin's "quagmire of desolation." Women and men experienced the publicity accorded their lives very differently, however, because different stories tended to be appropriated. Whereas men were celebrated as public heroes, women were often shamed by the exposure of their private lives.

This chapter explores the use of privacy law by individuals in the first half of the twentieth century to make a proprietary claim over the stories of their lives. It reveals the way in which motion picture studios constructed masculine stories of heroism and achievement but, by contrast, framed women's personal histories as scandalous or marginal. Three of the motion pictures I discuss featured a male hero, but the female characters were cloaked in shame, either as a result of their unconventional sexual relationships, their vocations as prostitutes, or their status as divorcees. The privacy cases I discuss reveal that these "shameful" women were used by the film industry as cautionary tales (such as Darley in *The Red Kimono* or Mary in *The Sands of Iwo Jima),* or written into roles of dutiful respectability as supportive wives (such as the character Mary in *Yankee Doodle Dandy,* 1942) or completely marginalized (as happened to Ethel Levey). As these privacy cases relied on a plaintiff establishing the truth of the film narrative, the court documents also demonstrate the extent to which production studios selected the facts of "true" stories to shape the appeal to audiences or please the Motion Picture Production Code of 1930, also known as the Hays

Code. These cases tell us not only about constructions of femininity and masculinity within the popular American film industry in the early decades of the twentieth century but also of the ways in which gender influenced the objectives and outcomes of legal privacy claims.

The other significant aspect of these cases involving the exploitation of personal stories is the way they reflected the geographic and economic shift in the moving picture industry from the East to the West Coast. Until the establishment of the studio system in Hollywood in the 1920s, the vast majority of privacy cases concerning pictures occurred in New York State—the home of Eastman Kodak, the beginnings of American cinema, and the first U.S. "right to privacy." The particular historical development of privacy law in New York, originating in 1903 after the *Roberson v. Rochester Folding Box Co.*[4] decision, can be contrasted with the battle for recognition of "a right to privacy" in California in 1931. The language used in the case of *Melvin v. Reid*,[5] evident in the parties' arguments and the court's reasoning, shaped a specific idea of privacy, reflecting not only the facts of the cases but a utopian philosophy of self-improvement and renewal. The right to privacy in these cases was based not on appropriation of a photographic "likeness" but on the right of each individual "to pursue and obtain happiness."

Binns v. Vitagraph Company of America

The first privacy case in the United States concerning the unauthorized appropriation of a person's life story was *Binns v. Vitagraph Company of America* in 1911.[6] The plaintiff, John R. Binns, brought an action against the Vitagraph Company of America, one of the major film studios operating during the silent film era, in relation to their motion picture film *CQD Or Saved by Wireless; A True Story of the Wreck of the Republic* (*Saved by Wireless*). The short film dramatically recounted the 1909 collision between two steamships, the *Republic* and the *Florida,* in the Atlantic and the plaintiff's heroic efforts in saving the vast majority of passengers and crew on board. The plaintiff, a British citizen, was the operator of a wireless telegraphy machine on board the *Republic.* Immediately following the collision, he sent the international distress signal "CQD" by wireless, which was received by a wireless operator on Nantucket Island, Massachusetts, and relayed to the nearby steamship *Baltic.* As a result of the distress signal, the *Baltic* arrived to rescue passengers from the two sinking steamships and transported them to New York City. It was the first time wireless telegraphy had been used to save lives on a sinking ship. The *Republic* was a luxury ocean liner, owned and operated by the White Star Line, which also owned the RMS *Titanic,* which would sink in dramatic circumstances in the same area of the Atlantic three years later. As the film *Saved by Wireless* has been lost, the court documents that describe its content are particularly important to both film history and legal history.

The collision between the steamships in 1909 and John Binns's efforts in saving those on board understandably attracted immense publicity in New York, with newspapers and newsreels circulating accounts of the "heroic" action "in great vividness and at great length."[7] Binns's picture was also reproduced in connection with the news articles. To the plaintiff's apparent dismay, however, in February 1909, the defendant produced a motion picture dramatizing the events. Evidence given by one of Vitagraph's employees during the trial described the process of making the film: "We purchased all the newspapers we could find, everything that had any bearing on the story, and we sat down and wrote out what we called a scenario. . . . We produced in our studio the interiors of the captain's cabin, the wireless operator's room on the *Republic,* the wireless operator's room on the *Baltic,* and the operator's room at Siasconset [on Nantucket Island]. . . . We assigned various actors and actresses in our employ to take various parts. . . . The part of Mr. Binns was assigned to one of our actors."[8]

The court in this case was required to tackle a number of difficult issues. The facts were vastly different from contemporary privacy cases, including that which led to New York's statutory privacy laws[9] being so narrowly framed (*Roberson v. Rochester Folding Box Co.*). It did not involve a private individual but rather involved someone thrust into the limelight by a particular incident. In relation to the use of Binns's "picture," it was not a photograph or motion picture footage of him but rather a depiction of him by an actor. The valuable asset appropriated by the defendant was not the plaintiff's attractive form or features but rather an interesting biographical tale. This was the first case in the United States to consider a right to privacy in the context of motion pictures. Applying New York's statutory privacy laws, the court was faced with the question of whether the use of the plaintiff's name or likeness in a dramatic motion picture could be defined as being for the purposes of "advertising or trade."

At first, Binns was successful in his privacy action. The jury found that the Vitagraph film studio had used his name and likeness contrary to New York's privacy laws. It awarded him the sum of $12,500 in damages (half of the $25,000 he was claiming). The defendant appealed and found the sympathetic ear of Justice Greenbaum, who stated that despite instructions from the court, the jury seemed to have been "either swayed by passion or prejudice, or was perhaps affected by the quite natural admiration one has for the heroic act of the plaintiff."[10] Justice Greenbaum did not believe the plaintiff had been "seriously hurt" by the defendant's acts.[11] He stated that Binns had not objected to the wide publicity afforded to his name and image by newspapers and magazines as a result of his heroic act, that he was not adverse to reaping the pecuniary advantages now attaching to his name and likeness, and that rather than belittling or ridiculing him, the defendant's motion picture glorified his deeds. Justice Greenbaum ordered a retrial, unless the plaintiff agreed to the reduced sum of $2,500 damages.

After a number of cross-appeals, the case finally reached the New York Court of Appeals. Delivering judgment for a unanimous bench, Justice Chase accorded a strict legal reading to the New York privacy laws. Unlike Justice Greenbaum, he avoided any discussion of the harm inflicted upon Binns by stating immediately that this was not an action for libel and so it was "immaterial whether the defendant's use of the plaintiff's name and picture held him up to public ridicule and contempt"[12] or in fact glorified him. The essence of the privacy provisions, he explained, was to prohibit a person using the name or likeness of a private individual "for his own selfish purposes."[13] The defendant's motion picture was a "matter of business and profit," designed "to amuse those who paid to be entertained," rather than to "instruct or educate" its audience.[14] It was unnecessary in judgment on the case, Justice Chase commented, to discuss whether the same laws would prohibit the name or likeness of an individual incidentally captured within a motion picture of an "actual" event.[15] As I showed in chapter 5, this issue was decided by the court in the cases of *Humiston v. Universal Film Manufacturing Co.*[16] and *Blumenthal v. Picture Classics, Inc.*[17]

The Court of Appeals also turned its attention to the fact that the picture of Binns was not photographic, as had been the case in *Roberson v. Rochester Folding Box Co.*[18] and the vast majority of privacy cases since. The motion picture used an actor to portray Binns, and so this was not a case of lifting and reproducing someone's own unique appearance. Nonetheless, Justice Chase held that "a picture within the meaning of the statute is not necessarily a photograph of the living person, but includes any representation of such person."[19] The defendant, he stated, was in no position to argue that the picture was only another person made up to look like and impersonate the plaintiff. This clarification by the New York Court of Appeals widened the possible application of the statutory privacy laws and led to new privacy suits involving narrative feature films.

Even though the issue of "harm" was not considered relevant by the New York Court of Appeals, it is important to examine why Binns brought the action and the particular grievance he had with the defendant's motion picture, particularly given that the story of his efforts in saving passengers from the *Republic* and the *Florida* was already well known and well publicized. The complaint stated that he was "greatly damaged in his business and occupation and suffered great anxiety of mind, humiliation and mortification, and [was] exposed to public ridicule and contempt."[20] The harm allegedly sustained by Binns closely resembled that occurring in cases of common law defamation, that is, reputational loss for which plaintiffs could recover compensatory damages to vindicate their reputation and console their hurt feelings. As pointed out by Justice Greenbaum, however, the depiction of Binns could not be a case of libel, as the motion picture represented the plaintiff in a glowing light. A further complication was the fact the plaintiff had not seen the film himself but had relied on a reading of the screenplay and the reports of others about the film's content.

During the trial, the defendant attacked the plaintiff's claims of harm during a lengthy cross-examination. Mr. Allen, counsel for the defendant, asked Binns whether there was any particular part of the film that he found objectionable. The plaintiff singled out a scene referring to "Jack Binns and his Good American Smile," which apparently featured a shot of the actor playing Binns smiling broadly after having saved passengers on the *Republic* and the *Florida*.[21] Allen questioned Binns as to whether he disliked this description because it suggested he was American when in fact he was British. Binns replied: "No, no; simply because it described a state of being that I only exhibit to my friends or to my immediate associates . . . the question is whether the public should see me smile or not . . . my smile is my smile, of course."[22] Clearly, Binns believed that the motion picture, displayed for a large, anonymous public audience, depicted a personal "state of being"—his smile was his smile[23]—not appropriate for wider consumption. It did not matter to Binns that it was not a picture of his actual self; it nonetheless diminished his "dignity," as it put his emotions on show, whereas, from all accounts, he was a reserved man.

Allen also questioned Binns as to why motion picture coverage of the incident upset him when extensive coverage within newspapers and magazines did not. Binns replied: "I immediately found that I was in the public eye and in the public mouth and in the public press all over the world following this occurrence."[24] He respected the right of local newspapers and magazines to cover the story and inform the public of what had happened but saw the motion picture produced by the defendants as low-class entertainment. This view of the "movies" was not uncommon at the time. Motion pictures were yet to gain respectability as an art form and were associated with a lower class of uncultured and uneducated patron. Indeed, according to historian David Cook, it became obligatory in many parts of the country for "ministers, businessmen and politicians to inveigh against the movies as a corruptor of youth and a threat to public morality."[25] An editorial in the *Chicago Tribune,* for example, accused the "Five Cent Theatre" of "ministering to the lowest passions of children" and being "wholly vicious."[26] The courageous and reserved Britisher Mr. Binns seemingly felt humiliated by association with this vulgar industry.

Mr. Allen, Vitagraph's attorney, attempted to discredit Binns's apparent distaste for crude publicity by pressing him for details of his involvement in a stage play, called *Saved by Wireless,* at Luna Park on Coney Island in the months following the release of the film. Binns repeatedly answered that the play concerned the collision of the steamships. He was employed to operate the wireless machine but had no other role in the production. His contract with Thompson, the owner and operator of Luna Park, had stipulated "[t]hat under no circumstances should I be asked to do anything that I considered lowering to my dignity; that I should not be asked to do anything in the theatrical line and that I should be attached only to the electrical and wireless apparatus."[27] Allen pressured Binns to agree to his proposition that by virtue of participating in the play he had "capitalized and commercialized the fame and celebrity" that he had achieved through the rescue.[28] Binns disagreed, stating that he had simply been employed in his occupation as a wireless operator: "My connection with it was simply of a scientific character, in charge of the wireless apparatus . . . this machine is of a certain technical mechanism and can only be taken care of by a man who understands that mechanism."[29]

At the conclusion of giving evidence, Binns made a final statement on the stand regarding the harm he felt as a result of the motion picture: "The objection that I had was on the ground that the pictures tended to lead the public to believe that I had been—that I had given the right for their production. I did not want to do this thing myself, and I did not like anyone else to do it, and the fact somebody else had done it, it hurt me very much."[30] Binns considered participation in a dramatic motion picture undignified and boastful. The harm he felt was, in part, reputational. He believed he had been lowered in the estimation of others.

This case indicates how the context, circumstances, and medium of communication could impinge in different ways on a person's reputation (or be perceived to), even when the content itself did not. Even when a film or photograph presented an individual in a positive light, merely being rendered the object of the cinematic camera's gaze in the early decades of the twentieth century was, for some, enough to undermine one's standing in the community. As in a number of other privacy cases, *Binns* shows that privacy laws could be invoked to ameliorate reputational harm, when existing defamation laws could not. Privacy law could address the circumstances of a specific type of reputational harm, whereas defamation, restricted to the content of the representation, could not.

Binns also felt aggrieved by the motion picture, as it was based upon him and the events of his life, yet the film producers did not consult with him or request his permission to use his experience. Unlike in *Roberson v. Rochester Folding Box Co.* and the privacy cases I discussed earlier in this book, Binns did not claim a sense of ownership over his image or likeness as such, he claimed it over the deeds and narrative of his life. This case and the others I discuss below raised the question of who should have the right, ethical or legal, to retell people's personal stories. Should the subject of events—the agent—have a particular right to allow or refuse the representation and exploitation of those events before another party? Such questions have received little discussion, as they clash with the principle of freedom of expression. However, privacy cases involving motion pictures in the first half of the twentieth century did frequently propose that biographical subjects did have rights, and one example was the California case of *Melvin v. Reid*,[31] discussed below.

Privacy and the Californian "Pursuit of Happiness"

Until the early 1920s, the motion picture industry in the United States was based in the state of New York. This was the location of technological developments in photography and early cinematography, as well as the home of numerous creative professionals employed in the thriving artistic and theatrical communities of Broadway. During the years just prior to World War I, however, various film studios and producers began moving westward, and by the 1920s nearly all of them had relocated to the suburb of Hollywood in California, lured by the promise of light, space, and lower production costs.[32]

As most filming still occurred out of doors due to the relative unavailability of electric light, filmmaking on the East Coast was restricted during the long winter months. California offered not only a warm, bright climate year round but also cheap land for the construction of studios and proximity to a variety of landscapes for use as backdrops: ocean, forests, mountains, lakes, and deserts. As one newsman declared at the time: "Clear air and sunshine are available three hundred days out of the year, perfect conditions for picture making. The scenic advantages are unique. From the heights of Edendale one can see the stock ranches, its snow-capped mountains and its tropical vegetation to the east, north and south. Within a short distance of Edendale may be found every known variety of national scenery, seemingly arranged by a master producer expressly for the motion picture camera."[33] In 1911 the Nester Company and the Universal Company established the first film studios in Hollywood. By 1913 every major motion picture company except Edison was working in California, either permanently or at least during the winter months.[34]

Hollywood's global success was assured by the outbreak of world war in 1914, which crippled European film producers, as the same chemicals used to make celluloid were required for the production of gunpowder. By 1915 capital investment in the American movie industry—"the business of artisanal craftsmen and fairground operators only a decade before"—had exceeded five hundred million dollars.[35] By 1918 the United States (in particular Hollywood) dominated the world cinema market, and growth accelerated into the 1920s and 1930s. By leaving the East, film producers also escaped the application of increasingly restrictive privacy laws, particularly those operating in New York State. In 1931, however, this expanding body of law caught up with the relocation of the "pictures," as the question of whether or not to recognize a right of privacy reached the courts of California. But the nature of pictures had changed since *Roberson v. Rochester Folding Box Co.*,[36] and so too had the issues facing privacy jurisprudence.

The case of *Melvin v. Reid* concerned the right of film producers to exploit the life stories of others in feature films and thus was particularly relevant to California's lucrative motion picture industry, with potentially far-reaching consequences. The plaintiff, Gabrielle Darley Melvin, sought not only recognition of her right to privacy but also a determination on whether she held property rights in her life story—a question only raised implicitly in *Binns v. Vitagraph Company of America*.

The Red Kimono, the film at the center of the *Melvin v. Reid* litigation, was released in late 1925. It was the directorial debut of Walter Lang but the artistic and inspired creation of its producer, Mrs. Wallace Reid, previously known as Dorothy Davenport. After her film-star husband, Wallace Reid, who starred in D. W. Griffith's *Birth of a Nation* (1915) and Cecil B. DeMille's *Affairs of Anatol* (1921), died of morphine addiction in 1923, she capitalized on his famous name and formed a feature film production company. She also founded the Wallace Reid Foundation Sanatorium in Santa Monica for the treatment of drug addicts. Her first film, entitled *Human Wreckage* (directed by John Griffith Wray in 1923), told the story of an attorney (played by James Kickwood) who became addicted to morphine and only found the strength to give it up when his wife, played by Mrs. Wallace Reid, also showed signs of addiction. Her second film, *Broken Laws* (directed by Roy William Neill in 1924), concerned the neglect of children and expounded a strict law-and-order approach to parenting. Reid demonstrated a particular interest in educating audiences about contemporary social issues within the framework of an entertaining morality tale.

The Red Kimono opened inside a domed newspaper library, with Mrs. Wallace Reid being handed a giant folder of old newspapers. As she turned the pages, the camera focused on a particular headline: "Story of Gabrielle Darley: Startling Human Document—I didn't know what to do I loved him so." Mrs. Wallace Reid then turned to the camera to state (via intertitle): "This is a true story. Much of it is on record in the Superior Court of California. If it contains bitter truths, remember that I only turn the pages of the past." She then explained: "I cite you the case of Gabrielle from the files of this newspaper office, with the hope that you will help—rather than hinder—the upward struggle of such unfortunates." The first few minutes of the film made it plain that it was based on the true story of a woman called Gabrielle Darley. The solemnity of the library, the weathered look of the newspapers, and the reference to the Supreme Court of California all worked to underline the authority and authenticity of the film's narrative. Both *Saved by Wireless* and *The Red Kimono* were stories taken by film producers directly from the pages of newspapers. But in that the former celebrated a hero and the second shamed a hooker, they were vastly different films in their purposes and consequences.

The Red Kimono opens with the sad and sordid tale of Gabrielle Darley: "In the beginning, a child—trusting, believing—had committed the sin of loving too well. Ground in the mire, numb with heartache, we find her in New Orleans—deserted." The camera then cuts to Darley looking wan and disheartened in a New Orleans "crib," wearing only a slinky kimono. Clara, "the girl next door," then appears on the screen to tell her that Howard (Darley's lover and pimp) has left for Los Angeles to get married. Clara reassures her he will be back, as otherwise he would have taken her rings. Gabrielle decides to follow him to Los Angeles and traces him to a jewelry story, where he is purchasing an engagement ring for his new fiancée. She creeps up behind him, with a black veil over her face, her eyes mad and staring. She speaks, he turns, looks her up and down contemptuously, and turns away to continue his transaction. Gabrielle backs away, her hands shaking. She reaches into her coat pocket, takes aim with her gun, and shoots him in the back. Remorseful, she falls on the ground wringing her hands over what she has done and saying, "Speak to me." She sees the wedding ring, picks it up, and puts it on her finger, while tears run down her cheeks. She turns to God and pleads. A policeman places his hand on her shoulder.

Then follows the trial, during which she gives evidence of growing up in a poor, unloving home before meeting Howard, who whirled her into romance and promised to marry her but instead led her into a life of prostitution. In one scene in flashback showing her working as a prostitute in New Orleans, she stares dreamily into the mirror, where she sees an image of herself in a white bridal dress. Suddenly, the dress turns into a bright red kimono, and she reels in horror from her transformed image. After relaying her sad tale in court, Darley is acquitted by a sympathetic jury.

While her case was unfolding, however, a wealthy Los Angeles society matron had taken a keen interest in her story and offered Gabrielle a place to stay. Gabrielle was grateful and moved in with the woman, but it soon became clear that the matron was more interested in exhibiting her unfortunate houseguest to friends. Gabrielle decided to leave, but with no money or place to go, she decided to return to work in New Orleans. At the last minute she was rescued from this life of shame by the society matron's chauffeur, who declared his love and proposed to her before being sent off to war. The feature film stuck closely to the "real" past of Darley, apart from the romance with the chauffeur, which was wholly invented.

Mrs. Wallace Reid's film was a commercial success but a critical flop. A review in the *New York Times* stated: "There have been a number of wretched pictures on Broadway during the last year, but none seem to have quite reached the low level of 'The Red Kimono,' a production evidently intended to cause weeping, wailing and gnashing of teeth. . . . Mrs. Wallace Reid, who supervised this photoplay, has turned her attention from stories of drug addicts to those of abandoned women."[37] Another review commented: "This is a very lurid tale, very plainly and sordidly presented. It is quite evident that Mrs. Wallace Reid, producer, intended to preach a sermon and one not falling into the sugar-coated type. And she does from the first reel to the last. There is much truth, though not pleasant to dwell upon, in this picture, but there is little entertainment."[38]

It is interesting that Mrs. Wallace Reid decided to use the real name of Gabrielle Darley. She clearly calculated that the film would have greater impact if the truth of the morality tale were underlined, and indeed the marketing material for *The Red Kimono* emphasized its "truth" as a selling point.[39] These "truth" claims, however, could have been accomplished without the use of Darley's actual name, by simply referring to a California Supreme Court case or stating that the film was based upon a story reported in the pages of the *Los Angeles Times.* The use of Darley's real name did not add anything to the narrative for the vast majority of viewers. Only those who knew the real Gabrielle Darley knew its significance, but it was the use of her name that caused her the most reputational harm. Reid's message at the beginning of the film that we should help, rather than hinder, the upward struggle of such unfortunates thus seemed like hypocrisy. Reid's conduct mirrored that of the villainous society matron of her film, appearing sympathetic and virtuous while exploiting the public's curiosity in the sordid story of a "fallen" woman.

The complaint filed by the plaintiff claimed that the defendant emphasized the truth of the film's narrative for the purposes of profit: "The said moving picture film was stated and advertised to be the true story of a portion of the past life of the plaintiff as Gabrielle Darley; the principal commercial and market value of the picture to said defendants was its truth; the picture featured and advertised that the main attraction was the truth of the plot, and that the characters bore the names of actual persons."[40] At the time of the film's release, the plaintiff was apparently a "respected" member of the community and married to a wealthy businessman, Bernard Melvin of St. Louis. Her circle of acquaintances knew nothing of her former life as a prostitute or her trial for murder in 1917. As a result of the film's release, the plaintiff's friends and acquaintances "became apprised of the stigma attached to her name" and subjected her to "ridicule, obloquy and contempt," from which she suffered in "body and mind."[41]

Gabrielle (Darley) Melvin brought an action against Reid on four legal grounds. First, she argued that her right to privacy had been invaded and claimed both damages and an injunction prohibiting the defendant from screening the film. Second, she sought an account of profits from the box office proceeds made by the defendant. Third, she argued "conversion of property," that is, that the defendant had appropriated and exploited her property, her name, and her life story, without consent. Fourth, she claimed a constructive trust over all profits that continued to be made by the defendant. The defendant submitted a demurrer to the complaint, arguing that it disclosed no recognized cause of action. The court initially agreed, ordering that Melvin amend her complaint within ten days. After Melvin failed to amend the complaint, the court granted judgment for Reid. Melvin then appealed.

In their brief to the court, the plaintiff's attorneys (M. W. Purcell, Ben F. Griffith, and Hugh W. Darling) submitted that "the primary question which this Honorable Court is called upon to decide is whether or not remedy exists in this state for the violation of a person's right of privacy."[42] This was the fundamental legal ground upon which Melvin's three other claims rested. And so, the plaintiff's attorneys endeavored to convince the court that it was time for the state of California to recognize this "comparatively recent" common law right, first articulated by Warren and Brandeis in 1890. The plaintiff's attorneys then canvassed the "New York Cases" involving claims of privacy and those authorities sustaining the right. They expressed disappointment at Chief Justice Parker's "unintellectual and unphilosophical" judgment in *Roberson v. Rochester Folding Box Co.*,[43] which exposed a deplorable lack of appreciation and understanding of the spirit and principle underlying the common law. They argued that the New York legislature's act in passing narrow privacy laws in 1903[44] was simply meant to remedy "the evils of an erroneous decision," rather than to exercise exclusive jurisdiction over the subject.

The plaintiff's attorneys conceded that cases in New York were not binding on the court in California but stated that they could be instructive as to what constituted a breach of privacy. They cited the case of *Binns v. Vitagraph Company of America*[45] as one in which "the rights therein violated were apposite to the rights involved in this appeal."[46] Describing the facts and outcome of the *Binns* case, Melvin's attorneys concluded: "The case is convincing proof that one who makes a moving picture based upon a portion of the past life of an individual without that individual's consent is a violation of the right of privacy. If a person's privacy is invaded by augmenting his heroism, *a fortiori,* it is an even greater invasion when he is exposed on the screen in a most disreputable light."[47] The masculine pronoun in this statement obscured the kinds of disreputable light that might be cast by such films.

In legal terms, this was not entirely accurate. The *Binns* decision was based upon New York's statutory privacy laws, which prohibited the use of an individual's name or likeness by another for trade or advertising purposes. It was the use of Binns's name and a motion picture image of an actor playing him that violated the statute, not the representation of a story from his life. Nonetheless, Melvin's attorneys' argument clearly acknowledged the wrong perpetrated as the appropriation of an individual's life narrative. They did not simply attempt to convince the court that a right to privacy should be recognized as part of the common law, they also fashioned a clever argument based on the California Constitution. A right to privacy was essential, they claimed, for the protection of fundamental rights and liberties conferred by the state. In particular, they quoted article 1, section 1: "All men are by nature free and independent, and have certain inalienable rights, among which are those of enjoying and defending life and liberty; acquiring, possessing and protecting property; and pursuing and obtaining safety and happiness."[48] It was this last segment—the right to pursue and obtain happiness—which the plaintiff's attorneys argued would be "nullified" without the right to privacy.[49] The wording of this section of the California Constitution echoes, of course, the United States Declaration of Independence: "We hold these truths to be self-evident, that all men are created equal, that they are endowed by their Creator with certain unalienable Rights, that among these are Life, Liberty and the pursuit of Happiness." California in the late nineteenth century seemed to emphasize this promise.

Melvin's attorneys linked the recognition of a right to privacy not merely to the welfare of the individual but also to the constitutional rights of the state and the nation. Good citizens, they argued, were produced by laws encouraging their pursuit of happiness through redemption and self reinvention. The plaintiff, they submitted, struggled to overcome and transcend the mistakes of her "depraved" and "ignominious" life and for sixteen years had led an "exemplary" existence, only to find that her "buried secret" was "blazoned across the screen for the purpose of amusing the public."[50] In passionate language, they described the necessity of allowing citizens to leave shameful mistakes behind:

> Who among us, in our childhood, if not later, has not done something . . . which, if searched out, embellished and published in motion pictures or otherwise, would not only humiliate and embarrass us, but hold us up to ridicule and forever blast our future? This would not be news or public interest. . . . If there was no protection against such acts no one could ever correct or live down the slightest error. We would forever be driven to our lowest level, with no hope of ever raising ourselves

> to an equity with our better selves. If such were the law, we would soon become a hopelessly depraved nation, our only hope or ambition in life would be to discover something on the other fellow with which to tear him down to our lowest, meanest level. We would become little more than a detective and scavenger agency for political and financial purposes and gain.[51]

Despite the defendant's objections, this passionate appeal to citizens' better natures convinced the District Court of Appeal, with Justice Marks holding that *The Red Kimono* invaded the plaintiff's inalienable right to pursue and obtain happiness. He agreed with the plaintiff's attorneys that "it is our object to lift up and sustain the unfortunate rather than tear him down,"[52] a commitment that ironically echoed that stated by Mrs. Wallace Reid at the beginning of *The Red Kimono.* He refused, however, to determine whether or not this constitutional right founded or related to a right to privacy, commenting: "[W]hether we call this a right of privacy or give it any other name is immaterial, because it is a right guaranteed by our Constitution that must not be ruthlessly and needlessly invaded by others."[53] He stated that Melvin's first cause of action (privacy) stated facts sufficient for a cause of action, but the reluctance of the court to clearly articulate its reasoning created confusion regarding whether a right to privacy was recognized in the state of California.

The other interesting argument put forward by the plaintiff's attorneys related to property. However, unlike in the early New York privacy cases, such as *Roberson v. Rochester Folding Box Co.,* they did not argue the plaintiff had property rights in her own photographic likeness. Instead, they submitted that the plaintiff owned her name and life story, which were appropriated and exploited without consent by the defendants, instantiating the tort of "conversion." Traditionally, conversion only applied to "tangible" property capable of being "converted" by another. It is easier to understand, therefore, how a photograph or the imprinted likeness of a person could be regarded as property for the sake of the action. In this case, however, the plaintiff claimed property in something ephemeral and immaterial: the stories, incidents, and events from her past life. In support of this point, the plaintiff's attorneys pointed to section 655 of the Civil Code of California, which stated: "[T]here may be ownership of all inanimate things which are capable of appropriation."[54] Further, they submitted: "Surely a person's name and the incidents of his past life are capable of appropriation by him and usable to the exclusion of others. If such insistence were set forth in manuscript form no one would deny but that the result would be property. Is it, then, any less property before it has been committed to paper? Many of the cases discussed above conclude that a person's privacy is a property right as well as a personal right."[55]

This argument highlighted the intimate and tense relationship between copyright and the right to privacy, also evident in the early New York cases. In both *Melvin v. Reid* and *Roberson v. Rochester Folding Box Co.* it was argued that the subject of the image should also be a rights holder in the image. In *Roberson* the plaintiff submitted that the individual pictured should have property rights in her photograph. In *Melvin v. Reid* it was proposed that the individual who lived the incidents depicted should own them, as much as the person who committed them to material form. Such arguments threatened the basic premise of copyright law: that protection is provided only to an expression (a tangible item), not the ideas or substance contained in that expression. Further, copyright assigned all rights to the creator of that expression, not the subject of them.

In their submissions, the defendant's attorneys focused squarely on the plaintiff's privacy claim and did not respond to the arguments regarding property, which they probably considered to be far-fetched. Equally, the District Court of Appeal was dismissive of the property claims, with Justice Marks stating in no uncertain terms: "[W]e have found no authorities sustaining such a property right in the story of one's life . . . the appellant's cause of action must rest on tort and tort alone."[56] As noted earlier, however, the plaintiff did win her privacy case on the basis of "the right to pursue and obtain happiness" enshrined in the California Constitution. Mrs. Wallace Reid was ordered to pay substantial damages to Melvin. As a result she lost her house in West Hollywood and entered the next decade penniless.[57]

Melvin v. Reid was a significant decision for the way in which it brought together the utopian aspirations of early twentieth-century California, particularly Hollywood, with the doctrine of a right to privacy. The arguments of Melvin's legal counsel and the court's findings, that a right to privacy was necessary for one's full enjoyment of the constitutional right to pursue happiness, and society's commitment to "lift up" and "sustain" its unfortunates, arguably reflected the contemporary circumstances and aspirations of the West Coast. In *Hollywood Utopia*,[58] Justine Brown explores the utopian spirit evident in late nineteenth-century California, with the founding of theosophical communities at Point Loma in San Diego Bay and their links to L. Frank Baum's imagined land of Oz in the *Wonderful Wizard of Oz* (first published in 1900).[59]

Hollywood attracted those who believed they shared visions for a better world, such as director D. W. Griffith and actress Lillian Gish, and shaped the utopian visions that influenced the development of the film industry. Griffith, Gish, and others believed that silent motion pictures had the ability to uplift and improve society. Griffith once stated: "We've gone beyond Babel, beyond words. We've found a universal language—a power that can make men brothers and end war forever."[60] Such encomiums to human brotherhood sat rather uneasily with Griffith's film *The Birth of a Nation* that celebrated the Ku Klux Klan, whose utopianism focused rather more on the triumph of white supremacy. Griffith, like many filmmakers of his day, believed in the power of films to shape the future.

Mrs. Wallace Reid shared Griffith's belief in film as a force for reform and tried to contribute to this redemptive project with her instructive morality tales. However, just as *The Birth of a Nation* was criticized for its derogatory portrayal of African Americans, Mrs. Wallace Reid's *Red Kimono* was condemned for its appropriation of Gabrielle Melvin's life and subjecting her to calumny. But whereas the National Association for the Advancement of Colored People tried to have Griffith's film banned and lost, the California court upheld Melvin's constitutional right to pursue happiness and awarded her damages.

Privacy under the Production Code

In the late 1920s and early 1930s the Hollywood studios came under increasing pressure from powerful Catholic, Protestant, and Jewish organizations to sanitize the content of motion pictures. These religious groups, such as the American Bishops of the Roman Catholic Church, were concerned that cinema was corrupting the morality and values of citizens and children. The groups exerted such political pressure that many states began drafting and passing censorship legislation.[61] In 1915 the U.S. Supreme Court decision of *Mutual Film Corporation v. Industrial Commission*[62] upheld the validity of Ohio's censorship laws.[63] Film producers faced the onerous task of producing motion pictures capable of meeting each state's varying legal requirements. In addition, municipal and local authorities (and often the police) exercised censorship over motion pictures in those states without statutes. As a response to increasing legislative regulation and the mass boycotting of films, advocated, for example, by the Catholic Legion of Decency, the Motion Picture Producers and Distributors of America (MPPDA) set up the Hays Office in 1922, headed by William Hays Sr., to regulate the content of Hollywood pictures. Hays created the Production Code Administration (PCA) in 1930 and appointed a prominent Catholic, Joseph Breen, to its helm in 1934. Breen would enforce the Production Code until 1954.

The Production Code of 1930 shared the expectation of many that motion pictures should exercise a reforming influence on the nation, but it developed a particular focus on improving morality. Acknowledging that motion pictures were "primarily regarded as entertainment," the code held that they should also work to "improve the race," rather than "harm human beings, or lower their standards of life and living."[64] The code saw a particular responsibility in safeguarding the "moral standards" of film audiences and prescribed rules for the depiction of those subjects at greatest risk of harming morality, including "crime," "sex," "obscenity," "profanity," "religion," and "national feelings." It was sex, however, that attracted the greatest attention. With regard to "Sex," the

Production Code stated: "The sanctity of the institution of marriage and the home shall be upheld. Pictures shall not infer that low forms of sex relationship are the accepted or common thing."[65]

When one reviews the code in the context of privacy law, it might appear at first glance that it would uphold privacy by banning the depiction of "scenes of passion," "adultery," "seduction," and "white slavery." And it's doubtful that Mrs. Wallace Reid's *Red Kimono* would have been released under its aegis. However, the Production Code's deliberate manipulation of film scripts actually worked against privacy plaintiffs. Film studios, which borrowed the life stories of others, were also required to meet the rules of the code. The resultant manipulation of plot lines and the introduction of fictional material made it more difficult for plaintiffs to claim that the films were an appropriation of their life stories.

The first privacy case centered on a feature film that occurred after the introduction of the Production Code was *Levey v. Warner Bros. Pictures, Inc.*, concerning the motion picture *Yankee Doodle Dandy* (directed by Michael Curtiz).[66] In a review of the 1942 Hollywood hit, one critic stated: "The film is a biography of Cohan's public life, rather than his private one—a cavalcade of song and show. For dramatic convenience and because George M. wanted it that way, his two wives—Ethel Levey and Agnes Nolan—have become a fairly fictional girl named Mary. I don't think anybody will quarrel with this substitution, and the rest of the book is straight enough."[67]

In fact, Ethel Levey did quarrel with her removal from the telling of Cohan's life story. *Yankee Doodle Dandy* purported to tell the biographical story of the Broadway star George M. Cohan and did so in the form of a musical, recreating the most popular stage productions of Cohan's career. The film glorified him as a national treasure. It opened with him receiving a Congressional Medal of Honor from the White House, when he was invited to tell his life story. It is perhaps not surprising, therefore, that the film received Cohan's cooperation and approval. In a letter to Hedda Hopper (the *Los Angeles Times* gossip columnist), Warner Brothers producer Robert Bruckner wrote: "I spent seven months in the preparation and writing of Yankee Doodle Dandy. This included six weeks in New York with George M. Cohan, during which I overcame all his many objections to the entire project and finally secured his enthusiastic approval of a finished screenplay."[68] The screenwriting process also included an enormous amount of research into Cohan's life. The production notes for the film include an extensive collection of material on his life and career, including a vast number of newspaper clippings.[69]

Yankee Doodle Dandy was a box office hit and received overwhelmingly positive reviews. Many critics commended the "realism" of the picture and its biographical accuracy. In August 1942 the *American Cinematographer* stated: "So often, in sequences of this nature, the temptation in motion pictures is to splurge on something so impressive no stage could possibly house it. But in *Yankee Doodle Dandy* both the directors and cinematographer Howe have hewed to a line of strict realism."[70] A review by *Variety* magazine in June 1942 included the observation: "It is so steeped in the life and the legend of George M. Cohan as to have substantial accuracy about the man & Broadway figure who might appropriately be termed the music laureate of his American day."[71] A few critics did seem aware of the fictional basis of the character Mary, with another *Variety* review remarking, "Joan Leslie as the romantic vis-à-vis [?], if perhaps not strictly of biography born, is certainly a fetching and reasonable facsimile thereof."[72] It is likely that Warner Brothers producers adapted the screenplay to eclipse Levey and the Cohans' divorce, not only to further idealize Cohan, but also to please the Hays Office, which would no doubt have preferred the depiction of a happy marriage on the screen rather than serial relationships.

Levey, however, was incensed by her removal from the personal and professional life of her husband and replacement by a fictional, blended character called Mary. As her relationship with Cohan had been badly misrepresented, she brought an action against Warner Brothers in the State of New York[73] for invasion of her right to privacy under the New York statutory privacy laws, as had John Binns three decades earlier.[74] Like Binns, the plaintiff claimed the defendants had appropriated her "likeness" for the purposes of trade.

In order to demonstrate that the motion picture misrepresented her, Levey gave evidence at trial of her life with George M. Cohan. She described how she met him when she was seventeen and establishing her career as an actress and singer in vaudeville. Cohan was then twenty years of age and appearing in a show with his father, mother, and sister. He gave her two songs he had composed, and she sang them the following Monday at the opening of the show in which she had a part. They became a couple, and she continued to sing his compositions. In July 1899 they married, and thereafter she took a leading part in plays, which he wrote and produced. She stated that it was largely through her efforts that in 1904 Sam H. Harris, a theatrical producer, was induced to finance the play *Little Johnny Jones.* The next year at the opening in Chicago of the musical play *Forty-Five Minutes from Broadway,* written by Cohan, she was in a box with him and his parents and heard the popular song "Mary" sung by well-known actress Fay Templeton. In December 1906 the couple separated, and in June 1907 she obtained a divorce on grounds of adultery. In the same year, Cohan married Agnes Mary Nolan, with whom he lived until his death on 9 November 1942.

In many ways, the character of Mary in the film represented Levey, in the sense that she occupied the position and place of Levey in depictions of actual incidents in the life of Cohan. Mary met Cohan at a young age as an ambitious stage star. He wrote songs for her to perform. They married. She helped in acquiring funding for the production of *Little Johnny Jones.* She and Cohan were shown together at the first production of *Forty-Five Minutes from Broadway,* in which the actress Fay Templeton sang the song "Mary." But there were also significant differences between Mary and Ethel Levey. Not only was the character's name invented, Mary was not made up to look like or physically resemble Levey. Moreover, Mary was a member of the chorus and did not have the professional standing or status that Levey enjoyed. Furthermore, no reference was made in the film to Cohan's adultery, divorce, and remarriage. Mary was depicted as his sole sweetheart into old age.

The District Court of New York found that *Yankee Doodle Dandy* did not represent the plaintiff and therefore did not invade her right to privacy under the Civil Rights Laws. The similarities between Mary and Levey, they stated, were too insignificant and incidental to the theme of the motion picture. While the picture might remind some audience members of Levey, this did not mean Mary represented her. District Judge Bondy referred to such previous New York privacy decisions as *Roberson v. Rochester Folding Box Co.,*[75] *Binns v. Vitagraph Company of America,*[76] and *Humiston v. Universal Film*

Manufacturing Co.[77] and held that the words "portrait or picture" in the New York statutory privacy laws required a "clear representation of a person" by "photograph, statue, imitation or word painting," a representation at least approaching a "likeness."[78] Such a representation, he held, could not be found in the present film: "In the photoplay and in its press exploitation book, the defendant states that 'Yankee Doodle Dandy' is based on the story of George M. Cohan or that it is the life story of George M. Cohan. These statements do not suggest that Mary in appearance, personality, character, mannerism or action resembles the plaintiff or represents the plaintiff."[79]

The court dismissed Levey's complaint on the basis that the film did not depict her and therefore was not a breach of her right to privacy under the statute. The conclusion sounds logical, because a film substituting a fictional character for a real person could not be a breach of that real person's privacy. If anything, the substitution would surely ensure, rather than erode, an individual's privacy. In *Melvin v. Reid,* the plaintiff's primary concern was that her real name and details were used, when a fictional characterization would have sufficed.

The court in *Levey* did, however, recognize that, although deemed irrelevant to Levey's cause of action, "the reproduction in the picture of songs the plaintiff sang and of scenes in which she took part and the introduction of fictional characters and a largely fictional treatment of Cohan's life may hurt her feelings."[80] The film effectively wrote Levey out of Cohan's life, thus diminishing her professional career and the significance of her personal relationships in the interests of honoring him and suppressing his acts of adultery. Her contribution to his work and contribution to his life story were removed from popular history. It was not difficult to understand Levey's frustration. With no other cause of action available to redress the harm done, Levey framed her wrong as one involving a breach of privacy, when in fact it could perhaps be better described as too little publicity.

The next privacy case to involve a claim regarding the use of an individual's life story by a motion picture was *Stryker v. Republic Pictures Corporation* in California.[81] Like *Levey v. Warner Bros. Pictures, Inc.*, this case concerned a mixture of appropriation and misrepresentation. Louis Stryker asserted that the 1949 Hollywood war film *The Sands of Iwo Jima* (directed by Allan Dwan) used his name and participation in the battles of Guadalcanal and Iwo Jima as a U.S. marine in 1945, but that the film fictionalized parts of his private life.

The Sands of Iwo Jima tells the story of a U.S. Marine Corps squadron led by the demanding and taciturn Sergeant John Stryker, played by John Wayne. It follows the various squad members as they are trained and tested by Stryker and engage in the fierce battles of Guadalcanal and, finally, Iwo Jima. The film delves intermittently into the marines' personal lives and reveals the reasons Stryker is plagued by unhappiness: his wife has left him, and he rarely (if ever) sees his young son. Stryker wins the respect and love of his fellow marines and his country, by claiming the island of Iwo Jima and erecting the U.S. flag (the moment immortalized by the Marine Corps War Memorial in Arlington, Virginia), but is tragically shot by the Japanese.

The plaintiff, who shared the last name of the main character and was a marine sergeant during the battles of Guadalcanal and Iwo Jima in 1945, claimed the film invaded his right to privacy. Since *Melvin v. Reid* in 1931, a number of cases in California had affirmed the existence of the right to privacy at common law,[82] a point conceded by the defendants. *Melvin v. Reid*, however, was the only Californian precedent concerning the use of an individual's life narrative as the plot for a motion picture. The other two cases relied upon by Stryker, *Binns v. Vitagraph Company of America* and *Levey v. Warner Bros. Pictures, Inc.*, were both decided under New York's statutory privacy laws. The plaintiff's attorney, David J. Sachs, argued that *Melvin v. Reid*, as well as *Binns v. Vitagraph Company of America* and *Levey v. Warner Bros. Pictures, Inc.*, provided authority for the principle that unlike the case with newspapers and newsreels, the "public interest" or "public figure" exception to the right to privacy did not apply to fictional "photoplays": "The *Binns* case, as well as *Melvin v. Reid*, demonstrate with forceful clarity that where the production of a motion picture photoplay is involved, it is no defense that the subject is a public figure or concerns a matter of public or general interest."[83]

If the plaintiff, Stryker, had featured in a newsreel depiction of the events at Iwo Jima, Sachs conceded, he would have no valid claim for breach of privacy. In the present case, however, the film in question was partly fictional, was entertaining, not educational, and was produced for the purpose of profit. This argument was supported by New York case law, as *Binns v. Vitagraph Company of America* and *Blumenthal v. Picture Classics* had held that "a right to privacy" did apply to dramatic motion pictures mixing fact with fiction. The argument was vehemently opposed by counsel for Republic Pictures, however, who submitted that the public interest or public figure exception was not restricted to traditional news publications such as newspapers, newsreels, and nonfiction books. Information could be disseminated as valuable knowledge by the dramatic and literary arts as much as by straight factual reporting. They argued: "The biography, the critical or retrospective essay published long after current news value has been disseminated, the historical or sociological play or novel, are certainly as potent a force in the spread of knowledge as the newspaper or the technical history."[84] They cited a number of examples: the influence of *Uncle Tom's Cabin* by Harriet Beecher Stowe (first published in 1852) on the abolition of slavery; the reform of judicial procedure in England in the nineteenth century as a result of Charles Dickens's *Bleak House* (first published in 1852); the function of the motion picture biographies of Louis Pasteur,[85] Émile Zola[86] and Oliver Wendell Holmes Sr.[87] in introducing these famous figures to otherwise ignorant audiences.

The plaintiff's attorneys also put forward another argument. Even if Stryker "waived" his right to privacy in respect to his service during World War II, the defendants' motion picture was not confined to recounting his military action but also represented, or rather misrepresented, his personal life. "They proceeded with a fictionalized and re-created account of the Appellant's life, activities and name in their exploitation. This was . . . beyond 'the matters pertaining to his professional activities,' and therefore beyond the saving graces of the defense of waiver."[88]

However, the dramatic fictionalization by Republic Pictures of parts of Sergeant Stryker's personal life actually worked to hinder rather than help the plaintiff's case. This was because, as in *Levey v. Warner Bros. Pictures, Inc.*, identification was a key issue. Sachs (the plaintiff's attorney) asserted that the fact that the defendants used Stryker's name and title in relation to a battle in which he participated amounted to identification. Republic Pictures submitted that mere use of the plaintiff's last name and not his first name (the film's character was called John, not Louis), in conjunction with the title of sergeant and nothing more, was not sufficient to identify him.

Unlike in *Melvin v. Reid*[89] the plaintiff's actual relationships, temperament, and personal life were not represented on screen but were fictionalized, which made it more difficult to demonstrate the plaintiff was the character represented in the motion picture. Nor was this similar to *Blumenthal,* where a fictional narrative framing sequences of actual people and scenes on the streets of New York stripped the film of the public interest exception to privacy law. In that case, Miriam Blumenthal had her likeness appropriated, and she was clearly recognizable. Nor was the present case similar to *Binns,* where the dramatic portrayal of the steamship rescue and the fictionalization of some elements of the story worked to deny the film the public interest exception to privacy law, as John Binns was clearly identified by name and through his explicit connection with the specific event recounted.

The plaintiff struggled to define his case. This was in part due to the public interest argument in relation to the representation of the battle of Iwo Jima but also due to the difficulty in claiming that the film appropriated *his* life stories. As a consequence, the defendants were successful in their demurrer. The District Court of Appeal held that "men who are called to the colors subject their activities in that particular field to the public gaze and may not contend that in the discharge of such activities their actions may not be publicized."[90] The court conceded that servicemen do retain a right to privacy over incidents in their personal lives, but that in the present case the plaintiff failed to articulate in the complaint what parts of the film, if any, depicted his personal life (and therefore invaded his privacy) and what parts were simply a work of fiction. Justice Hanson (giving the opinion for the majority) also stated that both *Binns v. Vitagraph Company of America* and *Levey v. Warner Bros. Pictures, Inc.,* "so heavily relied upon by plaintiff,"[91] were not relevant to the present case, as "recovery was permitted by reason of a New York statute for which no counterpart rests in California."[92] Further, they corrected, *Melvin v. Reid* was not authority, "as the appellant seem[ed] to think," as a motion picture "photoplay" depicting the incidents of a person's life was in and of itself actionable.[93]

When I reviewed the production notes for *The Sands of Iwo Jima,* the control exercised by the Production Code over the script and plot of the film became clear.[94] In response to Republic Pictures' first submission of the script to the Production Code Administration (PCA), Joseph Breen wrote to Allen Wilson (of Republic Pictures) to say that the following alterations were required: "All dress needs to be modest, kisses not lustful or open mouthed, violence not brutal or gruesome." Stryker was not to be "shown as drunk [and] no sequences with prostitutes."[95] Changes were accordingly made to the script, and it was resubmitted to the PCA. The revisions were generally approved, but one scene in particular continued to trouble Breen. This was where (in the final film version) an off-duty Sergeant Stryker was drinking in a bar and was approached by a woman, called Mary, who attempted to engage him in conversation and persuade him to buy her a drink. She then suggested they go back to her place for a drink, to which proposition Stryker agreed. When they arrived Mary realized she had no liquor, and so Stryker gave her money to purchase a bottle at a nearby store. While she was out, Stryker discovered her baby son in an adjacent room. When she returned, he gave her some money and left. The scene was seemingly designed to demonstrate the challenges of personal and family life during the war.

In the revised script submitted to Breen in early June 1949, the woman's child was not a baby but a six-year-old boy, and it was "obvious" the woman was a prostitute. Breen wrote to Wilson: "Before this picture [can] be approved it will be necessary to change this sequence entirely to eliminate any suggestion of a prostitute."[96] Again the script was revised and sent to the PCA, but in a later letter, Breen continued to insist that the scene was still "unacceptable," suggesting to Republic Pictures that it consider rather "characterizing the woman as a cheap café hostess who does not take Stryker to her apartment." Instead the scene should be "played entirely in the bar, with the woman's ragamuffin child running off the street to see his mother for some reason or other, and having her rebuff him, possibly much in the same way as she presently does."[97]

Republic Pictures refused to amend the plot in this way but did undertake extensive rewriting of the script. After it was again submitted to the PCA, Breen responded that he recognized "great change had been made to the scenes," but it was still unacceptable and could only be remedied by giving Mary some definite occupation, such as a "chantoosie" (a singer) or a "photographer."[98] After Republic Pictures made further changes, Breen finally approved the script on 22 August 1949.[99] The final film did not provide Mary with an alternate occupation, but the script was carefully crafted to avoid any innuendo. Despite Breen's best efforts, however, many film critics still read between the lines. An article in *Variety* magazine commented that "Julie Bishop makes a bit role memorable as a girl of the streets who takes up a life of shame to feed her infant baby,"[100] and a review in the magazine referred to Mary as the "Pearl Harbor hustler with a baby to support."[101]

In their court submissions, Republic Pictures pushed Stryker to identify those scenes of the film concerning the main character's personal life that were factual as opposed to fictional. This request was understandable given the laborious task it had undertaken in rewriting the script to please Joseph Breen and the PCA. The production notes for the film also included the decision to include the following disclaimer within the credits: "While this photoplay is based on the battle for Iwo Jima, most of the incidents and, except where true names are knowingly used, all of the characters are fictitious. Any resemblance between any such events or characters and actual events or persons is coincidental."[102]

It is unclear whether "Sergeant Stryker" was one of the "true names . . . knowingly used" by the film. When the film was finally approved by the PCA, however, a form was completed by Republic Pictures entitled "Analysis of Film Content." One of the sections was headed "Material Source" and offered a variety of options, including "Biography." Republic Pictures did not mark this box, choosing rather "Original Screen Story" and wrote a note next to "Other": "Based in part on the battle for Iwo Jima."[103] These documents suggest that long before litigation commenced, Republic Pictures did not consider the film *The Sands of Iwo Jima* to be biographical or based strictly on actual events.

These, then, are among the distinctive ways in which masculinity and femininity were constructed by film studios in the early twentieth century with implications for legal claims of "privacy" and/or "property." Three of the films discussed in this chapter portrayed male heroes—saving passengers from sinking ships, building a celebrated career on stage, and leading a squadron during two iconic battles for their country at war. These films congratulated and commemorated the protagonists, reinforcing the idea that to be an ideal man was to achieve something extraordinary in the public domain and in one's professional life. Their private lives were either ancillary or entirely absent.

In contrast, the films at the center of life-story cases brought to court by women focused on their personal relationships and within this context characterized them as either marginal or shameful. In *Yankee Doodle Dandy,* George M. Cohan's fictional wife, Mary, is constructed as a star-struck, supportive, and loyal wife, whose stage talents never threaten the primacy of the protagonist. Ethel Levey's professional accomplishments and Cohan's adultery followed by their divorce were, much to Levey's distress, omitted from the screenplay. In *The Red Kimono,* Gabrielle Darley's seduction and corruption as a child, her work in a New Orleans brothel, and her trial for murder were presented explicitly by Mrs. Wallace Reid in the form of a sordid morality tale. In *The Sands of Iwo Jima,* despite pressure from the Production Code Administration, Sergeant Stryker was shown consorting with Mary, a woman who drinks and prostitutes herself to soldiers while her infant child sleeps in the next room. Women were mostly defined by the film studios through their personal relationships, usually with their sexuality safely contained by marriage or held up to public condemnation.

These films also point to another theme evident in many of the legal cases examined in this book. Women could appeal more successfully for the protection of their privacy than could men, because they were still defined primarily by their private lives despite the economic and social changes that saw new generations entering the workforce in unprecedented numbers. In this way, a right to privacy helped to reinforce the connection of femininity with private life by seeking to return women's portraits, bodies, and narratives to the private sphere. At the same time, however, the right to privacy also worked to provide women with some respite from voyeurism and exploitation and offered some control over the terms of their public appearance. For women in the early twentieth century, forging lives of greater agency and autonomy than did their predecessors, a "right to privacy" proved to be a double-edged doctrine in a legal system that continued to institutionalize men's authority and men's interests.

My investigation into how and why the advent of the nineteenth-century technologies of photography and cinema led to the development of a right to privacy in the United States concludes in the mid-twentieth century. By 1950 a right of privacy was recognized by a majority of states either at common law, by statute, or constitutionally, as in California.[104] My research suggests that by the middle decades of the twentieth century, women and men began to bring privacy suits in numbers approaching equality. In circumstances in which looking and being looked at remained highly gendered activities, however, their reasons for doing so were quite different. John Binns, Gabrielle Melvin, Ethel Levey, and Louis Stryker all used "a right to privacy" to argue that a motion picture unfairly exploited their life story, but whereas the women took issue with being shamed or marginalized by films because of their private lives (as hookers or divorcees), men protested about the implications of being publicly framed as national heroes.

In this book I have been examining the reasons plaintiffs brought privacy claims in relation to the use of their images. I have also suggested what these claims reveal about the history of "a right to privacy" as a legal vehicle and the ways in which an examination of the cases contributes to a richer understanding of the history of visual culture. In this chapter I have shown that plaintiffs also used a right to privacy to claim ownership over their life experiences and to protest against the appropriation and exploitation of those experiences by film studios. "A right to privacy" took a particular direction in California, the location of the Hollywood film studios, in response to the ascendant feature film industry, a cultural investment in self-invention, and the influence of the Hays Production Code. These cases highlighted the perceived possibilities of "privacy" in the context of an expanding and voracious film industry but also pointed to the limits of plaintiff success when confronted by opposing claims to copyright, free speech, and public interest. The cases also show the different kinds of claims made by men and women on the ever-evolving doctrine of privacy.

Conclusion

During the nineteenth century, technological innovations radically changed the nature of portraiture. The public unveiling of photography, in 1839, by William Henry Fox Talbot and Louis Daguerre, allowed the "likeness" of an individual to be lifted with uncanny precision and fixed upon paper, thence to be copied, appropriated, and circulated among an endless number of viewers. The pictured subject thus became an object, able to be reproduced, published, handled, and distributed on a massive scale with relative ease. The accuracy and autonomy of the photographic portrait were hailed by institutions of government and agencies of science as providing a valuable resource and embraced by communities and families wishing to keep their loved ones close.

As an artifact of self-expression, individuals welcomed the invention of the photographic portrait. Meanwhile, at a time when photography still necessitated expensive equipment and special technical ability, the professional photographer secured his position as image authority and owner through the doctrine of copyright. But with the transformation of photography into an amateur pastime in the late nineteenth century, a development led by the New York entrepreneur George Eastman, the experiences, expectations, and interests of those who "snapped" or "shot" pictures began to diverge from the interests of those "caught" on film. As their images began to be used in advertisements, for example, without their knowledge or permission, women, especially, began to express alarm and anger. They pointed to a new type of harm that current laws were inadequate to address: the unauthorized circulation and publication of their likenesses.

This was one of the harms identified by Samuel D. Warren and Louis D. Brandeis in their influential article "A Right to Privacy" in 1890,[1] in which they advocated that the common law recognize a "right to privacy" as a new tort. They did not identify the issue as a gendered one, but, as I have shown, their advocacy followed widespread public debates about how to "protect" "ladies" from the circulation and publication of their photographic images without their consent. The most high-profile case that preceded the Warren and Brandeis article was the use of the image of the First Lady of the United States, Frances Cleveland, for a "nostrum" advertisement. This had provoked the introduction in the House of Representatives of a Bill to Protect Ladies by Republican Congressman John Robert Thomas, intended to prohibit the use of images of women (in their capacity as the wives, daughters, mothers, and sisters of "American citizens") without their consent in advertisements.[2] As a result of protests by professional (male) photographers,[3] however, the bill was referred to the Judiciary Committee and subsequently disappeared. It was the press publicity surrounding this initiative that first connected the issue of the unauthorized circulation of women's photographic portraits with the idea of a right to privacy in the United States.

In 1902 the first superior state court in the United States, the New York Court of Appeals, was called on to consider recognition of such a right in the case of *Roberson v. Rochester Folding Box Co.*[4] Brought by the young and attractive Abigail Roberson over the use of her surreptitiously taken photograph within extensive national and international marketing material for a flour mill, the case failed, but it led to the enactment of the first "privacy" laws in the United States,[5] prohibiting the use of an individual's "name" or "likeness" for trade or advertising purposes without the individual's written consent.

The Face That Launched a Thousand Lawsuits has shown that the "right to privacy" was formulated primarily in response to complaints by women about the unauthorized publication of their photographic portraits. The first attempt was informed by paternalistic attempts to keep "ladies" out of the public gaze, but beginning with *Roberson v. Rochester Folding Box Co.,* women themselves acted to wrest control and ownership of images of their faces and bodies from the (mostly male) copyright holders of such images. The "right to privacy" doctrine may have initially employed conservative language upholding feminine virtues, such as "modesty" and "reserve," but the women who brought privacy actions were far from timid, as Abigail Roberson showed when she took the chief justice of the New York Court of Appeals to task in a letter to the *New York Times.* Women began to use the concept of a right to privacy as an instrument to question the masculine prerogatives of copyright law and argue that the value in a "pretty portrait" was as much in the person's face as the paper upon which it was printed. Far from representing a retreat to nineteenth-century ideals of passive femininity, a right to privacy is best understood as part of women's broader political struggle for citizenship rights at the turn of the twentieth century.

The Face That Launched a Thousand Lawsuits does not attempt to define the concept of privacy, as if it had a fixed meaning, but rather charts its historical evolution as a legal vehicle for women and its changing connotations and uses in the cases in which it was used. Abigail Roberson, Felicity Riddle, Mary Almind, Mabel Colyer, and others invoked a right to privacy to protest against the public exploitation of their photographic portraits by others in ways which reduced them to anonymous objects of consumption. These cases were brought by a generation of young women who grew up in the late nineteenth and early twentieth centuries with novel ambitions for education and freedom, embodied in the figure of the New Woman. They entered adulthood at a time when images were overtaking words as the primary resource of advertising and self-definition. When men brought actions in relation to the use of their images in advertisements or motion pictures, they usually referred to representations of the plaintiffs as public and professional figures. As their masculine reputation was at issue, a right to privacy was not the primary basis for their claims: instead they usually pleaded defamation.

Katherine Feeney, Dorothy Barber, Ina Banks, and others used a "right to privacy" to protest against the optic violation of their bodies (or the bodies of their deceased, deformed infants) by the photographic and cinematic camera that transformed them from patients receiving medical treatment into spectacles of "monstrosity." These cases illustrate the extent to which the technological conditions of modernity radically altered the ways in which bodies were inspected, exhibited, and exposed to the eyes of others. Traditional laws "protecting" the bodies of women and children from unwelcome looking (such as trespass and nuisance) were grounded in a reification of "the four walls of a man's home." The camera was able to penetrate private spaces and places and carry its images of the "monstrous" bodies of women and the dead deformed products of their wombs to the outside world to become objects of mass voyeurism and morbid curiosity. The law shifted from a focus on the masculine investment in private property to the feminine concern with protecting privacy in the use of women's images.

As well as filming bodies in private settings, cinematic cameras were able to roam urban streets looking for subjects to capture in their lenses and project upon the silent screen. The cases of *Kunz v. Allen,*[6] *Humiston v. Universal Film Manufacturing Co.,*[7] and *Blumenthal v. Picture Classics, Inc.,*[8] provide privileged insights into the experience of being an unwilling cinematic subject at the beginning of the twentieth century. These important privacy law decisions, adjudicating upon early nonfiction films, and the distinctions between newsreels, newspapers, and documentaries, also highlight the cinematic camera's unique invasion of the person through close-ups. Stella Kunz, Grace Humiston, Gertrude Sweenek, and Miriam Blumenthal used a right to privacy to protest against becoming objects of the mass gaze and provided disturbing accounts of the ways in which the details of their mannerisms, expressions, clothing, and movements loomed large upon the big screen. Their cases also reveal the limits of "privacy" as a discourse of resistance, with court judgments anchored in the public/privacy dichotomy that privileged the "public interest" in the distribution of nonfiction films over the individual rights claimed by the women who found themselves under surveillance.

As a doctrine used to assert control over photographic and cinematic images, "a right to privacy" also began to be used by women for professional purposes. As women entered the paid workforce in the early decades of the twentieth century, pursuing occupations defined by "techniques of appearance," in Liz Conor's words—as actresses, models, and dancers—their ability to own and control images of themselves became crucially important. Women such as Gladys Loftus, Beatrice Lillie, Gloria Middleton, and Judy Lane used a right to privacy to protect their professional integrity and earnings that depended on their skill and stature. These cases pushed a "right to privacy" in the direction of recognizing a separate "right of publicity." It was in this context that Pauline Myers, an African American dancer from Harlem, asserted her right to determine the meaning of her display as a "modern" woman adopting "primitive" adornment and won her case. Men also utilized these new understandings of "a right to privacy" as a way to safeguard the earnings flowing from what I term their "professions of performance"—their masculine pursuits conducted out of doors. The U.S. Supreme Court first identified a distinctive "right of publicity" in 1953 in *Haelen Laboratories, Inc. v. Topps Chewing Gum*,[9] and the relationship of this right to a "right to privacy" has long since preoccupied legal scholars. As I've shown, however, if one recognizes a "right to privacy" as a doctrine established primarily by women in the late nineteenth and early twentieth centuries to assert control over the use of their images, the emergence of a right of publicity in relation to those images was logical and inevitable.

Subjects caught on film were not the only ones who brought cases seeking legal redress against the activities of filmmakers. People whose life stories were appropriated as plot material for films also felt aggrieved. The emergence of narrative motion pictures increased the demand for exciting, marketable stories. In addition to pillaging plays, novels, and historical events for fictional fodder, the film industry looked to the lives of living persons. Women and men used a right to privacy from the 1920s through the 1940s to claim ownership over life stories depicted on the screen without their consent. Not surprisingly, the types of narratives borrowed and manipulated by film studios depended on the gender of the filmed subject. Whereas *Saved by Wireless*, *The Sands of Iwo Jima*, and *Yankee Doodle Dandy* celebrated the public achievements of male protagonists, *The Red Kimono* cast shame on the scandalous life of Gabrielle Melvin. Women were framed and shamed by their "private" lives, whereas men's professional achievements were honored. Darley forged a right to privacy in California, successfully arguing that *The Red Kimono* invaded her right to privacy by denying her "pursuit of happiness" as guaranteed by the state constitution. Whereas New York's privacy laws were born of the practical task of addressing the court's dismissal of Abigail Roberson's objection to the use of her image in advertising, Californian interpretations were framed by more utopian visions of the possibilities of personal redemption and self-reinvention.

My historical investigation ends mid-century, but a review of recent "privacy" cases suggests that it is still a doctrine connected intimately with the use of "pictures," still and moving. Television and the online circulation of images now account for many contemporary privacy cases. As legal scholars have noted, however, "a right to privacy" no longer affords plaintiffs the same degree of control over the use of their images and narratives that it once promised.[10] In the 1960s and 1970s, its application was restricted by a number of U.S. Supreme Court decisions stressing the importance of the First Amendment guaranteeing freedom of speech.[11]

In another development, men have become more active in invoking a discourse on privacy to quite different ends. Whereas women were central to the doctrine's development in the United States, protesting against the use and abuse of their images by others, it now seems that "privacy" as a right and a discourse is more frequently deployed by men, albeit for different purposes in quite different circumstances. In recent times, the focus of privacy law has shifted to the role of organizations—corporations and governments—in gathering and distributing private information about individuals, from numerous sources, including medical records, sales receipts, communication networks, and political affiliations. "Data mining" and "data-veillance" are new terms synonymous with recent claims to rights to privacy on the part of citizens and consumers.

Nevertheless, the circulation of women's pictures continues to be a major issue of concern, and privacy cases involving images continue to point to gendered harms. As the *Leviston* case, discussed at the opening of my book, highlights, ubiquitous technologies, including smart phones and the Internet, have resulted in the proliferation of new offenses involving injuries suffered by women and generally perpetrated by men. Images now circulate globally. In June 2015 it was reported by the *Adelaide Advertiser* in South Australia that nude and revealing images of more than four hundred Australian women and girls were being shared online, without their consent, on a United States website.

These mass "photo hacks" attract media attention and shine a light on the increasing occurrence of "revenge pornography"—a phrase used to describe the action of a person (usually a man) who uploads explicit images of someone else (usually a woman) in order to humiliate, shame, or ridicule the victim. Whether done with revenge in mind, nonconsensual pornography can ruin lives, leaving the women involved subject to unwanted sexual harassment, threats, and taunts, unable to find or continue in their employment, and shunned by acquaintances, friends, and family. As a consequence they often suffer from depression, anxiety, and thoughts of self-harm. The images can be easily found when a victim's name is entered online, and they spread with lightning speed across the Internet, making their suppression and containment almost impossible. Victims of nonconsensual pornography, their lawyers, and some lawmakers are currently campaigning across the United States to criminalize this practice, and as a result twenty-six states now outlaw it.

Some victims of nonconsensual pornography and their lawyers have also brought civil privacy suits, relying on laws first forged in relation to the unauthorized circulation and publication of images at the turn of the twentieth century. In January 2013 more than twenty-three women brought a class action for invasion of privacy in the state of Texas against revenge pornography websites where their ex-partners posted nude photographs of them without their consent.[12] Other young women are bringing individual lawsuits, such as Lastonia Leviston and twenty-nine-year-old Holly Jacobs, who on 18 April 2013 became the first person in the state of Florida to sue an ex-partner for the circulation and publication of sexually explicit photographs of her on the Internet without her consent.[13] She claimed the defendant breached her right to privacy and intentionally inflicted emotional distress upon her.

Jacobs, now founder and executive director of the Cyber Civil Rights Initiative, a group dedicated to criminalizing nonconsensual pornography and providing aid to victims, is actively trying to raise the profile of this issue within the legal community. Echoing the protests of privacy plaintiffs in the early twentieth century, Jacobs has said of her efforts: "I hope that I'll set an example and show this is how you overcome this: by coming forward. . . . If it's in the name of the cause and to change the laws about this, then I'm happy to do it."[14] The campaign to end nonconsensual online pornography, led by violated women and their attorneys, continues the fight for recognition of a right to privacy begun by women more than a hundred years ago. The unauthorized circulation and publication of still and moving images still disproportionately affects young women, "privacy" remains the primary discourse used to protest such practices, and legal change is advocated as the preferable remedy.

The cases analyzed in this book lead us to consider the ways in which gender and privacy rights are inextricably linked through their interconnected history. When the circulation of private portraits became a social and legal problem in the late nineteenth century, it was primarily a practice that affected women because their photographs (used in advertising, newsreels, and feature films) held greater voyeuristic appeal for both men and women. Their photographs also gave women a public presence at a time when debates about a woman's place, whether in the home, the workplace, the streets, or political system, were gathering public momentum.

"A right to privacy" appealed to both sides of the New Woman question. Through its discourse it appeared to reinforce traditional feminine ideals of passivity, reserve, domesticity, and modesty, but through the legal doctrine it granted greater autonomy to women determined to control the terms of their public presence. A right to privacy might have returned women's faces, bodies, and narratives to the private realm, but it also allowed women to voice their outrage and provide their perspectives. It also began to be used to advance their professional prospects. The "right to privacy" was an ambiguous doctrine, seeming to confirm traditional feminine virtues while also lending itself for use as a weapon to promote women's rights.

When the landmark case of *Roberson v. Rochester Folding Box Co.* was decided, the court might have awarded individuals a "property" rather than a "privacy" right in their images (as advocated by Abigail Roberson's progressive lawyer, Milton E. Gibbs). Such a move would have broken the link between image rights and privacy rights and allowed women in the twentieth century to protect their dignity, autonomy, and earnings without needing to appeal to a conservative ideal of femininity. But as it transpired, the legal right to control images of one's face or body or life story within pictures proceeded very narrowly in the form of common law or statutory rights to privacy in step with the facts of the case law. It encountered obstacles in arguments about free speech, the public interest, and competing copyright interests.

The failure of Gibbs's proposition and other arguments in favor of a property right derived perhaps as much from the hesitation of the court to embrace a more radical legal proposition as it did from the feminine character of the concerns in the case law. Had more male plaintiffs acted to prohibit the use and abuse of their images by others in the early decades, the courts may have been more comfortable in recognizing individuals' property rights in their image. In fact, only when men really began to use the "right to privacy" doctrine to a significant degree toward the middle of the twentieth century to protect their masculine "professions of performance"—as discussed in chapter 6—did the courts first declare that individuals held a property right in their image in the form of "a right to publicity."

The conviction on the part of early privacy plaintiffs and their lawyers that individuals should have an enforceable right to decide how and when their photographic or cinematic images were used by others now seems utopian as our images proliferate across the Internet without our knowledge or consent. In 1905 Justice Cobb mused prophetically that if one's form and features were not one's own, "one's picture may be reproduced and exhibited anywhere. If it may be used in a newspaper, it may be used in a poster or placard. It may be posted upon the walls of private dwellings or upon the streets. It may ornament the bar of the saloon keeper or decorate the walls of a brothel. By becoming a member of society, neither man nor woman can be presumed to have consented to such uses of the impression of their faces and features upon paper." Such scenarios have indeed eventuated, and the images of victims of nonconsensual pornography do, in effect, decorate the walls of (online) brothels. Diluted common law and statutory, state-based rights to privacy and rights of publicity, together with other doctrines such as defamation and intentional infliction of emotional distress, provide today's victims of the use and abuse of their images with only limited control.

Yet, as victims' lawyers and activists fight, state by state and at the federal level, to criminalize the practice of nonconsensual pornography, "privacy" is still invoked as the preferred discourse to protect women against the abuse of their images by others. Nonconsensual pornography shames and humiliates young women by transporting their sexualized bodies from the private domain of the home to the public pandemonium of the Web. Naked or explicit images of men do not, it seems, humiliate or disgrace them to the same degree. Men's sexuality is not regarded as intrinsically shameful. Naming the problem as a "violation of privacy" (as did the actor Jennifer Lawrence) and calling for greater privacy rights for women suggests that "a right to privacy" still works to protect women's dignity in at least a residual respect. But privacy remains a double-edged doctrine for women in a society in which men continue to dominate public life, the professions, public platforms, and media outlets. In the absence of fundamental social and legal change, men retain the power to abuse and demean women by circulating sexualized or otherwise private images, and women continue to rely on legal rights to privacy both to contest men's sense of entitlement and to protect their reputations and basic sense of self.

In this book I have suggested that it is just as important to understand the reasons plaintiffs brought lawsuits as it is to understand the legal content of their claims and the outcomes. In conclusion, I also wish to emphasize that an approach to legal history focused on the experiences of plaintiffs has methodological implications. Deep archival research is necessary to sustain such analysis. For it was often the case that legal doctrines at common law or within statute were used as tools to achieve an end, not because they defined or encapsulated the plaintiff's particular experience and sense of grievance. It would be wrong to assume, without further evidence, that women such as Abigail Roberson were modest and retiring types seeking paternal protection simply because their attorneys used this language to further their claims. It is even more necessary to investigate the experiences of actual plaintiffs in an area of law renowned for its lack of precise definition. To identify the circumstances and desires of plaintiffs (particularly those long dead) and analyze the eloquent arguments of their lawyers requires extensive research in dispersed primary sources. Primary court documents, including affidavits, pleadings, records of testimony, and exhibits, can only be understood, moreover, in their cultural and historical contexts. To pursue this kind of inquiry necessarily requires a commitment to interdisciplinary scholarship.

Serious scholarship at the intersection of law, film studies, and history is still in its relative infancy. Legal scholars are often skeptical as to what an understanding of film and history can contribute to their disciplinary knowledge, while the disciplines of film studies and history regard law in turn as a separate and self-contained domain. I have sought to bring these distinct disciplines into conversation in ways that advance knowledge in all three areas. By examining the primary records of some thirty court cases in detail, I have been able to highlight the perspectives of previously inaudible and invisible women, and of some men, who sought to negotiate the implications of the new inventions of photography and cinema for their lives and livelihoods. These are rich sources with a wealth of material that one hopes will be further researched to illuminate the intersecting histories of law, film, and gender.

The Face That Launched a Thousand Lawsuits has shown that women forged a right to privacy in the United States by protesting against the new harms occasioned by the use and abuse of photographic and cinematic images of their faces and bodies by others. At a time when they lacked basic civil and political rights, women asserted the right to control the circulation, publication, and exploitation of their images. Their aims were diverse and complex: to avoid being reduced to anonymous objects, to prevent their transformation into spectacles of monstrosity, to halt their exposure on the big screen to the mass gaze of audiences, to assert control of their careers as models, dancers, and actors and to reclaim the story of their lives from the exploitation of others. The outcomes of their actions were mixed. Still, the cases they brought to court shaped the doctrine of privacy that continues to be invoked by women in courts today.

Notes

Introduction

1. Leviston also sued Curtis for intentional infliction of emotional distress. See *Leviston v. Curtis James Jackson III,* No. 102449 of 2010 (NY Sup Ct, 2015); see also Dareh Gregorian, "50 Cent to Pay Another $2 Million for Sex Tape," *New York Daily News* (New York) (online), 24 July 2015, at http://nydn.us/1MpwfS5, and Andres Peterson, "50 Cent Filed for Bankruptcy Days after Losing a Revenge Porn Lawsuit," *Washington Post* (Washington, D.C.) (online), 14 July 2015, at https://www.washingtonpost.com/news/the-switch/wp/2015/07/14/50-cent-filed-for-bankruptcy-days-after-losing-a-revenge-porn-lawsuit/

2. See *Roberson v. Rochester Folding Box Co.* 64 NE 442 (NY, 1902).

3. Leviston quoted in Gregorian, "50 Cent to Pay Another $2 Million for Sex Tape." Jackson subsequently filed for bankruptcy, so it is unlikely Leviston will recover the full amount of damages ordered by the court. See Peterson, "50 Cent Filed for Bankruptcy Days after Losing a Revenge Porn Lawsuit."

4. For a detailed discussion of a few of the cases individually, see, for example, Caroline Danielson, "The Gender of Privacy and the Embodied Self: Examining the Origins of the Right to Privacy in U.S. Law" (1999), 25 (2) *Feminist Studies* 311; Dorothy Glancy, "Privacy and the Other Miss M." (1989–1990), 10 *Northern Illinois University Law Review* 401; Anita L. Allen, and Erin Mack, "How Privacy Got Its Gender" (1990), 10 (Spring) *Northern Illinois University Law Review* 441, and Anita L. Allen, "Natural Law, Slavery and the Right to Privacy Tort" (2012), 81 *Fordham Law Review* 1187. Otherwise, these cases mostly feature only as footnotes.

5. Samuel D. Warren and Louis D. Brandeis, "The Right to Privacy" (1890), 4 *Harvard Law Review* 193.

6. William Prosser, "Privacy" (1960), 48 (3) *California Law Review* 383, 423. Prosser cited as authority for this story in Alpheus Thomas Mason, *Brandeis: A Free Man's Life* (Viking Press, 1946), 70.

7. Legal historians subsequently disproved this story and explained that Warren's daughter would have been no more than six or seven years old when "A Right to Privacy" was published in 1890. See, e.g., James H. Barron, "Warren and Brandeis, The Right to Privacy, 4 *Harv. L. Rev.* 193 (1890): Demystifying a Landmark Citation" (1979), 13 *Suffolk University Law Review* 875, 891–907; K. Gormley, "A Hundred Years of Privacy" (1992), *Wisconsin Law Review* 1335, 1349; Amy Gajda, "What if Samuel D. Warren Hadn't Married a Senator's Daughter? Uncovering the Press Coverage That Led to 'The Right to Privacy'" (2008), 35 (Spring) *Michigan State Law Review* 35.

8. For histories that have recognized the gendered nature of "a right to privacy," see Danielson, "The Gender of Privacy and the Embodied Self," and Allen and Mack, "How Privacy Got Its Gender."

9. See newspaper articles discussing the cases of *Manola v. Stevens* (1890) and *Roberson v. Rochester Folding Box Co.* (1902): "Miss Manola's Tights," *Atlanta Constitution* (Atlanta), 21 June 1890, 4; "'Flour of the Family' Case: The Pretty Plaintiff Whose Picture Was Used for Advertising Purposes Non-suited," *New York Tribune* (New York), 28 June 1902, 10; "No Right of Privacy," *Salt Lake Herald* (Salt Lake City), 23 July 1902, 4.

10. Jonathan L. Hafetz, "A Man's Home Is His Castle: Reflections on the Home, the Family, and Privacy during the Late Nineteenth and Early Twentieth Centuries" (2001), 8 *William & Mary Journal of Women and the Law* 175, 184.

11. See, e.g., Giuliana Bruno, *Atlas of Emotion: Journeys in Art, Architecture and Film* (Verso, 2002); Jonathan Crary, *Techniques of the Observer: On Vision and Modernity in the Nineteenth Century* (MIT Press, 1990); Anne Friedberg, *The Virtual Window: From Alberti to Microsoft* (MIT Press, 2006); Scott McQuire, *Visions of Modernity: Representation, Memory, Time and Space in the Age of the Camera* (Sage, 1998); Patrice Petro (ed.), *Fugitive Images: From Photography to Video* (University of Wisconsin Press, 1995); John Tagg, *The Burden of Representation: Essays on Photographies and Histories* (University of Massachusetts Press, 1988).

12. Warren and Brandeis, "A Right to Privacy" (1890).

13. See Barron, "Warren and Brandeis, The Right to Privacy" (1979), 876; Frederick Davis, "What Do We Mean by 'Right to Privacy?'" (1959), 4 *South Dakota Law Review* 1, 3: "It is doubtful if any other law review arti-

cle, before or since, has achieved greater fame or recognition"; Harry Kalven Jr., "Privacy in Tort Law: Were Warren and Brandeis Wrong?" (1966), 31 *Law and Contemporary Problems* 326, 327: "that most influential law review article of all."

14. Warren and Brandeis, "A Right to Privacy" (1890), 195.

15. Justice Cobb quoted in *Pavesich v. New England Life Insurance Co.*, 50 SE 68 (Ga, 1905). *Pavesich* was the first superior court case in the United States to recognize a right to privacy.

16. "Parker Taken to Task by an Indignant Woman—If I Can Be Photographed, Why Not You? Asks Miss Roberson," *New York Times* (New York), 27 July 1904, 1; also reported in "Girl Asks Parker How He Likes It," *St. Louis Post-Dispatch* (St. Louis), 27 July 1904.

17. Prosser's article "Privacy" identified four types of privacy tort operating within the case law that are now reflected in the American Law Institute, *Restatement (Second) of Torts* (1977) §§ 652A–E. These are (1) intrusion upon the plaintiff's seclusion or solitude; (2) public disclosure of embarrassing private facts about the plaintiff; (3) publicity that places the plaintiff in a false light in the public eye; and (4) appropriation, for the defendant's advantage, of the plaintiff's name or likeness.

18. For work discussing gendered history of a "right to privacy" see Allen and Mack, "How Privacy Got Its Gender," and Danielson, "The Gender of Privacy and the Embodied Self." For general history of "a right to privacy" see, for example, "The Right to Privacy in Nineteenth Century America" (1981), 94 (8) *Harvard Law Review* 1892; Samantha Barbas, "The Laws of Image" (2012), 47 *New England Law Review* 23; Morris Leopold Ernst and Alan U. Schwartz, *Privacy: The Right to Be Let Alone* (Greenwood Press, 1977); David H. Flaherty, *Privacy in Colonial New England* (University Press of Virginia, 1967); Gajda, "What if Samuel D. Warren Hadn't Married a Senator's Daughter?" (2008), 35; Glancy, "Privacy and the Other Miss M.," 401; Gormley, "A Hundred Years of Privacy" (1992), 1335; Hafetz, "A Man's Home Is His Castle" (2001); Samuel H. Hofstadter and George Horowitz, *The Right of Privacy* (Central Book Co., 1964); Thomas McCarthy, *The Rights of Publicity and Privacy* (West Group, 2nd ed., 2008), vol. 1; Louis Nizer, "The Right of Privacy: A Half Century's Developments" (1941), 39 (4) *Michigan Law Review* 526; Prosser, "Privacy"; James Q. Whitman, "The Two Western Cultures of Privacy: Dignity versus Liberty" (2004), 113 *Yale Law Journal* 1151.

19. See Elizabeth Otto and Vanessa Rocco (eds.), *The New Woman International: Representations in Photography and Film from 1870s through the 1960s* (University of Michigan Press, 2012), and Martha H. Patterson (ed.),

The American New Woman Revisited: A Reader 1894–1930 (Rutgers University Press, 2008).

20. See Allen and Mack, "How Privacy Got Its Gender," and Danielson, "The Gender of Privacy and the Embodied Self."

21. See Liz Conor, *The Spectacular Modern Woman* (Indiana University Press, 2004), and Otto and Rocco (eds.), *The New Woman International.*

22. I use the term "monstrosity" to draw upon the work of the film studies scholar Barbara Creed. See Barbara Creed, *The Monstrous-Feminine: Film, Feminism and Psychoanalysis* (Routledge, 1993).

23. See Conor, *The Spectacular Modern Woman.*

24. In their book, Sarat, Lawrence, and Umphrey provide an excellent review of interdisciplinary work on film and law to that date. See Austin Sarat, Lawrence Douglas, and Martha Merrill Umphrey, "On Film and Law: Broadening the Focus," in Austin Sarat, Lawrence Douglas, and Martha Merrill Umphrey (eds.), *Law on the Screen* (Stanford University Press, 2005), 1.

1
Setting the Scene

1. "The Rights and Tights of an Actress," *Baltimore Sun* (Baltimore), 19 June 1890, 3.

2. French researcher Nicéphore Niépce, who later collaborated with Daguerre, is credited with producing the first "photograph," on a pewter plate in 1826 with a camera supplied by Parisian optician Charles Chevalier. It required an exposure time of eight hours. He labeled his invention "héliographie," or "sun drawing." See Helmut Gernsheim and Alison Gernsheim, *A Concise History of Photography* (Thames and Hudson, 1965), 20.

3. Jonathan Crary, *Techniques of the Observer: On Vision and Modernity in the Nineteenth Century* (MIT Press, 1990), 13.

4. See Scott McQuire, *Visions of Modernity: Representation, Memory, Time and Space in the Age of the Camera* (Sage, 1998).

5. Ibid., 15.

6. Fox Talbot quoted in Allan Sekula, "The Body and the Archive" (1986), 39 (Winter) *October* 3, 6.

7. "Strange Uses for Photographs" (1879), 13 *Western Jurist* 484, 484.

8. See ibid.; H. J. Witmore, "Photographs as Instruments of Evidence" (1890), 31 (21) *The Central Law Journal* 414; J. A. J., "The Legal Relations of Photographs" (1869), 17 (3) *American Law Register* 1, 4: "The principal object

of this paper, however, is, to determine the evidentiary rank of the products of the photographic art. Is a photograph, considered as a narration or delineation of facts, a piece of hearsay, or of original and direct evidence?"; "The Photograph as a False Witness" (1886), 10 *Virginia Law Journal* 644.

9. J. A. J., "The Legal Relations of Photographs" (1869), 5.

10. "The Photograph as a False Witness" (1886), 647.

11. Janssen quoted in McQuire, *Visions of Modernity* (1998), 34.

12. Carlyle quoted in Helmut Gernsheim and Alison Gernsheim, *The History of Photography from the Camera Obscura to the Beginning of the Modern Era* (McGraw-Hill, 2nd ed., 1969), 239.

13. Letter to Mary Russel Mitford quoted in Mark Haworth-Booth et al. (eds.), *The Golden Age of British Photography, 1839–1900: Photographs from the Victoria and Albert Museum, London, with Selections from the Philadelphia Museum of Art, Royal Archives, Windsor Castle, The Royal Photographic Society, Bath, Science Museum, London, Scottish National Portrait Gallery, Edinburgh* (Aperture, the Philadelphia Museum of Art, and Viking Penguin, 1984), 22.

14. Walter Benjamin, "The Work of Art in the Age of Mechanical Reproduction," in Walter Benjamin and Hannah Arendt, *Illuminations* (Harcourt, 1st ed., 1968), 223.

15. Roland Barthes, *Camera Lucida: Reflections on Photography* (Hill and Wang, 1981), 15.

16. Sekula, "The Body and the Archive" (1986).

17. Ibid., 7.

18. Tom Gunning, "Tracing the Individual Body: Photography, Detectives and Early Cinema," in Leo Charney and Vanessa R. Schwartz (eds.), *Cinema and the Invention of Modern Life* (University of California Press, 1995), 15.

19. Tagg, *The Burden of Representation* (1988), 66–102.

20. Sekula, "The Body and the Archive," 10.

21. Quentin Bajac, *The Invention of Photography: The First Fifty Years* (Thames & Hudson, 2002), 37.

22. Tagg, *The Burden of Representation* (1988), 43.

23. Ibid.

24. Bajac, *The Invention of Photography* (2002), 37.

25. See C. Edwards Lester and Mathew B. Brady, *The Gallery of Illustrious Americans, Containing the Portraits and Biographical Sketches of Twenty-four of the Most Eminent Citizens of the American Republic, Since the Death of Washington* (M. B. Brady, F. D'Avignon, and C. E. Lester, 1850).

26. Bajac, *The Invention of Photography* (2002), 58.

27. See Richard Rogers Bowker, *Copyright: Its History and Its Law, Being a Summary of the Principles and Practice of Copyright with Special Reference to the American Code of 1909 and the British Act of 1911* (Houghton Mifflin, 1912).

28. This phrase is taken from an 1895 advertisement for the Pocket Kodak, included in the George Eastman Archives held by the George Eastman House International Museum of Photography and Film (Rochester, N.Y.). It reads: "'One Button Does It, You Press It.' The Pocket Kodak offers the easiest, simplest, cheapest way of taking up that delightful pastime—amateur photography. It does every thing photographic, yet slips into the pocket easily and weighs only 5 ounces. Makes pictures big enough for contact printing and good enough to enlarge to any size. Made of aluminum, covered with fine leather. Rich and dainty in finish."

29. This advertisement is included in the Kodak Historical Collection held by the Rush Rhees Library at the University of Rochester (Rochester, N.Y.).

30. This advertisement is included in the Kodak Historical Collection held by the Rush Rhees Library at the University of Rochester (Rochester, N.Y.).

31. This advertisement is included in the Kodak Historical Collection held by the Rush Rhees Library at the University of Rochester (Rochester, N.Y.).

32. This advertisement is included in the Kodak Historical Collection held by the Rush Rhees Library at the University of Rochester (Rochester, N.Y.).

33. This advertisement was published on 20 October 1888 in *Scientific American*. It is included in the Kodak Historical Collection held by the Rush Rhees Library at the University of Rochester (Rochester, N.Y.).

34. This quote is taken from an advertisement for the Kodak Camera published on 18 April 1889 in the *Youth's Companion*. In the July 1889 edition of *Life* magazine, an advertisement for the Kodak Camera uses the famous slogan: "You press the button, we do the rest." Both advertisements are included in the Kodak Historical Collection held by the Rush Rhees Library at the University of Rochester (Rochester, N.Y.).

35. This advertisement is included in the Kodak Historical Collection held by the Rush Rhees Library at the University of Rochester (Rochester, N.Y.).

36. This advertisement is included in the Kodak Historical Collection held by the Rush Rhees Library at the University of Rochester (Rochester, N.Y.).

37. This advertisement is included in the Kodak Historical Collection held by the Rush Rhees Library at the University of Rochester (Rochester, N.Y.).

38. This advertisement is included in the George Eastman Archives held by the George Eastman House International Museum of Photography and Film (Rochester, N.Y.).

39. This advertisement is included in the George Eastman Archives held by the George Eastman House International Museum of Photography and Film (Rochester, N.Y.).

40. *New York Tribune*, 5 September 1889, 6, quoted in Robert Mensel, "Kodakers Lying in Wait" (1991) 43 (1) *American Quarterly* 24, 28.

41. B. F. McManus, "Amateur Photographers" (1890), 27 (370) *Wilson's Photographic Magazine* 296.

42. "The Kodac [*sic*] Camera" (1889), 6 (December) *The Detective*. This article is included in the Kodak Historical Collection held by the Rush Rhees Library at the University of Rochester (Rochester, N.Y.).

43. A selection of cameras included in the Technology Archive held by the George Eastman House International Museum of Photography and Film (Rochester, N.Y.). See also "Cameras from the Mees Gallery Exhibit: Enhancing the Illusion: The Process and Origins of Photography" at http://www.geh.org/technology.html

44. A line at the bottom of this advertisement states: "Sole agents for Australia: Baker & Rouse, 375 George Street, Sydney." There is no further information identifying when and where the advertisement was published. The advertisement is included in the Kodak Historical Collection held by the Rush Rhees Library at the University of Rochester (Rochester, N.Y.).

45. This advertisement is included in the Kodak Historical Collection held by the Rush Rhees Library at the University of Rochester (Rochester, N.Y.).

46. Mensel, "Kodakers Lying in Wait" (1991), 34.

47. This article is included in the Kodak Historical Collection held by the Rush Rhees Library at the University of Rochester (Rochester, N.Y.). The precise date of its publication was not provided in the archives.

48. Ibid.

49. McManus, "Amateur Photographers" (1890), 296.

50. Ibid.

51. These advertisements are included in the Kodak Historical Collection held by the Rush Rhees Library at the University of Rochester (Rochester, N.Y.).

52. This advertisement is included in the George Eastman Archives held by George Eastman House International Museum of Photography and Film (Rochester, N.Y.).

53. This advertisement is included in the Kodak Historical Collection at the Rush Rhees Library at the University of Rochester (Rochester, N.Y.).

54. *New York Times,* 15 June 1889, 8.

55. The Phenakistoscope, designed in 1832 by Belgian scientist Joseph Plateau and Austrian geometry professor Simon Stampfer, featured a spinning disc of pictures, which if viewed through a slot in an adjacent disc would appear to be moving. The Zoetrope, invented in 1833, contained a series of pictures set along the inner rim of a spinning drum, which would give the impression of movement if viewed through a slot in the side of the drum. In 1877, Frenchman Émile Reynaud built the Praxinoscope, similar to the Zoetrope but with the moving images projected upon mirrors for an audience, and later upon a screen. See Kristin Thompson and David Bordwell, *Film History: An Introduction* (McGraw-Hill, 2nd ed., 2003) 14–16.

56. Tom Gunning, "From the Kaleidoscope to the X-Ray: Urban Spectatorship, Poe, Benjamin and Traffic in Souls (1913)" (1997), 19 (4) *Wide Angle* 25, 33–34.

57. See British Film Institute, *Screen Online: Street Scenes* (British Film Institute, 2003–12), at http://www.screenonline.org.uk/film/id/748489/index.html (accessed 29 April 2013).

58. Benjamin, "The Work of Art in the Age of Mechanical Reproduction," 229.

59. Ibid., 223.

60. Ibid., 231.

61. Gunning, "Tracing the Individual Body," 18.

62. Jonathan Auerbach, *Body Shots: Early Cinema's Incarnations* (University of California Press, 2007).

63. Ibid., 56.

64. Munsterberg quoted in Gustavus A. Rogers, "The Law of the Motion Picture Industry," speech delivered at the College of the City of New York on 28 November 1916, 6. The manuscript is held by Yale University Law Library (New Haven).

65. Robert Stam, *Film Theory: An Introduction* (Blackwell, 2000), 29.

66. See Bruno, *Atlas of Emotion* (2002); Giuliana Bruno, "Film, Aesthetics, Science: Hugo Munsterberg's Laboratory of Moving Images" (2009), 36 (Summer) *Grey Room* 88.

67. *New York Times,* 15 June 1889, 8.

2
"Has a Beautiful Girl the Right to Her Own Face?"

1. *Roberson v. Rochester Folding Box Co.*, 65 NYS 1109 (Sup Ct, 1900), Record and Briefs ("Complaint"); for details of the back story, see "Her Picture on Flour Packages So Miss Abigail Roberson Brings Suit for $15,000," *Richmond Dispatch* (Richmond), 28 June 1900, 2.

2. 65 NYS 1109 (Sup Ct, 1900).

3. A photograph of Abigail Roberson was used in advertisements (within the United States and abroad) for Franklin Mills' flour. This case is discussed in detail later in this chapter.

4. J. A. J., "The Legal Relations of Photographs" (1869), 8.

5. Ibid.

6. See "A Handsome Card," *St. Louis Post-Dispatch* (St. Louis), 31 July 1886, 6; "Women in Politics," *St. Louis Post-Dispatch* (St. Louis), 8 April 8 1888, 23; "Not Miss Halford's Picture" *Washington Post* (Washington, D.C.), 29 August 1889, 2.

7. "A Chivalrous Congressman," *San Francisco Chronicle* (San Francisco), 6 March 1888, 1.

8. A Bill to Protect Ladies, HR 8151, 50th Congress (1888).

9. Ibid.

10. New York Laws, Ch 132 §§ 1–2 (1903) (subsequently became NY Civil Rights Law §§ 50–51) (McKinney 2004).

11. See Prosser, "Privacy" (1960).

12. Sir William Blackstone quoted in Barbara Young Welke, "Law, Personhood, and Citizenship in the Long Nineteenth Century: The Borders of Belonging," in Michael Grossberg and Christopher Tomlins (eds.), *The Cambridge History of Law in America, Volume II: The Long Nineteenth Century (1789–1920)* (Cambridge University Press, 2008), 348.

13. See Welke, "Law, Personhood, and Citizenship in the Long Nineteenth Century" (2008); Linda Kerber, *No Constitutional Right to Be Ladies* (Hill and Wang, 1998).

14. Welke, "Law, Personhood, and Citizenship in the Long Nineteenth Century" (2008).

15. Kerber, *No Constitutional Right to Be Ladies*, 305.

16. Charles Parker, "A Danger Ahead" (1888), (April 7) *Philadelphia Photographer* 218, 218.

17. Petition against a bill (No. 3516), held by the Legislative Branch of the National Archives (Washington, D.C.).

18. "Our Representative Women," *Albany Journal* (Albany, N.Y.), 16 March 1888.

19. "A Question of Personal Right," *Sacramento Daily Record-Union* (Sacramento), 31 March 1888, 4.

20. Ibid. (emphases added).

21. Robert Mensel mentions the Bill to Protect Ladies very briefly (although not by its title) but not the Petition Against the Bill or the other circumstances or debate surrounding the Bill; see Mensel, "Kodakers Lying in Wait" (1991) 34. No other references to the Bill to Protect Ladies, its introduction in the House, the Petition Against the Bill, or the surrounding media debate could be found in any publication.

22. See Gajda, "What if Samuel D. Warren Hadn't Married a Senator's Daughter?" (2008)

23. *Pollard v. Photographic Co.* (1889) LR 40 Ch D 345.

24. Ibid., 347 (North J).

25. Ibid., 345 (North J).

26. Ibid., 347 (North J).

27. Ibid., 349–353 (North J).

28. Ibid., 346 (North J) (emphasis added).

29. A. Bogardus, "A Caution to Women Who Intend Sitting for Their Photographs" (1890), VII (9) *Ladies' Home Journal* 11.

30. Ibid.

31. 46 NW 141 (Minn, 1890); "Photographs Use of Negative" (1890), 34 (10 Oct.) *The Central Law Journal* 15, 292.

32. *Moore v. Rugg*, 46 NW 141, 141 (Collins J) (Minn, 1890).

33. Ibid.

34. Julius F. Sachse, "Photographic Jurisprudence in Germany" (1891) 12 (133) (1 Jan.) *American Journal of Photography* 12.

35. Ibid.

36. See, e.g., *Mackenzie v. Soden Mineral Springs Co.*, 18 NYS 240 (Sup Ct, 1891); *Corliss v. E. W. Walker Co.*, 64 Fed 280 (D Mass, 1894); *Dockrell v. Dougal* (1899) 80 *Law Times* 556; *Atkinson v. John E. Doherty & Co.*, 80 NW 285 (Mich, 1899); *Edison v. Edison Polyform Manufacturing Co.*, 67 A 392 (NJ, 1907); *Foster-Milburn Co. v. Chinn*, 120 SW 364 (Ky Ct App, 1909).

37. NY Sup Ct [unpublished opinion] (June 1890).

38. Warren and Brandeis, "A Right to Privacy" (1890), 195–196.

39. "Photographed in Tights," *New York Times* (New York), 15 June 1890, 2.

40. "The Rights and Tights of an Actress" (1890), 3.

41. "Will Not Be Photographed in Tights," *Chicago Daily Tribune* (Chicago), 13 June 1890, 6.

42. "Miss Manola's Tights" (1890), 4.

43. Glancy, "Privacy and the Other Miss M." (1989–1990).

44. "Miss Manola's Tights" (1890), 4; "Photographed in Tights" (1890), 2; "The Rights and Tights of an Actress" (1890), 3; "Will Not Be Photographed in Tights" (1890), 6.

45. *Roberson v. Rochester Folding Box Co.*, 64 NE 442 (NY, 1902), Record and Briefs ("Complaint").

46. Ibid.

47. See "Predict Monroe Lost to Suffrage," *New York Times* (New York), 29 October 1915: "The suffragists will in all probability get a greater number of Democratic votes for their amendment than Republican. . . . The new Democratic organization is now in the hands of a more progressive set of leaders. The active leader is Milton E. Gibbs, a Rochester lawyer. . . . Mr. Gibbs is an ardent believer in votes for women. . . . Mr. Gibbs said today that the suffragists had conducted a splendid campaign and that the vote might be close in Rochester."

48. *Roberson v. Rochester Folding Box Co.*, 64 NE 442 (NY, 1902), Record and Briefs ("Brief of Respondent") (emphases added).

49. *Roberson v. Rochester Folding Box Co.* 65 NYS 1109, 1111 (Davy J) (Sup Ct, 1900).

50. See Allen and Mack, "How Privacy Got Its Gender" (1990).

51. Ibid., 444.

52. Ibid., 466.

53. Mack and Allen, "How Privacy Got Its Gender" (1990), 469.

54. *Roberson v. Rochester Folding Box Co.*, 64 NE 442 (NY, 1902), Record and Briefs ("Brief of Respondent") (emphasis in original)

55. "Judge Milton E. Gibbs, Jurist, Named to Claims Court in 1936, Dies in Rochester NY," *New York Times* (New York), 22 August 1940, 19.

56. Kathleen S. Sullivan, *Constitutional Context: Women and Rights Discourse in Nineteenth-Century America* (Johns Hopkins University Press, 2007), 69.

57. Karen Manners Smith, "New Paths to Power: 1890–1920," in Nancy F. Cott (ed.), *No Small Courage* (Oxford University Press, 2000), 369.

58. Ibid., 364.

59. Sarah Grand, "The New Aspects of the Woman Question," *North American Review*, March 1894, 270–276, republished in Martha H. Patterson (ed.), *The American New Woman Revisited: A Reader (1894–1930)* (Rutgers University Press, 2008), 30.

60. Ibid.

61. Ouida, "The New Woman," *North American Review,* May 1894, 610–619, republished in Patterson (ed.), *The American New Woman Revisited* (2008), 40.

62. Ibid.

63. *Roberson v. Rochester Folding Box Co.,* 65 NYS 1109, 1112 (Davy J) (Sup Ct, 1900).

64. Ibid.

65. *Pollard v. Photographic Co.* (1889) LR 40 Ch D 345.

66. *Roberson v. Rochester Folding Box Co.,* 65 NYS 1109, 1113 (Davy J) (Sup Ct, 1900).

67. *Corliss v. E. W. Walker Co.,* 64 F 280 (D Mass, 1894).

68. *Roberson v. Rochester Folding Box Co.,* 65 NYS 1109, 1114 (Davy J) (Sup Ct. 1900).

69. *Roberson v. Rochester Folding Box Co.,* 64 NE 442, 546 (Parker CJ) (1902).

70. Ibid., 546.

71. See NY Laws Ch 132 § 1 (1903). It subsequently became NY Civil Rights Law § 50 (McKinney 2004).

72. See NY Laws Ch 132 § 2 (1903). It subsequently became NY Civil Rights Law § 51 (McKinney, 2004).

73. *Roberson v. Rochester Folding Box Co.,* 64 NE 442, 544 (Parker CJ) (1902).

74. "Parker Taken to Task by an Indignant Woman—If I Can Be Photographed, Why Not You? Asks Miss Roberson," *New York Times* (New York), 27 July 1904, 1.

75. Ibid.; also reported in "Girl Asks Parker How He Likes It," *St. Louis Post-Dispatch* (St. Louis), 27 July 1904.

76. Regina Graycar, "The Gender of Judgments: Some Reflections on Bias" (1998), 32 *University of British Columbia Law Review* 1, 14; see also Regina Graycar, "The Gender of Judgments: An Introduction," in Margaret Thornton (ed.), *Public and Private: Feminist Legal Debates* (Oxford University Press, 1995), 262.

77. Sullivan, *Constitutional Context* (2007), 87.

78. "Has Not Right to Her Own Face," *Boston Daily Globe* (Boston), 7 July 1902, 6.

79. "Publishing a Woman's Picture," *New York Times* (New York), 13 July 1902, 8.

80. "'Flour of the Family' Case" (1902), 10.

81. "Her Picture on Boxes: A Handsome Young Woman Brings Suit for Damages," *Evening Times* (Little Falls, N.Y.), 27 June 1900, 3.

82. "Your Feelings Hurt? Sue: Justice Rumsey Decides Abigail Roberson Picture Case" *Sun* (New York), 24 July 1901, 7.

83. "Fair Girl's Plea Vain: Fails to Get Picture Declared Individual Property," *Saint Paul Globe* (Saint Paul), 20 July 1902, 7.

84. "No Right of Privacy," *Salt Lake Herald* (Salt Lake City), 23 July 1902, 4.

85. See Tagg, *The Burden of Representation* (1988), 56: "First used in the *New York Daily Graphic* in 1880, [photographs] rapidly displaced illustrations which required the intervention of artist or engraver and, by 1897, were in regular use in the *New York Tribune*."

86. See, e.g., *Riddle v. MacFadden,* 101 NYS 606 (AD, 1906); *Almind v. Sea Beach Co.,* 139 NYS 559 (Sup Ct, 1912); *Colyer v. Richard K. Fox Pub. Co.,* 146 NYS 2d 999 (AD, 1914); *Humiston v. Universal Film Manufacturing Co.,* 167 NYS 98 (Sup Ct, 1917); *Loftus v. Greenwich Lithographing Co.,* 182 NYS 428 (AD, 1920); *Blumenthal v. Picture Classics,* 257 NYS 800 (AD, 1932); *Sweenek v. Pathe News, Inc.,* 16 F Supp 746 (ED NY, 1936); *Myers v. Afro-American Publishing Co.,* 5 NYS 2d 223 (Sup Ct, 1938); *Semler v. Ultem Publications,* 9 NYS 2d 319 (City Ct, 1938); *Lane v. F. W. Woolworth Co.,* 12 NYS 2d 352 (Sup Ct, 1939).

87. 50 SE 68 (Ga, 1905).

88. Following *Pavesich v. New England Life Insurance Co.,* 50 SE 68 (Ga, 1905), two other cases involved the use of a man's picture without his consent in an advertisement simply because it was attractive: *Henry v. Cherry & Webb,* 73 A 97 (RI, 1909), and *Munden v, Harris,* 134 SW 1076 (Kan Ct App, 1911). In *Henry,* the plaintiff's picture was used to advertise "auto-coats" (driving coats) in the *Providence Evening Bulletin.* In *Munden,* the plaintiff was a five-year-old boy, whose photograph was used in a jewelry advertisement. With respect to the claim of breach of privacy, Justice Ellison held in *Munden* (at 1079): "We therefore conclude that one has an exclusive right to his picture, on the score of its being a property right of material profit. We also consider it to be a property right of value, in that it is one of the modes of securing to a person the enjoyment of life and the exercise of liberty, and that novelty of the claim is no objection to relief."

89. Ibid., 70 (Cobb J).

90. "Each person has a liberty of privacy, and every other person has, as against him, liberty in reference to other matters, and the line where these liberties impinge upon each other may in a given case be hard to define; but that such a case may arise can afford no more reason for denying to one his liberty of privacy than it would to deny to another his liberty, whatever it may be": ibid., 72 (Cobb J); at 77 (Cobb J).

91. Susan E Gallagher, *Reading New England: The Right to Privacy* (University of Massachusetts Press, 2010), 27, at http://readingnewengland.org/app/books/righttoprivacy/

92. *Roberson v. Rochester Folding Box Co.*, 64 NE 442, 451 (Gray J) (1902), cited with approval in *Pavesich v. New England Life Insurance Co.*, 50 SE 68, 79 (Cobb J) (Ga, 1905).

93. *Pavesich v. New England Life Insurance Co.*, 50 SE 68, 79 (Cobb J) (Ga, 1905).

94. Ibid., 80 (Cobb J).

95. Ibid.

96. For an interesting discussion of Justice Cobb's analogy between deprivations of privacy and slavery see Anita L. Allen, "Natural Law, Slavery and the Right to Privacy Tort" (2012), 81 *Fordham Law Review* 1187.

97. The highest appeal court in each state of the United States is the Supreme Court, except in Maine (the Supreme Judicial Court), Massachusetts (the Supreme Judicial Court), New York (the Court of Appeals), and West Virginia (the Supreme Court of Appeals).

98. NY Laws Ch 132, §§ 1–2 (1903) (subsequently became NY Civil Rights Law §§ 50–51 (McKinney 2004)).

99. *Edison v. Edison Polyform Manufacturing Co.*, 67 A 392 (NJ, 1907).

100. *Foster-Milburn Co. v. Chinn*, 120 SW 364 (Ky Ct App, 1909).

101. 101 NYS 606 (AD, 1906).

102. NY Laws Ch 132 §§ 1–2 (1903) (subsequently became NY Civil Rights Law §§ 50–51 (McKinney 2004)).

103. Publication details for the book subject to proceedings are not provided by the court or the court documents. But for an earlier edition of the book see Bernarr Macfadden, *Macfadden's New Hair Culture: Rational, Natural Methods for Cultivating Strength and Luxuriance of the Hair* (Physical Culture Publishing Co., 3rd ed., 1901).

104. *Riddle v. MacFadden*, 94 NE 644 (1911), Records and Briefs ("Amended Complaint").

105. *Riddle v. MacFadden*, 94 NE 644 (1911), Records and Briefs ("Answer to the Complaint").

106. *Riddle v. MacFadden*, 94 NE 644 (1911), Record and Brief ("Testimony" given by Emil Philip Grenz on 16 June 1908).

107. *Riddle v. MacFadden*, 94 NE 644 (1911), Record and Brief ("Amended Complaint").

108. *Riddle v. MacFadden*, 94 NE 644 (1911), Record and Brief ("Testimony" given by Felicite Skiff Riddle on 16 June 1908) (emphases added).

109. Otto and Rocco (eds.), *The New Woman International* (2012).

110. *Riddle v. MacFadden*, 94 NE 644 (1911), Record and Brief ("Testimony" given by Felicite Skiff Riddle on 16 June 1908).

111. *Riddle v. MacFadden*, 94 NE 644 (1911), Record and Brief ("Testimony" given by Cass B. Riddle on 16 June 1908) (emphasis added).

112. *Manola v. Stevens*, NY Sup Ct [unpublished opinion] (June 1890).

113. NY Civil Rights Law §§ 50–51 (McKinney 2004).

114. *Almind v. Sea Beach Co.*, 139 NYS 559 (Sup Ct, 1912).

115. *Almind v. Sea Beach Co.*, 141 NYS 842 (AD, 1913), Record and Brief ("Trial Decision").

116. *Almind v. Sea Beach Co.*, 141 NYS 842 (AD, 1913), Record and Brief ("Complaint").

117. *Almind v. Sea Beach Co.*, 141 NYS 842 (AD, 1913), Record and Brief ("Answer").

118. *Almind v. Sea Beach Co.*, 141 NYS 842 (AD, 1913), Record and Briefs ("Testimony" of Mary Clarissa Almind given on 7 November 1912).

119. Ibid.

120. *Almind v. Sea Beach Co.*, 141 NYS 842 (AD, 1913), Record and Briefs ("Testimony" of George H. Pierce given on 12 November 1912).

121. *Almind v. Sea Beach Co.*, 141 NYS 842 (AD, 1913), Record and Briefs ("Testimony" of Charles B. Attelsey, Joseph J. Dilgen, Eugene C. Clarke, and Henry Muller given on 12 November 1912).

122. *Almind v. Sea Beach Co.*, 139 NYS 559, 560 (Kapper J) (Sup Ct, 1912).

123. *Almind v. Sea Beach Co.*, 141 NYS 842, 843 (Thomas J) (AD, 1913).

124. NY Laws Ch 132 §§ 1–2 (1903) (subsequently became NY Civil Rights Law §§ 50–51 (McKinney 2004)).

125. Ibid. (emphases added).

126. *Almind v. Sea Beach Co.*, 141 NYS 842 (AD, 1913), Record and Briefs ("Brief of Appellant").

127. *Almind v. Sea Beach Co.*, 141 NYS 842, 843 (Thomas J) (AD, 1913).

128. NY Civil Rights Law §§ 50–51 (McKinney 2004).

129. *Colyer v. Richard K. Fox Publishing Co.*, 146 NYS 2d 999 (AD, 1914).

130. *Colyer v. Richard K. Fox Publishing Co.*, 146 NYS 2d 999 (AD, 1914), Record and Briefs ("Complaint").

131. Ibid.

132. *Colyer v. Richard K. Fox Publishing Co.*, 146 NYS 2d 999 (AD, 1914), Record and Briefs ("Testimony" of Mabel Colyer given on 12 December 1913).

133. *Colyer v. Richard K. Fox Publishing Co.*, 146 NYS 2d 999 (AD, 1914), Record and Briefs ("Respondent's Brief on Appeal from Judgment Dismissing Complaint").

134. Ibid.

135. *Colyer v. Richard K. Fox Publishing Co.*, 146 NYS 2d 999 (AD, 1914), Record and Briefs ("Case"—statements made by Frank Davis, plaintiff's attorney, during argument).

136. Ibid.

137. Ibid.

138. Ibid.

139. Ibid. (emphasis added).

140. *Colyer v. Richard K. Fox Publishing Co.*, 146 NYS 2d 999 (AD, 1914), Record and Briefs ("Case"—decision of trial judge).

141. Ibid.

142. Ibid. (emphasis added).

143. *Colyer v. Richard K. Fox Publishing Co.*, 146 NYS 2d 999, 1001 (Carr J) (AD, 1914).

144. NY Civil Rights Law §§ 50–51 (McKinney 2004).

145. Nizer, "The Right of Privacy" (1941), 528.

146. "Acute Privacy," *Washington Post* (Washington, D.C.), 4 August 1904, 6.

3
Medical Men and Peeping Toms

1. 9 NW 146 (1881). The Michigan Supreme Court used the phrase "a right to privacy" in this case but was not considering whether such a right should be the basis for a separate tort as the New York Court of Appeals was in *Roberson v. Rochester Folding Box Co.*, 65 NYS 1109 (Sup Ct, 1900).

2. 181 NYS 481 (AD, 1920).

3. 9 NW 146 (1881).

4. Quoted in Danielson, "The Gender of Privacy and the Embodied Self" (1999), 322.

5. *DeMay v. Roberts,* 9 NW 146, 165–166 (Marston CJ) (1881) (emphasis added).

6. See Danielson, "The Gender of Privacy and the Embodied Self" (1999), 311 ("*DeMay v. Roberts* is the earliest case in the United States explicitly to name a right to privacy").

7. 50 SE 68 (Ga, 1905).

8. Danielson, "The Gender of Privacy and the Embodied Self" (1999), 314–315.

9. Ibid., 312.

10. Ibid., 323.

11. The principal English authority for the maxim is *Semayne's Case* (1605) 5 Co Rep 91a, 91b, 77 Eng Rep 194, 195. See a discussion of its wide application and usage in the United States during the nineteenth century in "The Right to Privacy in Nineteenth-Century America" (1981); Hafetz, "A Man's Home Is His Castle" (2001).

12. Hafetz, "A Man's Home Is His Castle" (2001), 184.

13. *Pavesich v. New England Life Insurance*, 50 SE 68, 69 (Ga, 1905).

14. Prosser, "Privacy" (1960), 389.

15. Prewett, "The Crimination of Peeping Toms and Other Men of Vision" (1950–1951) 3 *Arkansas Law Review* 388; "Right to Privacy in Nineteenth Century America" (1981).

16. *City of Grand Rapids v. Williams*, 70 NW 547, 547–548 (Mich, 1897).

17. See Elizabeth M. Schneider, "The Violence of Privacy" (1991), 23 *Connecticut Law Review* 973; Reva B. Siegel, "'The Rule of Love': Wife Beating as Prerogative and Privacy" (1995–1996), 105 *Yale Law Journal* 2117.

18. Elizabeth Arens, "The Elevated Railroad Cases: Private Property and Mass Transit in Gilded Age New York" (2005), 61 *NYU Annual Survey of American Law* 629.

19. 130 NYS 523, 528 (1892).

20. 181 NYS 481 (1920).

21. *Feeney v. Young*, 181 NYS 481 (AD, 1920), Record and Briefs ("Brief of Respondent").

22. *Feeney v. Young*, 181 NYS 481 (AD, 1920), Record and Briefs ("Brief of Appellant").

23. NY Civil Rights Law §§ 50–51 (McKinney 2004)

24. For discussions of this case as it concerns the "best evidence" rule see "Moving Pictures and the Right of Privacy" (1919) 28 (3) *Yale Law Journal* 269; "Right of Privacy. Injunction. Motion Pictures" (1920) 20 (1) *Columbia Law Review* 100; "Notes of Important Decisions" (1920), 91 (2) *The Central Law Journal* 23; "Evidence: Moving Pictures: Best Evidence Rule" (1920) 19 (1) *Michigan Law Review* 101; "Best and Secondary Evidence. Testimony That Motion Picture Represented Plaintiff" (1920), 6 (6) *Virginia Law Register* 460; "Motion Pictures in Court" (1924) 2 *New York Law Review* 96, 98; Carl M. Gray, "Motion Pictures in Evidence" (1939) 15 *Indiana Law Journal* 408, 430.

25. *Feeney v. Young,* 181 NYS 481 (AD, 1920), Record and Briefs ("Brief of Respondent").

26. *Feeney v. Young,* 181 NYS 481 (AD, 1920), Record and Briefs ("Brief of Appellant").

27. Ibid.

28. *Feeney v. Young,* 181 NYS 481 (AD, 1920), Record and Briefs ("Brief of Respondent") (emphases added).

29. Ibid. (emphasis added).

30. Ibid.

31. See, e.g., *Banks v. King Features Syndicate, Inc.*, 30 F Supp 352 (SD NY, 1939); *Barber v. Time, Inc.*, 159 SW 291 (Mo, 1942); *Bazemore v. Savannah Hospital,* 155 SE 194 (Ga, 1930); *Clayman v. Bertstein,* 38 Pa D & C 543 (Pa, 1940); *Douglas v. Stokes,* 149 SW 849 (Ky, 1912); *Feeney v. Young,* 181 NYS 481 (AD, 1920); *Griffin v. Medical Society of New York,* 11 NYS 2d 109 (Sup Ct, 1939). In *Griffin v. Medical Society of New York,* two doctors published photographs of a male patient's "saddle nose" in a professional journal. All the other medical cases involving claims to privacy prior to 1950 involved photographs or films of women or newborn infants. For a discussion of these cases and the nature and scope of the right to privacy as it affects medical practice see Theodore R. LeBlang, "Invasion of Privacy: Medical Practice and the Tort of Intrusion" (1978), 18 *Washburn Law Journal* 205.

32. See Lisa Cartwright, *Screening the Body: Tracing Medicine's Visual Culture* (University of Minnesota Press, 1995).

33. Ibid., 3.

34. Felicia Feaster, "The Woman on the Table: Moral and Medical Discourse in the Exploitation Cinema" (1994) 6 (3) *Film History* 340.

35. Ibid., 348.

36. Ibid., 349.

37. See *DeMay v. Roberts,* 9 NW 146 (1881); *Feeney v. Young,* 181 NYS 481 (1920); *Inderbitzen v. Lane Hospital,* 12 P 2d 744 (Cal, 1932). In *Inderbitzen,* a young pregnant woman, about to give birth, was poked, prodded, mocked, and insulted by ten to twelve male medical students at Lane Hospital. This case did not involve photography or cinema.

38. See *Banks v. King Features Syndicate, Inc.*, 30 F Supp 352 (SD NY, 1939).

39. See *Barber v. Time, Inc.*, 159 SW 291 (Mo, 1942).

40. See *Bazemore v. Savannah Hospital,* 155 SE 194 (Ga,1930); *Douglas v. Stokes,* 149 SW 849 (Ky, 1912).

41. Creed, *The Monstrous-Feminine* (1993).

42. Jane Ussher, *Managing the Monstrous-Feminine: Regulating the Reproductive Body* (Routledge, 2006).

43. *Banks v. King Features Syndicate, Inc.*, 30 F Supp 352 (SD NY, 1939).

44. Cartwright, *Screening the Body* (1995), 115.

45. 159 SW 291 (Mo, 1942).

46. Ibid., 293.

47. Ibid., 295.

48. See Prosser, "Privacy" (1960)

49. 65 NYS 1109 (Sup Ct, 1900).

50. 42 NE 22 (NY, 1895). In this case the action was brought by Philip Schuyler, nephew of Mary Hamilton Schuyler, on behalf of all her immediate relatives, to enjoin members of the Woman's Memorial Fund Association, a voluntary unincorporated association, from making a memorial statue of Mary Schuyler with the title "The Woman as Philanthropist" or from causing it to be exhibited at the World's Fair. For a contemporary discussion of the case see Augustus N. Hand, "Schuyler against Curtis and the Right to Privacy" (1897), 45 (12) *American Law Register* 745.

51. 80 NW 285 (Mich, 1899). John Atkinson was a well-known lawyer and politician, whose widow brought a "right to privacy" suit against the defendants to restrain them from using his picture and name to sell cigars.

52. The states of Oklahoma, Utah, and Virginia are the only ones to expressly allow heirs or next of kin to recover for a deceased's invasion of privacy. See Okla Stat Ann tit 21, §§ 839–840 (1958); Utah Code Ann §§ 76-4-8 and 76-4-9 (1953); Va Code Ann §§ 8–650 (1957).

53. Quoted in Hand, "Schuyler against Curtis and the Right to Privacy" (1897), 749.

54. *James v. Screen Gems, Inc.*, 344 P 2d 799 (Cal, 1959); *Kelly v. Johnson Publishing Co.*, 325 P 2d 659 (Cal, 1958); *Kelley v. Post Publishing Co.*, 98 NE 2d 286 (Mass, 1951).

55. Julia Kristeva, *Powers of Horror: An Essay on Abjection* (Columbia University Press, 1982).

56. Creed, *The Monstrous-Feminine* (1993).

57. *Douglas v. Stokes*, 149 SW 849 (Ky, 1912)

58. Ibid.

59. Ibid.

60. Ibid.

61. *Pollard v. Photographic Co.* (1889) LR 40 Ch D 345, 349–350 (Parker CJ) cited in *Douglas v. Stokes*, 149 SW 849, 849 (Hobson CJ) (Ky,

1912). The case of *Pollard v. Photographic Co.* is discussed in detail in chapter 2.

62. Ibid., 850.

63. Ibid.

64. "Right of Privacy—Relative's Interest in a Deceased's Name or Likeness" (1961), 22 *Ohio State Law Journal* 438, 439; see also "Publication of Photograph of Child's Mutilated Body Held Not to Violate Right of Privacy" (1956–1957), 5 *Utah Law Review* 265.

65. 155 SE 194 (Ga, 1930); see also "Right of Privacy: Publishing Picture of Deceased Child as Invasion of Parents' Rights" (1931) 17 (4) *Virginia Law Review* 393.

66. *Bazemore v. Savannah Hospital,* 155 SE 194, 195 (Ga, 1930) (emphasis added).

67. Ibid.

68. *Pavesich v. New England Life Insurance Co.*, 50 SE 68, 76 (Cobb J) (Ga, 1905) cited in *Bazemore v. Savannah Hospital,* 155 SE 194, 196 (Ga, 1930).

69. 28 NYS 271 (1894).

70. *Bazemore v. Savannah Hospital,* 155 SE 194, 197 (1930).

71. Ibid., 198 (Hill J).

72. Kristeva, *Powers of Horror* (1982), 3.

4
Privacy, the Celluloid City, and the Cinematic Eye

1. "Moving Pictures Used as an Aid to Education," *New York Tribune* (New York), 6 February 1910, 3.

2. See, e.g., Bruno, *Atlas of Emotion* (2002); Peter Conrad, *Modern Times, Modern Places* (Thames & Hudson, 1998); Friedberg, *The Virtual Window* (2006).

3. See Nezar AlSayyad, *Cinematic Urbanism: A History of the Modern from Reel to Real* (Routledge, 2006); Bruno, *Atlas of Emotion* (2002); Charney and Schwartz (eds.), *Cinema and the Invention of Modern Life* (1995); David B. Clarke, *The Cinematic City* (Routledge, 1997); Conrad, *Modern Times, Modern Places* (1998); Tony Fitzmaurice and Mark Shiel, *Cinema and the City: Film and Urban Societies in a Global Context* (Blackwell, 2001); Friedberg, *The Virtual Window* (2006); Richard Koeck and Les Roberts, *The City and the Moving Image: Urban Projections* (Palgrave Macmillan, 2010).

4. As I noted in chapter 1, the recent scholars who have done so include Tom Gunning and Jonathan Auerbach. See Gunning, "Tracing the Individual Body" (1995), and Auerbach, *Body Shots* (2007).

5. Bruno, *Atlas of Emotion* (2002), 7.

6. See Allan Langdale (ed.), *Hugo Munsterberg on Film: The Photoplay—A Psychological Study and Other Writings* (Routledge, 2002).

7. Ibid., 54.

8. The 1910 U.S. Copyright Office Rules and Regulations defined "photographs" to include "all possible prints from photographic negatives, including those from moving-picture films, the entire series being counted as a single photograph." On 24 August 1912, "motion pictures" became their own separate category of protected work under U.S. copyright law. See Bowker, *Copyright* (1912), 224.

9. See especially Christian Metz, *The Imaginary Signifier: Psychoanalysis and the Cinema* (Indiana University Press, first published 1977, 1982 ed.); Laura Mulvey, "Visual Pleasure and Narrative Cinema" (1975), 16 (3) *Screen* 6.

10. *La sortie des usines Lumière* was first shown to the Société d'Encouragement à l'Industrie Nationale in Paris on 22 March 1895. It was exhibited to a paying audience of thirty-three people on 28 December 1895 in the Salon Indien of the Grand Café in Paris. See Thompson and Bordwell, *Film History* (2003), 19; Simon Popple and Joe Kember, *Early Cinema: From Factory Gate to Dream Factory* (Wallflower, 2004), 7.

11. Thomas Y. Levin, "Rhetoric of Temporal Index: Surveillant Narration and the Cinema of 'Real Time'" in Peter Weibel et al. (eds.), *Ctrl [Space]: Rhetorics of Surveillance from Bentham to Big Brother* (ZKM and MIT, 2002), 581.

12. *Kunz v. Allen,* 172 P 532 (Kan, 1918).

13. *Kunz v. Allen,* 172 P 532 (Kan, 1918), Record and Briefs ("Amended Petition").

14. *Kunz v. Allen,* 172 P 532 (Kan, 1918), Record and Briefs ("Testimony of Stella Kunz given in Cross Examination").

15. *Kunz v. Allen,* 172 P 532 (Kan, 1918), Record and Briefs ("Amended Petition").

16. Ibid.

17. *Kunz v. Allen,* 172 P 532 (Kan, 1918), Record and Briefs ("The Trial").

18. *Kunz v. Allen,* 172 P 532 (Kan, 1918), Record and Briefs ("Journal Entry").

19. *Kunz v. Allen,* 172 P 532 (Kan, 1918), Record and Briefs ("Defendants' Demurrer to the Plaintiff's Evidence").

20. *Kunz v. Allen,* 172 P 532 (Kan, 1918), Record and Briefs ("Brief of Appellees").

21. *Kunz v. Allen,* 172 P 532 (Kan, 1918), Record and Briefs ("Testimony of Pearl Armstrong given in Direct Examination").

22. *Kunz v. Allen,* 172 P 532 (Kan, 1918), Record and Briefs ("Specifications of Error").

23. *Pavesich v. New England Life Insurance Co.,* 50 SE 68 (Ga, 1905).

24. *Kunz v. Allen,* 172 P 532 (Porter J) (1918).

25. "Moving Pictures and the Right of Privacy" (1919), 269.

26. *Binns v. Vitagraph Company of America,* 130 NYS 876 (Sup Ct, 1911).

27. *Kunz v. Allen,* 172 P 532 (Kan, 1918), Record and Briefs ("Amended Petition").

28. *Kunz v. Allen,* 172 P 532 (Kan, 1918), Record and Briefs ("Testimony of Mrs. Stella Kunz given in Direct Examination").

29. *Kunz v. Allen,* 172 P 532 (Kan, 1918), Record and Briefs ("Testimony of Mr Jacob Kunz given in Direct Examination").

30. *Kunz v. Allen,* 172 P 532 (Kan, 1918), Record and Briefs ("Testimony of Mr. Jacob Kunz given in Direct Examination").

31. Auerbach, *Body Shots* (2007), 105.

32. Ibid., 51.

33. *Kunz v Allen,* 172 P 532 (Kan, 1918), Record and Briefs ("Testimony of Mrs. Stella Kunz given in Direct Examination").

34. *Kunz v. Allen,* 172 P 532 (Kan, 1918), Record and Briefs ("Brief on Behalf of the Appellant").

35. Popple and Kember, *Early Cinema* (2004), 56.

36. There are a number of stories concerning individuals recognizing themselves within newsreel footage or being recognized by others. One such story from 1909 is reproduced in Popple and Kember, *Early Cinema* (2004), 60: "A man named Julian Boistard presented himself at the police station of Petit-Montrouge on Monday to give himself up for the murder of his wife. He had shot her with a revolver as the result of a quarrel, which arose in a curious way. Boistard had been to see a cinematograph display in the Rue de la Gaite and among the pictures was one representing the Rheims aviation week. On the films he recognized his wife, making merry at the buffet. His wife, who was by his side, also recognized the tell-tale picture and fainted, whilst the wronged husband cried out his woes to the audience. He had believed his wife to be spending a holiday with some relations, while he was doing military service."

37. *Humiston v. Universal Film Manufacturing Co.,* 167 NYS 98, 101 (Sup Ct, 1917).

38. *Humiston v. Universal Film Manufacturing Co.*, 178 NYS 752, 755 (AD, 1919).

39. NY Civil Rights Law §§ 50–51 (McKinney 2004).

40. *Humiston v. Universal Film Manufacturing Co.*, 167 NYS 98, 101 (Sup Ct, 1917).

41. See *Colyer v. Richard K Fox Publishing Co.*, 146 NYS 2d 999 (AD, 1914) (discussed at length in chapter 2); *Jeffries v. New York Evening Journal Publishing Co.*, 124 NYS 780 (Sup Ct, 1910).

42. See *Mutual Film Corporation v. Industrial Commission of Ohio*, 236 US 230 (1916): "It cannot be put out of view that the exhibition of moving pictures is a business pure and simple, originated and conducted for profit, like other spectacles, not to be regarded, nor intended to be regarded by the Ohio Constitution, we think, as part of the press of the country or as organs of public opinion."

43. *Humiston v. Universal Film Manufacturing Co.*, 167 NYS 98, 100 (Sup Ct, 1917).

44. *Humiston v. Universal Film Manufacturing Co.*, 178 NYS 752, 754 (Smith J) (AD, 1919).

45. Ibid., 755.

46. Ibid.

47. Ibid., 756.

48. Ibid., 757.

49. Ibid.

50. Ibid., 759.

51. Carl Zollman, "Moving Picture Abuses and Their Correction in the United States" (1937), 21 (3) *Marquette Law Review* 105, 108.

52. See Stam, *Film Theory* (2000), 29–31.

53. Munsterberg quoted in Langdale (ed.), *Hugo Munsterberg on Film* (2002), 129.

54. *Sweenek v. Pathe News, Inc.*, 16 F Supp 746 (ED NY 1936).

55. NY Civil Rights Law §§ 50–51 (McKinney 2004).

56. *Sweenek v. Pathe News, Inc.*, 16 F Supp 746, 747–748 (Moscowitz J) (ED NY 1936)

57. Ibid., 748.

58. Bruno, *Atlas of Emotion* (2002), 14.

59. Ibid., 21.

60. Conrad, *Modern Times, Modern Places* (1998), 462.

61. Jean-Paul Sartre quoted in Conrad, *Modern Times, Modern Places* (1998), 462.

62. Conrad, *Modern Times, Modern Places* (1998), 463.

63. NY Civil Rights Law §§ 50–51 (McKinney 2004).

64. *Blumenthal v. Picture Classics, Inc.*, 257 NYS 800 (AD, 1932).

65. *Blumenthal v. Picture Classics, Inc.*, 185 NE 713 (NY, 1933), Record and Briefs ("Affidavit of Miriam Blumenthal Sworn 14 January 1932").

66. Ibid.

67. *Blumenthal v. Picture Classics, Inc.*, 185 NE 713 (NY, 1933), Record and Briefs ("Complaint").

68. *Blumenthal v. Picture Classics, Inc.*, 185 NE 713 (NY, 1933), Record and Briefs ("Affidavit of Adele Blumenthal Sworn 15 January 1932").

69. *Blumenthal v. Picture Classics, Inc.*, 185 NE 713 (NY, 1933), Record and Briefs ("Affidavit of Max J. Weisfeldt Sworn 26 January 1932").

70. Ibid.

71. Ibid.

72. Ibid.

73. Ibid.

74. *Blumenthal v. Picture Classics, Inc.*, 257 NYS 800, 801 (McAvoy J) (AD, 1932).

75. *Blumenthal v. Picture Classics, Inc.*, 257 NYS 800, 804 (O'Malley J) (AD, 1932).

76. 130 NYS 876 (Sup Ct, 1911).

77. *Blumenthal v. Picture Classics, Inc.*, 185 NE 713 (NY, 1933), Record and Briefs ("Affidavit of Harry Roter Sworn 30 January 1932").

78. Ibid.

79. Ibid.

80. *Blumenthal v. Picture Classics, Inc.*, 185 NE 713 (NY, 1933), Record and Briefs ("Brief of the Defendants-Appellants to the Court of Appeals").

81. *Blumenthal v. Picture Classics, Inc.*, 185 NE 713 (NY, 1933), Record and Briefs ("Brief of the Plaintiff-Respondents to the Court of Appeals").

82. Lauren Rabinovitz, "Temptations of Pleasures: Nickelodeons, Amusement Parks and the Sights of Female Sexuality" (1990), 8 (2) *Camera Obscura* 71, 85.

83. Alison Griffiths, "'To the World the World We Show': Early Travelogues as Filmed Ethnography" (1999), 11 (3) *Film History* 282, 285.

84. *Blumenthal v. Picture Classics, Inc.*, 185 NE 713 (NY, 1933), Record and Briefs ("Brief of Defendants-Appellants to the Court of Appeals").

85. *Blumenthal v. Picture Classics, Inc.*, 185 NE 713 (NY, 1933), Record and Briefs ("Reply Affidavit of Harry Roter" sworn 30 January 1932).

86. *Blumenthal v. Picture Classics, Inc.*, 185 NE 713 (NY, 1933), Record and Briefs ("Brief of Defendants-Appellants to the Court of Appeals").

87. Ibid.

88. *Blumenthal v. Picture Classics, Inc.*, 185 NE 713 (NY, 1933), Record and Briefs ("Brief of Plaintiff-Respondents to the Court of Appeals").

89. See, e.g., Jean Bethke Elshtain, *Public Man, Private Woman: Women in Social and Political Thought* (Princeton University Press, 1981); Katherine O'Donovan, *Sexual Divisions in Law* (Weidenfeld and Nicolson, 1985); Ruth Gavison, "Feminism and the Public/Private Distinction" (1992) 45 (1) *Stanford Law Review* 1; Margaret Thornton (ed.), *Public and Private: Feminist Legal Debates* (Oxford University Press, 1995); Susan B. Boyd (ed.), *Challenging the Public/Private Divide: Feminism, Law and Public Policy* (University of Toronto Press, 1997).

90. Nicole Lacey, "Theory into Practice? Pornography and the Public/Private Dichotomy" (1993), 20 *Journal of Law and Society* 93, 100.

91. See Conor, *The Spectacular Modern Woman.*

5
Privacy for Profit and a Right of Publicity

1. *Myers v. African American Publishing Co.*, 7 NYS 2d 662 (Sup Ct, 1938), Record and Briefs ("Amended Complaint"), and *Myers v. African American Publishing Co.*, 5 NYS 2d 223, 224–225 (Noonan J) (Sup Ct, 1938).

2. McCarthy, *The Rights of Publicity and Privacy* (2008), 8.

3. *Roberson v. Rochester Folding Box Co.*, 64 NE 442 (NY, 1902), Record and Briefs. (In the "Brief of Respondent," the plaintiff's attorney, Milton E. Gibbs, argued: "The defendants are estopped from denying that the lithographic likenesses of [the] plaintiff are not of value and are not property. . . . Is it reasonable to suppose that the defendant corporations have sold 25,000 of these lithographs if they are not of value? *The value is not in the paper; it is in the picture*") (emphasis in original); for a detailed discussion of this case see chapter 2.

4. *Manola v. Stevens and Meyer*, NY Sup Ct [unpublished opinion] (1890). For a detailed discussion of this case see chapter 2.

5. Alice Kessler-Harris, *In Pursuit of Equity* (Oxford University Press, 2001), 38.

6. See Lois Banner, *Women in Modern America* (Harcourt Brace Jovanovich, 1984); Manners-Smith, "New Paths to Power" (2000); Alice Kessler-Harris, *Out to Work: A History of Wage-Earning Women in the United States* (Oxford University Press, 1982), 109: "In 1890, more than 90 percent of women over thirty-five were married and would spend their lives with 'husbands present.' That figure altered only slightly in the years

after 1900, but what women did with their lives changed dramatically. Up to 1890, the vast majority of these women remained outside the paid labor force, contributing to the family economy in other ways. After that married women began to take jobs with disconcerting frequency." Kessler-Harris, *In Pursuit of Equity* (2001), 37–38: "Eight million women worked for wages in 1920; of these fully a quarter were married with husbands present, and at least 15 per cent were widowed, divorced, or separated from their spouses. . . . More than half of all female workers were over twenty-five years old."

7. Karen Ward Mahar, *Women Filmmakers in Early Hollywood* (Johns Hopkins University Press, 2006), 1.

8. Conor, *The Spectacular Modern Woman* (2004), 29.

9. Ibid., 2: "Through what I will term *techniques of appearing*—the manners and means of execution of one's visual effects and status—women's bodies became a place of action in modern culture."

10. Ibid.

11. 202 F 2d 866 (1st Cir, 1953).

12. See Michael Madow, "Private Ownership of Public Image: Popular Culture and Publicity Rights" (1993) 81 *California Law Review* 125, 150.

13. Conor, *The Spectacular Modern Woman* (2004), 2.

14. *Loftus v. Greenwich Lithographing Co., Inc.*, 182 NYS 428 (AD, 1920).

15. *Loftus v. Greenwich Lithographing Co., Inc.*, 182 NYS 428 (AD, 1920), Record and Briefs ("Complaint").

16. NY Civil Rights Law §§ 50–51 (McKinney 2004).

17. *Loftus v. Greenwich Lithographing Co., Inc.*, 182 NYS 428, 430 (AD, 1920).

18. Ibid.

19. Ibid.

20. *Loftus v. Greenwich Lithographing Co., Inc.*, 182 NYS 428 (AD, 1920), Record and Briefs ("Appellant's Brief").

21. *Loftus v. Greenwich Lithographing Co., Inc.*, 182 NYS 428, 431 (Laughlin J) (AD, 1920).

22. Ibid.

23. 64 NE 442 (NY, 1902). This case is discussed at length in chapter 2.

24. *Lillie v. Warner Bros. Pictures, Inc.*, 34 P 2d 835 (Cal Ct App, 1934).

25. *Lillie v. Warner Bros. Pictures, Inc.*, 34 P 2d 835 (Cal Ct App, 1934), Record and Briefs ("Appellant's Third Amended Complaint").

26. Ibid.

27. Ibid.

28. Ibid.

29. 297 P 91 (Cal Ct App, 1931).

30. *Lillie v. Warner Bros. Pictures, Inc.*, 34 P 2d 835 (Cal Ct App, 1934), Record and Briefs ("Appellant's Brief").

31. Ibid.

32. Ibid.

33. Ibid.

34. *Lillie v. Warner Bros. Pictures, Inc.*, 34 P 2d 835 (Cal Ct App, 1934), Record and Briefs ("Respondent's Brief").

35. Ibid.

36. Ibid.

37. *Lillie v. Warner Bros. Pictures, Inc.*, 34 P 2d 835, 837 (Conrey J) (Cal Ct App, 1934).

38. See Gibbs's argument in chapter 2.

39. McCarthy, *The Rights of Publicity and Privacy* (2008), 8.

40. *Middleton v. News Syndicate*, 295 NYS 120 (Sup Ct, 1937).

41. *Semler v. Ultem Publications*, 9 NYS 2d 319 (City Ct, 1938).

42. *Semler v. Ultem Publications*, 9 NYS 2d 319, 320 (Conroy J) (City Ct 1938).

43. *Colyer v. Richard K. Fox Publishing Co.*, 146 NYS 2d 999 (AD, 1914).

44. NY Civil Rights Law §§ 50–51 (McKinney 2004).

45. *Lane v. Woolworth Co.*, 11 NYS 2d 199 (Sup Ct, 1939).

46. *Lane v. Woolworth Co.*, 11 NYS 2d 199 (Sup Ct, 1939), Record and Briefs ("Complaint").

47. Ibid.

48. Ibid.

49. *Lane v. Woolworth Co.*, 11 NYS 2d 199, 200 (Noonan, J) (Sup Ct, 1939).

50. 5 NYS 2d 223 (Sup Ct 1938).

51. *Roberson v. Rochester Folding Box Co.*, 65 NYS 1109, 1111 (Davy J) (Sup Ct, 1900).

52. Gail Bederman, *Manliness and Civilization* (University of Chicago Press, 1995).

53. Eden Osucha, "The Whiteness of Privacy" (2009), 24 (1) *Camera Obscura* 66.

54. Ibid., 73.

55. *Kunz v. Allen*, 172 P 532 (Kan, 1918). Record and Briefs ("Testimony of Pearl Armstrong given in Direct Examination"); see chapter 4 for a detailed discussion of this case.

56. Osucha, "The Whiteness of Privacy" (2009), 89.

57. *Myers v. African American Publishing Co.*, 7 NYS 2d 662 (Sup Ct, 1938).

58. NY Civil Rights Law §§ 50–51 (McKinney 2004).

59. *Myers v. African American Publishing Co.*, 7 NYS 2d 662 (Sup Ct, 1938), Record and Briefs ("Amended Complaint").

60. Ibid.

61. The story in *Afro-American* spells her surname "Meyers." In the case, however, she is referred to as Pauline Myers.

62. *Myers v. African American Publishing Co.*, 7 NYS 2d 662 (AD, 1938), Record and Briefs ("Exhibit Attached to Foregoing Amended Complaint").

63. *Myers v. African American Publishing Co.*, 5 NYS 2d 223, 224 (Noonan J) (Sup Ct, 1938).

64. Conor, *The Spectacular Modern Woman* (2004), 178.

65. *Myers v. African American Publishing Co.*, 5 NYS 2d 223, 224 (Noonan J) (Sup Ct 1938).

66. 1 NYS 2d 643 (AD, 1938).

67. 284 NYS 96 (Sup Ct, 1935).

68. Bederman, *Manliness and Civilization* (1995); John F. Kasson, *Houdini, Tarzan and the Perfect Man* (Hill and Wang, 2001).

69. *Redmond v. Columbia Pictures Corporation,* 14 NE 2d 636, 636 (NY, 1938).

70. NY Civil Rights Law §§ 50–51 (McKinney 2004).

71. 64 NE 442 (NY, 1902).

72. See Gibbs's argument in chapter 2.

73. *Franklin v. Columbia Pictures Corporation,* 284 NYS 96 (Sup Ct, 1935).

74. Ernest Hemingway, *Death in the Afternoon* (Scribner, 1932), 387.

75. NY Civil Rights Law §§ 50–51 (McKinney 2004).

76. *Franklin v. Columbia Pictures Corporation,* 2 NE 2d 691 (1936), Record and Briefs ("Amended Complaint").

77. Ibid.

78. Ibid.

79. Ibid.

80. NY Civil Rights Law §§ 50–51 (McKinney 2004).

81. *Franklin v. Columbia Pictures Corporation,* 2 NE 2d 691 (1936), Record and Briefs ("Amended Complaint").

82. NY Civil Rights Law §§ 50–51 (McKinney 2004).

83. 202 F 2d 866 (2nd Cir, 1953).

84. NY Civil Rights Law §§ 50–51 (McKinney 2004).

85. *Haelan Laboratories, Inc. v. Topps Chewing Gum, Inc.*, 202 F 2d 866, 868 (Frank J) (2nd Cir, 1953) (emphasis added).

86. See the Cal Civil Code §§ 3344, 3344.1 (West 1997 & Supp 2002). Section 3344(a) provides: "Any person who knowingly uses another's name, voice, signature, photograph, or likeness, in any manner, on or in products, merchandise, or goods, or for purposes of advertising or selling, or soliciting purchases . . . without such person's prior consent . . . shall be liable for any damages sustained by the person or persons injured as a result thereof." In addition, § 3344.1 regulates the use of the name, voice, signature, photograph, or likeness of a "deceased personality."

87. McCarthy, *The Rights of Publicity and Privacy* (2008).

88. See Gibbs's argument in chapter 2.

6
Hollywood Heroes and Shameful Hookers

1. *Melvin v. Reid*, 297 P 91 (Cal Ct App. 1931).

2. *Melvin v. Reid*, 297 P 91 (Cal Ct App. 1931), Record and Briefs ("Appellant's Brief").

3. John Belton, *American Cinema, American Culture* (McGraw-Hill, 2009) 13.

4. 64 NE 442 (NY, 1902).

5. 297 P 91 (Cal Ct App, 1931).

6. *Binns v. Vitagraph Company of America*, 130 NYS 876 (Sup Ct, 1911).

7. *Binns v. Vitagraph Company of America*, 103 NE 1108, 1110 (NY, 1913), Record and Briefs ("John R. Binns. Called by Plaintiff. Cross [Examination]").

8. *Binns v. Vitagraph Company of America*, 103 NE 1108, 1110 (NY, 1913).

9. NY Civil Rights Law §§ 50–51 (McKinney 2004).

10. *Binns v. Vitagraph Company of America*, 130 NYS 876, 878 (Greenbaum J) (Sup Ct, 1911).

11. Ibid., 879.

12. *Binns v. Vitagraph Company of America*, 103 NE 1108, 1109 (Chase J) (NY, 1913).

13. Ibid., 1110.

14. Ibid., 1111.

15. Ibid., 1110.

16. *Humiston v. Universal Film Manufacturing Co.*, 178 NYS 752 (AD, 1919).

17. *Blumenthal v. Picture Classics, Inc.*, 185 NE 713 (NY, 1933).

18. *Roberson v. Rochester Folding Box Co.*, 65 NYS 1109 (Sup Ct, 1900).

19. *Binns v. Vitagraph Company of America*, 103 NE 1108, 1110 (Chase J) (NY, 1913).

20. *Binns v. Vitagraph Company of America*, 103 NE 1108, 1110 (NY, 1913), Record and Briefs ("Complaint").

21. *Binns v. Vitagraph Company of America*, 103 NE 1108, 1110 (NY, 1913), Record and Briefs ("John R. Binns. Called by Plaintiff. Cross [Examination]").

22. Ibid.

23. Ibid.

24. Ibid.

25. David Cook, *A History of Narrative Film* (Norton, 1990), 36.

26. Quoted in ibid., 35.

27. *Binns v. Vitagraph Company of America*, 103 NE 1108, 1110 (NY, 1913), Record and Briefs ("John R. Binns. Called by Plaintiff. Cross [Examination]").

28. Ibid.

29. Ibid.

30. *Binns v. Vitagraph Company of America*, 103 NE 1108, 1110 (NY, 1913), Record and Briefs ("John R. Binns. Called by Plaintiff. Redirect").

31. 297 P 91 (Cal Ct App, 1931).

32. Cook, *A History of Narrative Film* (1990), 42.

33. Quoted in David Robinson, *From Peep Show to Palace: The Birth of American Film* (Columbia University Press, 1996), 115.

34. Ibid., 116–117.

35. Cook, *A History of Narrative Film* (1990), 44

36. *Roberson v. Rochester Folding Box Co.*, 64 NE 442 (1902).

37. Mordaunt Hall, "Justified Revenge," *New York Times* (New York), 3 February 1926.

38. This newspaper review was included within a "Scrapbook" about *The Red Kimono* held by Special Collections at the Academy of Motion Picture Arts and Sciences' Margaret Herrick Library in Beverly Hills (Los Angeles). Publication details of the particular newspaper review were not available.

39. Anthony Slide, *The Silent Feminists: America's First Women Directors* (Scarecrow Press, 1996), 91.

40. *Melvin v. Reid,* 297 P 91 (Cal Ct App. 1931), Record and Briefs ("Complaint").

41. Ibid.

42. *Melvin v. Reid,* 297 P 91 (Cal Ct App. 1931), Record and Briefs ("Appellant's Brief").

43. 64 NE 442 (NY, 1902).

44. NY Civil Rights Law §§ 50–51 (McKinney 2004).

45. *Binns v. Vitagraph Company of America,* 130 NYS 876 (1911).

46. *Melvin v. Reid,* 297 P 91 (Cal Ct App, 1931), Record and Briefs ("Appellant's Brief").

47. Ibid.

48. California Constitution art. I, § 1.

49. *Melvin v. Reid,* 297 P 91 (Cal Ct App, 1931), Record and Briefs ("Appellant's Brief").

50. Ibid.

51. *Melvin v. Reid,* 297 P 91 (Cal Ct App, 1931), Record and Briefs ("Answer to Petition for Hearing").

52. *Melvin v. Reid,* 297 P 91, 93 (Marks J) (Cal Ct App, 1931).

53. Ibid., 93–94.

54. Cal Civil Code § 655 (West).

55. *Melvin v. Reid,* 297 P 91 (Cal Ct App, 1931), Record and Briefs ("Appellant's Brief").

56. *Melvin v. Reid,* 297 P 91, 94 (Marks J) (Cal Ct App, 1931).

57. See Anthony Slide, *The Idols of Silence* (A. S. Barnes, 1976), 72, and Denise Lowe, *An Encyclopedic Dictionary of Women in Early American Films, 1895–1930* (Haworth Press, 2005), 158–159.

58. Justine Brown, *Hollywood Utopia* (New Star Books, 2002).

59. L. Frank Baum, *The Wonderful Wizard of Oz* (George M. Hill, 1900).

60. D. W. Griffith quoted in Brown, *Hollywood Utopia* (2002), 40.

61. See, e.g., Pennsylvania (1911), Pa Stat Ann tit 4 §§ 41–58, tit 71 §§ 12, 62, 119, 356 (Purdon 1930); Ohio (1913), Ohio Gen Code Ann §§ 871 (48–53), §§ 154 (46–47) (page 1937); Kansas (1913), Kan Rev Stat Ann c 51 §§ 101–112, c 74 §§ 2201–2209 (1935); Maryland (1916), Md Ann Code art 66A (Bagby 1924), amended Md Code Pub Gen Laws art 66A §§ 7, 10, 11 (Flack, Supp 1935), amended Laws 1939 c 430; New York (1921), NY Educ Law §§ 1080–1092; Florida (1921), Fla Comp Gen Laws Ann §§ 3584–3586, 7719 (Skillman 1927); Virginia (1922), Va Code Ann §§ 378b=-378j (Michie 1936). See also "Censorship of Motion Pictures" (1939) 49 (1) *Yale Law Journal* 87.

62. 236 US 230 (1915); See also the similar decision of *Mutual Film Corp. v. Hodges,* 236 US 248 (1915), upholding film censorship laws in Kansas. For a detailed discussion of these cases see John Wertheimer, "Mutual Film Reviewed: The Movies, Censorship and Free Speech in Progressive America" (1993), 37 *American Journal of Legal History* 158.

63. Justice McKenna held that moving pictures were not to be regarded in the same category as "the press of the country or as organs of public opinion" and therefore were not protected by the First Amendment to the U.S. Constitution guaranteeing freedom of expression: *Mutual Film Corp. v. Industrial Commission,* 236 US 230, 242–244 (McKenna J) (1915).

64. The Production Code reproduced in Thomas Doherty, *Pre-Code Hollywood: Sex, Immorality and Insurrection in American Cinema 1930–1934* (Columbia University Press, 1999), 348.

65. Ibid., 362.

66. 57 F Supp 40 (SD NY, 1944).

67. This review was written by John Chapman around the time of *Yankee Doodle Dandy*'s release in 1942. It is held by Special Collections at the Academy of Motion Picture Arts and Sciences' Margaret Herrick Library in Beverly Hills (Los Angeles). Further publication details are not provided.

68. Letter dated 29 June 1942 from Robert Buckner (producer of Warner Bros. Pictures) to Hedda Hopper regarding her review of *Yankee Doodle Dandy* published on Saturday 27 June 1942 in the *Los Angeles Times.* The letter is held by Special Collections at the Academy of Motion Picture Arts and Sciences' Margaret Herrick Library, Beverly Hills (Los Angeles).

69. Production notes for *Yankee Doodle Dandy* held by Special Collections at the Academy of Motion Picture Arts and Sciences' Margaret Herrick Library, Beverly Hills (Los Angeles).

70. "Yankee Doodle Dandy" (August 1942), *American Cinematographer.* Article held in Special Collections at the Academy of Motion Picture Arts and Sciences' Margaret Herrick Library, Beverly Hills (Los Angeles). No other publication details are provided.

71. "Yankee Doodle Dandy" (1 June 1942), *Variety.* Article held in Special Collections at the Academy of Motion Picture Arts and Sciences' Margaret Herrick Library, Beverly Hills (Los Angeles). No other publication details are provided.

72. "Yankee Doodle Dandy" (3 June 1942), *Variety.* Article held in Special Collections at the Academy of Motion Picture Arts and Sciences' Margaret Herrick Library, Beverly Hills (Los Angeles). No other publication details are provided.

73. *Levey v. Warner Bros. Pictures, Inc.*, 57 F Supp 40 (SD NY, 1944).

74. NY Civil Rights Law §§ 50–51 (McKinney 2004).

75. 64 NE 442 (NY, 1902).

76. 103 NE 1108 (NY, 1913).

77. 178 NYS 752 (AD, 1919).

78. *Levey v. Warner Bros. Pictures, Inc.*, 57 F Supp 40, 42 (Bondy J) (SD NY, 1944).

79. Ibid.

80. Ibid., 40–41.

81. *Stryker v. Republic Pictures Corporation*, 238 P 2d 670 (Cal Ct App, 1951).

82. *Metter v. L.A. Examiner*, 95 P 2d 491(Cal Ct App, 1939); *Kerby v. Hal Roach Studios*, 127 P 577 (1942); *Cohen v. Marx*, 211 P 2d 320 (Cal Ct App, 1949); *Mau v. Rio Grande Oil Co., Inc.*, 28 F Supp 845 (ND Cal, 1939).

83. *Stryker v. Republic Pictures Corporation*, 238 P 2d 670 (Cal Ct App, 1951), Record and Briefs ("Appellant's Opening Brief").

84. *Stryker v. Republic Pictures Corporation*, 238 P 2d 670 (Cal Ct App, 1951), Record and Briefs ("Respondents' Brief").

85. *The Story of Louis Pasteur* (directed by William Dieterle, 1936).

86. *The Life of Emile Zola* (directed by William Dieterle, 1937).

87. *Oliver Wendell Holmes* (directed by James A. Fitzpatrick, 1922).

88. *Stryker v. Republic Pictures Corporation*, 238 P 2d 670 (Cal Ct App, 1951), Record and Briefs ("Appellant's Opening Brief").

89. *Melvin v. Reid*, 297 P 91 (Ct Cal App, 1931).

90. *Stryker v. Republic Pictures Corporation*, 238 P 2d 670, 672 (Hanson J) (Cal Ct App, 1951).

91. Ibid., 673.

92. Ibid.

93. Ibid.

94. Production notes for *The Sands of Iwo Jima* held in Special Collections at the Academy of Motion Picture Arts and Sciences' Margaret Herrick Library, Beverly Hills (Los Angeles).

95. Letter from Joseph Breen (Production Code Administration) to Allen Wilson (Republic Pictures) dated 12 May 1949. Held in Special Collections at the Academy of Motion Picture Arts and Sciences' Margaret Herrick Library, Beverly Hills (Los Angeles).

96. Letter from Joseph Breen (Production Code Administration) to Allen Wilson (Republic Pictures) dated 21 June 1949. Held in Special Collections at the Academy of Motion Picture Arts and Sciences' Margaret Herrick Library, Beverly Hills (Los Angeles).

97. Letter from Joseph Breen (Production Code Administration) to Allen Wilson (Republic Pictures) dated 23 June 1949. Held in Special Collections at the Academy of Motion Picture Arts and Sciences' Margaret Herrick Library, Beverly Hills (Los Angeles).

98. Letter from Joseph Breen (Production Code Administration) to Allen Wilson (Republic Pictures) dated 5 August 1949. Held in Special Collections at the Academy of Motion Picture Arts and Sciences' Margaret Herrick Library, Beverly Hills (Los Angeles).

99. Letter from Joseph Breen (Production Code Administration) to Allen Wilson (Republic Pictures) dated 22 August 1949. Held in Special Collections at the Academy of Motion Picture Arts and Sciences' Margaret Herrick Library, Beverly Hills (Los Angeles).

100. "Sands of Iwo Jima" (14 December 1949), *Variety.* Article held in Special Collections at the Academy of Motion Picture Arts and Sciences' Margaret Herrick Library, Beverly Hills (Los Angeles). No other publication details are provided.

101. Herm, "Sands of Iwo Jima" (14 December 1949), *Variety.* Article held in Special Collections at the Academy of Motion Picture Arts and Sciences' Margaret Herrick Library, Beverly Hills (Los Angeles). No other publication details are provided..

102. Production notes for *The Sands of Iwo Jima* held in Special Collections at the Academy of Motion Picture Arts and Sciences' Margaret Herrick Library, Beverly Hills (Los Angeles).

103. Original document entitled "Analysis of Film Content" included in the production notes for *The Sands of Iwo Jima* held in Special Collections at the Academy of Motion Picture Arts and Sciences' Margaret Herrick Library, Beverly Hills (Los Angeles).

104. By 1950 "a right to privacy" had been recognized by the courts in the following jurisdictions: Alabama, Alaska, Arizona, California, District of Columbia, Florida, Georgia, Indiana, Kansas, Kentucky, Louisiana, Michigan, Missouri, Nevada, New Jersey, North Carolina, Ohio, Oregon, Pennsylvania, and South Carolina. In addition, the following states recognized "a right to privacy" via statute: New York, Oklahoma, Utah, and Virginia. See Prosser, "Privacy" (1960), 386–387.

Conclusion

1. Warren and Brandeis, "A Right to Privacy" (1890).
2. A Bill to Protect Ladies, HR 8151, 50th Congress (1888).

3. Petition against a bill (No. 3516), held by the Legislative Branch of the National Archives (Washington, D.C.).

4. 64 NE 442 (NY, 1902).

5. New York Laws Ch 132 §§ 1–2 (1903) (subsequently became NY Civil Rights Law §§ 50–51 (McKinney 2004)).

6. 172 P 532 (Kan, 1918).

7. 167 NYS 98, 101 (Sup Ct, 1917).

8. 257 NYS 800 (AD, 1932).

9. 202 F 2d 866 (1st Cir, 1953).

10. See, e.g., Jon L. Mills, *Privacy: The Lost Right* (Oxford University Press, 2008); David Anderson, "The Failure of American Privacy Law," in Basil Markesinis (ed.), *Protecting Privacy* (Oxford University Press, 1999); Megan Richardson, "Candid Camera" (2007) 66 *Meanjin* 83.

11. *New York Times v. Sullivan,* 376 US 254 (1964); *Time, Inc. v. Hill,* 365 US 374 (1967); *Cox Broadcasting v. Cohn,* 420 US 469 (1975).

12. Abby Rogers, "More Than 20 Women Are Suing a Texas 'Revenge Porn' Site and GoDaddy," *Business Insider Australia* (online), 24 January 2012, at http://au.businessinsider.com/class-action-lawsuit-against-texxxancom-2013-1; Erin Mulvaney, "GoDaddy.com Among Defendants in 'Revenge Porn' Law Suit," *Houston Chronicle* (online), 17 January 2013, at http://www.chron.com/news/houston-texas/houston/article/GoDaddy-com-among-defendants-in-revenge-porn-4202646.php

13. Woodrow Hartzog, "How to Fight Revenge Porn," *Atlantic* (online), 10 May 2013, at http://www.theatlantic.com/technology/archive/2013/05/how-to-fight-revenge-porn/275759

14. Jessica Roy, "A Victim Speaks: Standing Up to the Revenge Porn Tormentor," *BetaBeat* (online), 1 May 2013, at http://betabeat.com/2013/05/revenge-porn-holli-thometz-criminal-case

Bibliography

Articles, Books, and Reports

"Best and Secondary Evidence. Testimony That Motion Picture Represented Plaintiff" (1920). 6 (6) *Virginia Law Register* 460.

"The Casuistry of Photographic Ethics" (1899). 19 *American Journal of Photography* 81.

"Censorship of Motion Pictures" (1939). 49 (1) *Yale Law Journal* 87.

"Evidence: Moving Pictures: Best Evidence Rule" (1920). 19 (1) *Michigan Law Review* 101.

"The Kodac [*sic*] Camera" (1889). 6 (December) *The Detective.*

"Motion Pictures as Evidence" (1914). 22 *Law Student Helper.*

"Motion Pictures in Court" (1924). 2 *New York Law Review* 96.

"Moving Pictures and the Right of Privacy" (1919). 28 (3) *Yale Law Journal* 269.

"Notes of Important Decisions" (1920). 91 (2) *Central Law Journal* 23.

"The Photograph as a False Witness" (1886). 10 *Virginia Law Journal* 644.

"Photographs Use of Negative (1890). 34 (10 Oct.) *Central Law Journal* 15.

"Publication of Photograph of Child's Mutilated Body Held Not to Violate Right of Privacy" (1956–1957). 5 *Utah Law Review* 265.

"Right of Privacy. Injunction. Motion Pictures" (1920). 20 (1) *Columbia Law Review* 100.

"Right of Privacy. Nature and Extent. Biographical Motion Pictures" (1931). 44 (7) *Harvard Law Review* 1146.

"Right of Privacy. Publishing Picture of Deceased Child as Invasion of Parents' Rights" (1931). 17 (4) *Virginia Law Review* 393.

"Right of Privacy—Relative's Interest in a Deceased's Name or Likeness" (1961). 22 *Ohio State Law Journal* 438.

"The Right to Privacy in Nineteenth-Century America" (1981). 94 (8) *Harvard Law Review* 1892.

"Strange Uses for Photographs" (1879). 13 *Western Jurist* 484.

"Torts. Suit for Display of Motion Picture in Violation of Contract with Actress" (1934). 34 (8) *Columbia Law Review* 1565.

Abate, Corinne S. (ed.), *Privacy, Domesticity and Women in Early Modern England* (Ashgate, 2003).

Allen, Anita L. *Uneasy Access: Privacy for Women in a Free Society.* Rowman and Littlefield, 1988.

———. "Natural Law, Slavery and the Right to Privacy Tort" (2012). 81 *Fordham Law Review* 1187.

Allen, Anita L., and Erin Mack. "How Privacy Got Its Gender" (1990). 10 (Spring) *Northern Illinois University Law Review* 441.

AlSayyad, Nezar. *Cinematic Urbanism: A History of the Modern from Reel to Real.* Routledge, 2006.

American Law Institute. *Restatement (Second) of Torts.* American Law Institute Publishers, 1977.

Anderson, David. "The Failure of American Privacy Law." In Basil Markesinis (ed.), *Protecting Privacy.* Oxford University Press, 1999.

Arendt, Hannah (ed.). *Illuminations.* Harcourt, 1st ed., 1968.

Arens, E. "The Elevated Railroad Cases: Private Property and Mass Transit in Gilded Age New York" (2005). 61 *NYU Annual Survey of American Law* 629.

Armstrong, Meg. "'A Jumble of Foreignness': The Sublime Musayums of Nineteenth-Century Fairs and Expositions" (1992–1993). 23 (Winter) *Cultural Critique* 199.

Auerbach, Jonathan. *Body Shots: Early Cinema's Incarnations.* University of California Press, 2007.

Bajac, Quentin. *The Invention of Photography: The First Fifty Years.* Thames and Hudson, 2002.

Banner, Lois W. *Women in Modern America: A Brief History.* Harcourt Brace Jovanovich, 1984.

Barbas, Samantha. "The Laws of Image" (2012). 47 *New England Law Review* 23.

Barber, Stephen. *Projected Cities: Cinema and Urban Space.* Reaktion, 2002.

Barron, James H. "Warren and Brandeis, The Right to Privacy, 4 Harv. L. Rev. 193 (1890): Demystifying a Landmark Citation" (1979). 13 *Suffolk University Law Review* 875.

Barthes, Roland. *Camera Lucida: Reflections on Photography*. Hill and Wang, 1981.

Baum, L. Frank. *The Wonderful Wizard of Oz*. George M. Hill Company, 1900.

Bederman, Gail. *Manliness and Civilization: A Cultural History of Gender and Race in the United States 1880–1917*. University of Chicago Press, 1995.

Belton, John. *American Cinema, American Culture*. McGraw-Hill, 2009.

Benjamin, Walter. "The Work of Art in the Age of Mechanical Reproduction." In Hannah Arendt (ed.), *Illuminations*. Harcourt, 1st ed., 1968.

Birnbaum, Harold F. "Libel by Lens" (1966). 52 (September) *American Bar Association Journal* 837.

Bishop, J. P. *New Commentaries on the Criminal Law upon a New System of Legal Exposition*. T. H. Flood, 8th ed., 1892.

Bogardus, A. "A Caution to Women Who Intend Sitting for Their Photographs" (1890). VII (9) *Ladies' Home Journal* 11.

Bottomore, S. "That Bloomin' Cinematograph" (1995). 8 *Yale Journal of Criticism* 61.

Bowker, Richard Rogers. *Copyright: Its History and Its Law, Being a Summary of the Principles and Practice of Copyright with Special Reference to the American Code of 1909 and the British Act of 1911*. Houghton Mifflin, 1912.

Bowry, Kathy. "Who's Painting Copyright's History?" In Daniel McClean and Karsten Schubert (eds.), *Dear Images: Art, Copyright and Culture*, 256. Ridinghouse and the Institute of Contemporary Art, 2002.

Boyd, Susan B. (ed.). *Challenging the Public/Private Divide: Feminism, Law and Public Policy*. University of Toronto Press, 1997.

British Film Institute. *Screen Online: Street Scenes*. British Film Institute, at http://www.screenonline.org.uk/film/id/748489/index.html (accessed 29 April 2013).

Brown, Justine. *Hollywood Utopia*. New Star Books, 2002.

Bruno, Giuliana. *Atlas of Emotion: Journeys in Art, Architecture, and Film*. Verso, 2002.

———. "Film, Aesthetics, Science: Hugo Munsterberg's Laboratory of Moving Images" (2009). 36 (Summer) *Grey Room* 88.

Cartwright, Lisa. *Screening the Body: Tracing Medicine's Visual Culture* (University of Minnesota Press, 1995).

Charney, Leo, and Vanessa R. Schwartz (eds.). *Cinema and the Invention of Modern Life*. University of California Press, 1995.

Clarke, David B. *The Cinematic City.* Routledge, 1997.

Clemons, L. S. "The Right of Privacy in Relation to the Publication of Photographs" (1930). 14 (4) *Marquette Law Review* 193.

Collins, Douglas. *The Story of Kodak.* H. N. Adams, 1990.

Conor, Liz. *The Spectacular Modern Woman.* Indiana University Press, 2004.

Conrad, Peter. *Modern Times, Modern Places.* Thames and Hudson, 1998.

Cook, David. *A History of Narrative Film.* Norton, 1990.

Cott, Nancy F. *No Small Courage: A History of Women in the United States.* Oxford University Press, 2000.

Crangle, Richard. "Saturday Night at the X-Rays: The Moving Picture and 'The New Photography' in Britain, 1896." In John Fullerton (ed.), *Celebrating 1895: The Centenary of Cinema,* 138. John Libey, 1998.

Crary, Jonathan. *Techniques of the Observer: On Vision and Modernity in the Nineteenth Century.* MIT Press, 1990.

———. *Suspensions of Perception: Attention, Spectacle, and Modern Culture.* MIT Press, 1999.

Creed, Barbara. *The Monstrous-Feminine: Film, Feminism and Psychoanalysis.* Routledge, 1993.

Danielson, Caroline. "The Gender of Privacy and the Embodied Self: Examining the Origins of the Right to Privacy in U.S. Law" (1999). 25 (2) *Feminist Studies* 311.

Davis, Frederick. "What Do We Mean by 'Right to Privacy'?" (1959). 4 *South Dakota Law Review* 1.

Doane, Mary-Ann. *The Emergence of Cinematic Time: Modernity, Contingency, the Archive.* Harvard University Press, 2002.

Doherty, Thomas. *Pre-Code Hollywood: Sex, Immorality and Insurrection in American Cinema 1930–1934.* Columbia University Press, 1999.

Edelman, Bernard. *Ownership of the Image: Elements for a Marxist Theory of Law.* Routledge and Kegan Paul, 1979.

Elshtain, Jean Bethke. *Public Man, Private Woman: Women in Social and Political Thought.* Princeton University Press, 1981.

Ernst, Morris Leopold, and Alan U. Schwartz. *Privacy: The Right to Be Let Alone.* Greenwood Press, 1977.

Farley, Christine Haight. "The Lingering Effects of Copyright's Response to the Invention of Photography" (2003–2004). 65 *University of Pittsburgh Law Review* 385.

Feaster, Felicia. "The Woman on the Table: Moral and Medical Discourse in the Exploitation Cinema" (1994). 6 (3) *Film History* 340.

Felcher, D. L., and E. L. Rubin. "Privacy, Publicity and the Portrayal of Real People by the Media" (1979). 88 (8) *Yale Law Journal* 1577.

Fitzpatrick, John R. 'The Unauthorized Publication of Photographs" (1931–1932). 20 *Georgetown Law Journal* 134.

Flaherty, David H. *Privacy in Colonial New England.* University Press of Virginia, 1967.

Friedberg, Anne. *The Virtual Window: From Alberti to Microsoft* (MIT Press, 2006).

———. *Window Shopping: Cinema and the Postmodern.* University of California Press, 1993.

Frohlich, Louis D., and Charles Schwartz. *The Law of Motion Pictures, Including the Law of the Theatre Treating of the Various Rights of the Author, Actor, Professional Scenario Writer, Director, Producer, Distributor, Exhibitor and the Public, with Chapters on Unfair Competition, and Copyright Protection in the United States, Great Britain and Her Colonial Possessions.* Baker, Voorhis, 1918.

Gaines, Jane. *Contested Culture: The Image, the Voice, and the Law.* University of North Carolina Press, 1991.

Gajda, Amy. "What If Samuel D. Warren Hadn't Married a Senator's Daughter? Uncovering the Press Coverage That Led to 'The Right to Privacy'" (2008). 35 (Spring) *Michigan State Law Review* 35.

Gallagher, Susan E. *Reading New England: The Right to Privacy* (University of Massachusetts Press, 2010), at http://readingnewengland.org/app/books/righttoprivacy/

Gavison, Ruth. "Feminism and the Public/Private Distinction" (1992). 45 (1) *Stanford Law Review* 1.

———. "Privacy and the Limits of Law" (1980), 89 *Yale Law Journal* 421.

Gerety, Tom. "Redefining Privacy" (1977), 12 *Harvard Civil Rights—Civil Liberties Law Review* 233.

Gernsheim, Helmut, and Alison Gernsheim. *A Concise History of Photography.* Thames and Hudson, 1965.

———. *The History of Photography from the Camera Obscura to the Beginning of the Modern Era.* McGraw-Hill, 2nd ed., 1969.

Gever, Martha. "Photographs as Private Property: A Marxist Analysis" (1981). 8 (6) *Afterimage* 8.

Glancy, Dorothy. "Privacy and the Other Miss M." (1989–1990). 10 *Northern Illinois University Law Review* 401.

Gormley, K. "A Hundred Years of Privacy" (1992). *Wisconsin Law Review* 1335.

Gray, Carl M. "Motion Pictures in Evidence" (1939). 15 *Indiana Law Journal* 408.

Graycar, Regina. "The Gender of Judgments: An Introduction." In Margaret Thornton (ed.), *Public and Private: Feminist Legal Debates.* Oxford University Press, 1995.

——. "The Gender of Judgments: Some Reflections on Bias" (1998). 32 (1) *U.B.C. Law Review* 1.

Griffiths, Alison. "'To the World the World We Show': Early Travelogues as Filmed Ethnography" (1999). 11 (3) *Film History* 282.

Gross, Hyman. "The Concept of Privacy" (1967). 47 *New York University Law Review* 34.

Gross, Larry P., John Stuart Katz, and Jay Ruby (eds.). *Image Ethics: The Moral Rights of Subjects in Photographs, Film, and Television.* Oxford University Press, 1988.

Grossberg, Michael, and Christopher Tomlins (eds.). *The Cambridge History of Law in America, Volume II: The Long Nineteenth Century (1789–1920).* Cambridge University Press, 2008.

Grove, Allen W. "Rontgen's Ghosts: Photography, X-Rays and the Victorian Imagination" (1997). 16 (2) *Literature and Medicine* 141.

Gunning, Tom. "From the Kaleidoscope to the X-Ray: Urban Spectatorship, Poe, Benjamin and Traffic in Souls (1913)" (1997). 19 (4) *Wide Angle* 25.

——. "Tracing the Individual Body: Photography, Detectives and Early Cinema." In Leo Charney and Vanessa R. Schwartz (eds.), *Cinema and the Invention of Modern Life,* 15. University of California Press, 1995.

Hafetz, J. L., "A Man's Home Is His Castle: Reflections on the Home, the Family, and Privacy during the Late Nineteenth and Early Twentieth Centuries" (2001). 8 *William and Mary Journal of Women and the Law* 175.

Hand, Augustus N. "Schuyler against Curtis and the Right to Privacy" (1897). 45 (12) *American Law Register* 745.

Haworth-Booth, Mark, et al. (eds.). *The Golden Age of British Photography, 1839–1900: Photographs from the Victoria and Albert Museum, London, with Selections from the Philadelphia Museum of Art, Royal Archives, Windsor Castle, The Royal Photographic Society, Bath, Science Museum, London, Scottish National Portrait Gallery, Edinburgh.* Aperture, the Philadelphia Museum of Art, and Viking Penguin, 1984.

Hemingway, Ernest. *Death in the Afternoon*. Scribner, 1932.

Herm. "Sands of Iwo Jima" (14 December 1949). *Variety.*

Hoff, Joan. *Law, Gender and Injustice: A Legal History of U.S. Women*. New York University Press, 1991.

Hofstadter, Samuel H., and George Horowitz. *The Right of Privacy.* Central Book Company, 1964.

J., J. A. "The Legal Relations of Photographs" (1869). 17 (3) *American Law Register* 1.

Jay, Bill. "Photographer as Aggressor." In David Featherstone (ed.), *Observations: Essays on Documentary Photography.* Friends Photography, 1984.

Jay, Martin. *Downcast Eyes: The Denigration of Vision in Twentieth-Century French Thought.* University of California Press, 1993.

Kalven Jr., Harry. "Privacy in Tort Law: Were Warren and Brandeis Wrong?" (1966). 31 *Law and Contemporary Problems* 326.

Kerber, Linda K. *No Constitutional Right to Be Ladies: Women and the Obligations of Citizenship.* Hill and Wang, 1st ed., 1998.

Kessler-Harris, Alice. *In Pursuit of Equity: Women, Men, and the Quest for Economic Citizenship in 20th-Century America.* Oxford University Press, 2001.

———. *Out to Work: A History of Wage-Earning Women in the United States.* Oxford University Press, 1982.

Kitch, Carolyn. *The Girl On the Magazine Cover.* University of North Carolina Press, 2001.

Klasson, John F. *Houdini, Tarzan and the Perfect Man: The White Male Body and the Challenge of Modernity in America.* Hill and Wang, 2001.

Knight, Nancy. "The New Light: X-Rays and Medical Futurism." In Joseph J. Corn (ed.), *Imagining Tomorrow: History, Technology, and the American Future,* 10. MIT Press, 1986.

Koeck, Richard, and Les Roberts. *The City and the Moving Image: Urban Projections.* Palgrave Macmillan, 2010.

Krauss, Rosalind E. *The Optical Unconscious.* MIT Press, 1993.

Kristeva, Julia. *Powers of Horror: An Essay on Abjection.* Columbia University Press, 1982.

Lacey, Nicole. "Theory into Practice? Pornography and the Public/Private Dichotomy" (1993). 20 *Journal of Law and Society* 93.

Lane, Frederick S. *American Privacy: The 400-Year History of Our Most Contested Right.* Beacon Press, 2009.

Langdale, Allan (ed.). *Hugo Munsterberg on Film: The Photoplay—A Psychological Study and Other Writings*. Routledge, 2002.

Larremore, W. "Law of Privacy" (1912). 12 (8) *Columbia Law Review* 693.

Larremore, Wilbur. "The Right of Privacy" (1913). 21 (3) *Sewanee Review* 297.

LeBlang, Theodore R. "Invasion of Privacy: Medical Practice and the Tort of Intrusion" (1978). 18 *Washburn Law Journal* 205.

Lester, C. Edwards and Mathew B. Brady. *The Gallery of Illustrious Americans, Containing the Portraits and Biographical Sketches of Twenty-Four of the Most Eminent Citizens of the American Republic, Since the Death of Washington*. M. B. Brady, F. D'Avignon, and C. E. Lester, 1850.

Levin, David Michael. *Modernity and the Hegemony of Vision*. University of California Press, 1993.

Lowe, Denise. *An Encyclopedic Dictionary of Women in Early American Films, 1895–1930*. Haworth Press, 2005.

Macfadden, Bernarr. *Macfadden's New Hair Culture: Rational, Natural Methods for Cultivating Strength and Luxuriance of the Hair*. Physical Culture Publishing, 3rd ed., 1901.

Madow, Michael. "Private Ownership of Public Image: Popular Culture and Publicity Rights" (1993). 81 *California Law Review* 125.

Mahar, Karen Ward. *Women Filmmakers in Early Hollywood*. Johns Hopkins University Press, 2006.

Malkan, Jeffrey. "Stolen Photographs: Personality, Publicity and Privacy" (1996–1997). 75 *Texas Law Review* 779.

Mankiller, Wilma, et al. (eds.). *The Reader's Companion to U.S. Women's History*. Houghton Mifflin, 1998.

Manners Smith, Karen. "New Paths to Power: 1890–1920." In Nancy F. Cott (ed.), *No Small Courage*, 353. Oxford University Press, 2000.

Mason, Alpheus Thomas. *Brandeis: A Free Man's Life*. Viking Press, 1946.

McCarthy, Thomas. *The Rights of Publicity and Privacy*, volume 1. West Group, 2nd ed., 2008.

McManus, B. F. "Amateur Photographers" (1890). 27 (370) *Wilson's Photographic Magazine* 296.

McQuire, Scott. *Visions of Modernity: Representation, Memory, Time and Space in the Age of the Camera*. Sage, 1998.

Mensel, Robert E. "'Kodakers Lying in Wait': Amateur Photography and the Right of Privacy" (1991). 43 (1) *American Quarterly* 24.

Metz, Christian. *The Imaginary Signifier: Psychoanalysis and the Cinema*. Indiana University Press, first published 1977, 1982 ed.

Miller, Toby, and Robert Stam (eds.). *Film and Theory: An Anthology*. Blackwell, 2000.

Mills, Jon L. *Privacy: The Lost Right*. Oxford University Press, 2008.

Mulvey, Laura. "Visual Pleasure and Narrative Cinema" (1975). 16 (3) *Screen* 6.

Munsterberg, Hugo. "The X-Rays" (1896). 3 (57) *Science* 161.

Nizer, Louis. "The Right of Privacy: A Half Century's Developments" (1941). 39 (4) *Michigan Law Review* 526.

O'Donovan, Katherine. *Sexual Divisions in Law*. Weidenfeld and Nicolson, 1985.

O'Neill, William L. *Feminism in America: A History*. Transaction, 2nd ed., 1989.

Osucha, Eden. "The Whiteness of Privacy" (2009). 24 (1) *Camera Obscura* 66.

Otto, Elizabeth, and Vanessa Rocco (eds.). *The New Woman International: Representations in Photography and Film from 1870s through the 1960s*. University of Michigan Press, 2012.

Ouida. "The New Woman." *North American Review*, May 1894, 610–619. In Martha H. Patterson (ed.), *The American New Woman Revisited* (1894–1930), 40. Rutgers University Press, 2008.

Pamboukian, Sylvia. "'Looking Radiant': Science, Photography and the X-Ray Craze of 1896" (2001). 27 (2) *Victorian Review* 56.

Parker, Charles. "A Danger Ahead" (1888). (April 7) *Philadelphia Photographer* 218.

Patterson, Martha H. (ed.). *The American New Woman Revisited: A Reader 1894–1930*. Rutgers University Press, 2008.

Perkins Gilman, Charlotte. *Women and Economics: A Study of the Economic Relations between Men and Women as a Factor in Social Evolution*. Small, Maynard, 1898.

Petro, Patrice (ed.). *Fugitive Images: From Photography to Video*. University of Wisconsin Press, 1995.

Popple, Simon, and Joe Kember. *Early Cinema: From Factory Gate to Dream Factory*. Wallflower, 2004.

Post, Robert. "Three Concepts of Privacy" (2001). 89 *Georgia Law Journal* 2087.

Prewett, B. "The Crimination of Peeping Toms and Other Men of Vision" (1951). 5 *Arkansas Law Review* 388.

Prosser, William L. "Privacy" (1960). 48(3) *California Law Review* 383.

Rabinbach, Anson. *The Human Motor: Energy, Fatigue and the Origins of Modernity*. University of California Press, 1990.

Rabinovitz, Lauren. "Temptations of Pleasures: Nickelodeons, Amusement Parks and the Sights of Female Sexuality" (1990). 8 (2) *Camera Obscura* 71.

Richardson, Megan. "Candid Camera" (2007). 66 *Meanjin* 83.

Richardson, Megan, et al. *Breach of Confidence: Social Origins and Modern Developments.* Edward Elgar, 2012.

Riley, Glenda. *Inventing the American Woman: An Inclusive Story,* volume 2. Harlan Davidson, 2007.

Robinson, David. *From Peep Show to Palace: The Birth of American Film.* Columbia University Press, 1996.

Sachse, Julius F. "Photographic Jurisprudence in Germany" (1891). 12 (1 Jan.) *American Journal of Photography* 133.

Salmon, Marylynn. "The Legal Status of Women in Early America" (1983). 1 *Law and History Review* 129.

Sarat, Austin, Lawrence Douglas, and Martha Merrill Umphrey (eds.). *Law on the Screen.* Stanford University Press, 2005.

———. "On Film and Law: Broadening the Focus." In Austin Sarat, Lawrence Douglas, and Martha Merrill Umphrey (eds.), *Law on the Screen,* 1. Stanford University Press, 2005.

Schneider, Elizabeth M. "The Violence of Privacy" (1991). 23 *Connecticut Law Review* 973.

Schwartz, L. G. *Mechanical Witness: A History of Motion Picture Evidence in U.S. Courts.* Oxford University Press, 2009.

Sekula, Allan. "The Body and the Archive" (1986). 39 *October* 3.

Shiel, Mark, and Tony Fitzmaurice. *Cinema and the City: Film and Urban Societies in a Global Context.* Blackwell, 2001.

Siegel, Reva B. "'The Rule of Love': Wife Beating as Prerogative and Privacy" (1995–1996). 105 *Yale Law Journal* 2117.

Slide, Anthony. *The Idols of Silence.* A. S. Barnes, 1976.

———. *The Silent Feminists: America's First Women Directors.* Scarecrow Press, 1996.

Solove, Daniel J. "Conceptualizing Privacy" (2002). 90 (4) *California Law Review* 1087.

———. "A Taxonomy of Privacy" (2005–2006). 154 (3) *University of Pennsylvania Law Review* 477.

Sontag, Susan. *On Photography.* Penguin, 1977.

Staiger, Janet. *Bad Women: Regulating Sexuality in Early American Cinema.* University of Minnesota Press, 1995.

Stam, Robert. *Film Theory: An Introduction.* Blackwell, 2000.

Suid, Lawrence. "'The Sands of Iwo Jima,' The United States Marines, and the Screen Image of John Wayne" (1978). (May 1) *Film and History* 25.

Sullivan, Kathleen S. *Constitutional Context: Women and Rights Discourse in Nineteenth-Century America.* Johns Hopkins University Press, 2007.

Tagg, John. *The Burden of Representation: Essays on Photographies and Histories.* University of Massachusetts Press, 1988.

Thompson, Kristin, and David Bordwell. *Film History: An Introduction.* McGraw-Hill, 2nd ed., 2003.

Thompson III, Robert T. "Image as Personal Property: How Privacy Law Has Influenced the Right of Publicity" (2009). 16 (1) *UCLA Entertainment Law Review* 155

Thornton, Margaret (ed.). *Public and Private: Feminist Legal Debates.* Oxford University Press, 1995.

Ussher, Jane. *Managing the Monstrous-Feminine: Regulating the Reproductive Body.* Routledge, 2006.

Viera, John David. "Images as Property." In Larry P. Gross, John Stuart Katz, and Jay Ruby (eds.), *Image Ethics: The Moral Rights of Subjects in Photographs, Films and Television,* 135. Oxford University Press, 1988.

Wagner, W. J. "Photography and the Right to Privacy: The French and American Approaches" (1980). Summer *Catholic Lawyer* 195.

Wallach, Glenn. "'A Depraved Taste for Publicity': The Press and Private Life in the Gilded Age" (1998). 39 (1) *American Studies* 31.

Warren, Samuel D., and Louis D. Brandeis. "The Right to Privacy" (1890). 4 *Harvard Law Review* 193.

Weibel, Peter, et al. (eds.). *Ctrl [Space]: Rhetorics of Surveillance from Bentham to Big Brother.* ZKM and MIT Press, 2002.

Wells, J. A. "Motion Pictures in Evidence" (1938). 8 *Brooklyn Law Review* 290.

Wertheimer, John. "Mutual Film Reviewed: The Movies, Censorship and Free Speech in Progressive America" (1993). 37 *American Journal of Legal History* 158.

Whissle, Kristin. *Picturing American Modernity: Traffic, Technology and the Silent Cinema.* Duke University Press, 2008.

Whitman, James Q. "The Two Western Cultures of Privacy: Dignity versus Liberty" (2004). 113 *Yale Law Journal* 1151.

Witmore, H. J. "Photographs as Instruments of Evidence" (1890). 31 (21) *Central Law Journal* 414.

Young Welke, Barbara. "Law, Personhood, and Citizenship in the Long Nineteenth Century: The Borders of Belonging." In Michael Grossberg and Christopher Tomlins (eds.), *The Cambridge History of Law in America, Volume II: The Long Nineteenth Century (1789–1920)*. Cambridge University Press, 2008.

Zollman, Carl. "Moving Picture Abuses and Their Correction in the United States" (1937). 21 (3 [April]) *Marquette Law Review* 105.

Cases

Almind v. Sea Beach Co., 139 NYS 559 (Sup Ct, 1912); 141 NYS 842 (AD, 1913).

Atkinson v. John E. Doherty & Co., 80 NW 285 (Mich, 1899).

Banks v. King Features Syndicate, Inc., 30 F Supp 352 (SD NY, 1939).

Barber v. Time, Inc., 159 SW 291 (Mo, 1942).

Bazemore v. Savannah Hospital, 155 SE 194 (Ga, 1930).

Binns v. Vitagraph Company of America, 130 NYS 876 (Sup Ct, 1911); 103 NE 1108 (NY, 1913).

Blumenthal v. Picture Classics, Inc., 257 NYS 800 (AD, 1932); 185 NE 713 (NY, 1933).

City of Grand Rapids v. Williams, 70 NW 547 (Mich, 1897).

Clayman v. Bertstein, 38 Pa D & C 543 (Pa, 1940).

Cohen v. Marx, 211 P 2d 320 (Cal Ct App, 1949).

Colyer v. Richard K. Fox Pub. Co., 146 NYS 2d 999 (AD, 1914).

Corliss v. E. W. Walker Co., 64 F 280 (D Mass, 1894).

Cox Broadcasting v. Cohn, 420 US 469 (1975).

DeMay v. Roberts, 9 NW 146 (Mich, 1881).

Dockrell v. Dougal (1899), 80 *Law Times* 556.

Douglas v. Stokes, 149 SW 849 (Ky, 1912).

Edison v. Edison Polyform Manufacturing Co., 67 A 392 (NJ, 1907).

Feeney v. Young, 181 NYS 481 (AD, 1920).

Foster-Milburn Co. v. Chinn, 120 SW 364 (Ky Ct App, 1909).

Franklin v. Columbia Pictures Corporation, 284 NYS 96 (Sup Ct, 1935).

Griffin v. Medical Society of New York, 11 NYS 2d 109 (Sup Ct, 1939).

Haelan Laboratories v. Topps Chewing Gum, 202 F 2d 866 (1st Cir, 1953).

Henry v. Cherry & Webb, 73 A 97 (RI, 1909).

Humiston v. Universal Film Manufacturing Co., 167 NYS 98, 101 (Sup Ct, 1917); 178 NYS 752, 755 (AD, 1919).

Inderbitzen v. Lane Hospital, 12 P 2d 744 (Cal, 1932).

James v. Screen Gems, Inc., 344 P 2d 799 (Cal, 1959).

Jeffries v. New York Evening Journal Publishing Co., 124 NYS 780 (Sup Ct, 1910).

Kelley v. Post Publishing Co., 98 NE 2d 286 (Mass, 1951).
Kelly v. Johnson Publishing Co., 325 P 2d 659 (Cal, 1958).
Kerby v. Hal Roach Studios, 127 P 577 (1942).
Kunz v. Allen, 172 P 532 (Kan, 1918).
Lake v. Wal-Mart Stores, Inc., 582 NW 2d 231 (Minn, 1998).
Lane v. F. W. Woolworth Co., 12 NYS 2d 352 (Sup Ct, 1939).
Levey v. Warner Bros. Pictures, Inc., 57 F Supp 40 (SD NY, 1944).
Leviston v. Curtis James Jackson III, No. 102449 of 2010 (NY Sup Ct, 2015).
Lillie v. Warner Bros Pictures Inc, 34 P 2d 835 (Cal Ct App, 1934).
Loftus v. Greenwich Lithographing Co., Inc., 182 NYS 428 (AD, 1920).
Lugosi v. Universal Pictures, Inc., 603 P 2d 425 (Cal, 1979).
Mackenzie v. Soden Mineral Springs Co., 18 NYS 240 (Sup Ct, 1891).
Manola v. Stevens, NY Sup Ct [unpublished opinion] (June 1890).
Mau v. Rio Grande Oil Co., Inc., 28 F Supp 845 (ND Cal, 1939).
Melvin v. Reid, 297 P 91 (Cal Ct App, 1931).
Metter v. L.A. Examiner, 95 P 2d 491(Cal Ct App, 1939).
Middleton v. News Syndicate, 295 NYS 120 (Sup Ct, 1937).
Moore v. New York Elevated Railroad, 130 NYS 523 (1892).
Moore v. Rugg, 46 NW 141 (Minn, 1890).
Munden v. Harris, 134 SW 1076 (Kan Ct App, 1911).
Murray Lithographic Co., 28 NYS 271 (1894).
Mutual Film Corp. v. Hodges, 236 US 248 (1915).
Mutual Film Corporation v. Industrial Commission of Ohio, 236 US 230 (1916).
Mutual Film Corporation v. Industrial Commission, 236 US 230 (1915).
Myers v. Afro-American Publishing Co., 5 NYS 2d 223 (Sup Ct, 1938); 7 NYS 2d 662 (AD, 1938).
New York Times v. Sullivan, 376 US 254 (1964).
Pavesich v. New England Life Insurance Co., 50 SE 68 (Ga, 1905).
Pollard v. Photographic Co. (1889), LR 40 Ch D 345.
Redmond v. Columbia Pictures Corporation, 1 NYS 2d 643 (AD, 1938).
Riddle v. MacFadden, 101 NYS 606 (AD, 1906); 94 NE 644 (NY, 1911).
Roberson v. Rochester Folding Box Co., 65 NYS 1109 (Sup Ct, 1900); 64 NE 442 (NY, 1902).
Schuyler v. Curtis, 42 NE 22 (NY, 1895).
Semayne's Case (1605), 5 Co Rep 91a, 91b, 77 Eng Rep 194.
Semler v. Ultem Publications, 9 NYS 2d 319 (City Ct, 1938).
Shulman v. Group W. Productions, Inc., 955 P 2d 469 (Cal, 1998).
Stryker v. Republic Pictures Corporation, 238 P 2d 670 (Cal Ct App, 1951).
Sweenek v. Pathe News, Inc., 16 F Supp 746 (ED NY 1936).
Time, Inc. v. Hill, 365 US 374 (1967)

Legislation and Legislative Instruments

A Bill to Protect Ladies, HR 8151, 50th Congress (1888).
Cal Constitution art. I, § 1.
Cal Civil Code § 655 (West).
Cal Civil Code §§ 3344, 3344.1 (West 1997 & Supp 2002).
Fine Arts Copyright Act 1865 (U.K.).
Fla Comp Gen Laws Ann §§ 3584–86, 7719 (Skillman 1927).
Kan Rev Stat Ann c 51 §§ 101–112, c 74 §§ 2201–2209 (1935).
Md Ann Code art 66A (Bagby 1924), amended Md Code Pub Gen Laws art 66A §§ 7, 10, 11 (Flack, Supp 1935), amended Laws 1939 c 430.
NY Educ Law §§ 1080–1092.
NY Laws Ch 132 §§ 1–2 (1903) (subsequently NY Civil Rights Law §§ 50–51 (McKinney 2004)).
Ohio Gen Code Ann §§ 871 (48–53), §§ 154 (46–47) (page 1937).
Okla Stat Ann tit 21 §§ 839–840 (1958).
Pa Stat Ann tit 4 §§ 41–58, tit 71 §§ 12, 62, 119, 356 (Purdon 1930).
Utah Code Ann §§ 76-4-8 and 76-4-9 (1953)
Va Code Ann §§ 8–650 (1957) and §§ 378b–378j (Michie 1936).

Case Records and Briefs

Almind v. Sea Beach Co., 141 NYS 842 (AD, 1913) (held in Special Collections at the New York State Library in Albany, N.Y.).
Binns v. Vitagraph Co. of America, 103 NE 1108, 1110 (NY, 1913) (held in Special Collections at the New York State Library in Albany, N.Y.).
Colyer v. Richard K. Fox Publishing Co., 146 NYS 2d 999 (AD, 1914) (held in Special Collections at the New York State Library in Albany, N.Y.).
Feeney v. Young, 181 NYS 481 (AD, 1920) (held in Special Collections at the New York State Library in Albany, N.Y.).
Franklin v. Columbia Pictures Corporation, 2 NE 2d 691 (NY, 1936) (held in Special Collections at the New York State Library in Albany, N.Y.).
Humiston v. Universal Film Manufacturing Co., 178 NYS 752, 755 (AD, 1919) (held in Special Collections at the New York State Library in Albany, N.Y.).
Kunz v. Allen, 172 P 532 (Kan, 1918) (held by the Kansas Supreme Court Law Library in Topeka, Kans.)
Lane v. Woolworth Co., 12 NYS 2d 352 (Sup Ct, 1939) (held in Special Collections at the New York State Library in Albany, N.Y.).

Lillie v. Warner Bros. Pictures, Inc., 34 P 2d 835 (Cal Ct App, 1934) (held in Special Collections by the Witkin State Law Library in Sacramento, Calif.).

Loftus v. Greenwich Lithographing Company, Inc., 182 NYS 428 (AD, 1920) (held in Special Collections at the New York State Library in Albany, N.Y.).

Melvin v. Reid, 297 P 91 (Cal Ct App, 1931) (held in Special Collections by the Witkin State Law Library in Sacramento, Calif.).

Myers v. Afro-American Publishing Co., 5 NYS 2d 223 (Sup Ct, 1938) (held in Special Collections at the New York State Library in Albany, N.Y.).

Riddle v. MacFadden, 94 NE 644 (NY, 1911) (held in Special Collections at the New York State Library in Albany, N.Y.).

Roberson v. Rochester Folding Box Co., 64 NE 442 (NY, 1902) (held in Special Collections at the New York State Library in Albany, N.Y.).

Stryker v. Republic Pictures Corporation, 238 P 2d 670 (Cal Ct App, 1951) (held in Special Collections by the Witkin State Law Library in Sacramento, Calif.).

Other Archival Material

Kodak Advertisements included in the George Eastman Archives, held by George Eastman House International Museum of Photography and Film, Rochester, N.Y.

John Robert Thomas papers, 1846–1914, held in Manuscripts Reading Room (Madison Building) of the Library of Congress, Washington, D.C.

Petition against a bill (No. 3516), held by the Legislative Branch of the National Archives, Washington, D.C.

Production notes (including scripts, research materials, internal working documents, letters, articles, and reviews) for *The Red Kimono*, held in Special Collections at the Academy of Motion Picture Arts and Sciences' Margaret Herrick Library in Beverly Hills, Los Angeles.

Production notes (including scripts, research materials, internal working documents, letters, articles, and reviews) for *The Sands of Iwo Jima*, held in Special Collections at the Academy of Motion Picture Arts and Sciences' Margaret Herrick Library in Beverly Hills, Los Angeles.

Production notes (including scripts, research materials, internal working documents, letters, articles, and reviews) for *Yankee Doodle*

Dandy, held in Special Collections at the Academy of Motion Picture Arts and Sciences' Margaret Herrick Library in Beverly Hills, Los Angeles.

Various documents (advertisements, articles, internal working documents, transcripts of radio programs) included in Kodak Historical Collection, held in Special Collections at the Rush Rhees Library of the University of Rochester, Rochester, N.Y.

Gustavus A. Rogers. "The Law of the Motion Picture Industry," speech delivered at the College of the City of New York, 28 November 1916. The manuscript is held by the Yale University Law Library, New Haven.

Newspaper Articles

"Acute Privacy." *Washington Post* (Washington, D.C.), 4 August 1904, 6.

Barry, Doug. "A New Bill in Florida Would Make Non-Consensual 'Revenge Porn' a Felony." *Jezebel* (online), 7 April 2013, at http://jezebel.com/5993942/a-new-bill-in-florida-would-make-non+consensual-revenge-porn-a-felony

Buchanan, Rose Troup. "Jennifer Lawrence Nude Pictures Leak Sparks Fear of More Celebrity Hackings: 'A Flagrant Violation of Privacy.'" *Independent* (London), 1 September 2014.

"A Chivalrous Congressman." *San Francisco Chronicle* (San Francisco), 6 March 1888, 1.

"Fair Girl's Plea Vain: Fails to Get Picture Declared Individual Property." *Saint Paul Globe* (St. Paul), 20 July 1902, 7.

Fewster, Sean. "U.S. Website Exploits Hundreds of Adelaide Women and Girls—And Refuses Victims Pleas to Remove Nude Images." *Adelaide Advertiser* (Adelaide, Australia), 17 June 2015.

"'Flour of the Family' Case: The Pretty Plaintiff Whose Picture Was Used for Advertising Purposes Non-suited." *New York Tribune* (New York), 28 June 1902, 10.

"Girl Asks Parker How He Likes It." *St. Louis Post-Dispatch* (St. Louis), 27 July 1904.

Gregorian, Dareh. "50 Cent to Pay Another $2 Million for Sex Tape." *New York Daily News* (New York) (online), 24 July 2015, at http://nydn.us/1MpwfS5

Hall, Mordaunt. "Justified Revenge." *New York Times* (New York), 3 February 1926.

"A Handsome Card." *St. Louis Post-Dispatch* (St. Louis), 31 July 1886, 6.

Hartzog, Woodrow. "How to Fight Revenge Porn." *Atlantic* (online), 10 May 2013, at http://www.theatlantic.com/technology/archive/2013/05/how-to-fight-revenge-porn/275759

"Has Not Right to Her Own Face." *Boston Daily Globe* (Boston), 7 July 1902, 6.

"Her Picture on Boxes: A Handsome Young Woman Brings Suit for Damages." *Evening Times* (Little Falls, N.Y.), 27 June 1900, 3.

"Her Picture on Flour Packages So Miss Abigail Roberson Brings Suit for $15,000." *Richmond Dispatch* (Richmond, Va.), 28 June 1900, 2.

"Judge Milton E. Gibbs, Jurist, Named to Claims Court in 1936, Dies in Rochester N.Y." *New York Times* (New York), 22 Aug 1940, 19.

"Miss Manola's Tights." *Atlanta Constitution* (Atlanta), 21 June 1890, 4.

"Moving Pictures Used as an Aid to Education."' *New York Tribune* (New York), 6 February 1910, 3.

Mulvaney, Erin. "GoDaddy.com among Defendants in 'Revenge Porn' Law Suit." *Houston Chronicle* (online), 17 January 2013, at http://www.chron.com/news/houston-texas/houston/article/GoDaddy-com-among-defendants-in-revenge-porn-4202646.php

"Not Miss Halford's Picture." *Washington Post* (Washington, D.C.), 29 August 1889, 2.

"No Right of Privacy." *Salt Lake Herald* (Salt Lake City), 23 July 1902, 4.

"Our Representative Women." *Albany Journal* (Albany, N.Y.), 16 March 1888.

"Parker Taken to Task by an Indignant Woman—If I Can Be Photographed, Why Not You? Asks Miss Roberson." *New York Times* (New York), 27 July 1904, 1.

Peterson, Andrea. "50 Cent Filed for Bankruptcy Days after Losing a Revenge Porn Lawsuit." *Washington Post* (Washington, D.C.), 14 July 2015.

"Photographed in Tights." *New York Times* (New York), 15 June 1890, 2.

"A Plea for Privacy at Weddings." *San Francisco Chronicle* (San Francisco), 11 October 1874, 6.

"Predict Monroe Lost to Suffrage." *New York Times* (New York), 29 October 1915.

"Privacy in Railway Traveling." *Baltimore Sun* (Baltimore), 24 November 1868, 3.

"Privacy in Theatres." *Washington Post* (Washington, D.C.), 7 July 1889, 15.

"The Privacy of Executions." *Baltimore Sun* (Baltimore), 15 March 1870, 2.

"Publishing a Woman's Picture." *New York Times* (New York), 13 July 1902, 8.

"A Question of Personal Right." *Sacramento Daily Record-Union* (Sacramento), 31 March 1888, 4.

"The Rights and Tights of an Actress." *Baltimore Sun* (Baltimore), 19 June 1890, 3.

Rogers, Abby. "More Than 20 Women Are Suing a Texas 'Revenge Porn' Site and GoDaddy." *Business Insider Australia* (online), 24 January 2012, at http://au.businessinsider.com/class-action-lawsuit-against-texxxancom-2013-1

Roy, Jessica. "A Victim Speaks: Standing Up to the Revenge Porn Tormentor." *BetaBeat* (online), 1 May 2013, at http://betabeat.com/2013/05/revenge-porn-holli-thometz-criminal-case

"The Sacred Privacy of Home." *Zion's Herald and Wesleyan Journal* (Boston), 23 October 1850, 172.

"Will Not Be Photographed in Tights." *Chicago Daily Tribune* (Chicago), 13 June 1890, 6.

"Women in Politics." *St. Louis Post-Dispatch* (St. Louis), 8 April 1888, 23.

"Your Feelings Hurt? Sue: Justice Rumsey Decides Abigail Roberson Picture Case." *Sun* (New York), 24 July 1901, 7.

Films

The Affairs of Anatol (dir. Cecil B DeMille, 1921).

At the Foot of the Flatiron Building (American Mutoscope & Biograph Company, 1903).

Birth (dir. Alfred Warman, 1917).

Birth of a Nation (dir. D. W. Griffith, 1915).

Broken Laws (dir. Roy William Neill, 1924).

C.Q.D. Or Saved by Wireless; A True Story of the Wreck of the Republic (Vitagraph Company of America, 1911).

The Crowd (dir. King Vidor, 1928).

The Hollywood Revue of 1929 (directed by Charles Reisner).

Human Wreckage (dir. John Griffith Wray, 1923).

La sortie des usines Lumière (Workers Leaving the Lumière Factory) (dir. Louis Lumière, 1895).

The Life of Emile Zola (dir. William Dieterle, 1937).

Manhatta (dir. Paul Strand and Charles Sheeler, 1921).

Metropolis (dir. Fritz Lang, 1926).

Oliver Wendell Holmes (dir. James A. Fitzpatrick, 1922).

Panorama from Times Building, New York (American Mutoscope and Biograph Company, 1905).

The Red Kimono (dir. Walter Lang, 1925).
The Sands of Iwo Jima (dir. Allan Dwan, 1949).
The Show of Shows (directed by John G. Adolfi, 1929).
Site-Seeing in New York with Nick and Tony (Picture Classics, 1931).
The Story of Louis Pasteur (dir. William Dieterle, 1936).
Yankee Doodle Dandy (dir. Michael Curtiz, 1942).

Index